A God of One's Own

A God of One's Own

Religion's Capacity for Peace and
Potential for Violence

Ulrich Beck

Translated by Rodney Livingstone

polity

First published in German as *Der eigene Gott* © Suhrkamp Verlag Frankfurt am Main 2008

This English edition © Polity Press, 2010
Polity Press
65 Bridge Street
Cambridge CB2 1UR, UK

Polity Press
350 Main Street
Malden, MA 02148, USA

ISBN-13: 978-0-7456-4618-3
ISBN-13: 978-0-7456-4619-0(pb)

A catalogue record for this book is available from the British Library.

Typeset in 11 on 13 pt Sabon
by Toppan Best-set Premedia Limited
Printed and bound in Great Britain by MPG Books Group Limited, Bodmin, Cornwall

The publisher has used its best endeavours to ensure that the URLs for external websites referred to in this book are correct and active at the time of going to press. However, the publisher has no responsibility for the websites and can make no guarantee that a site will remain live or that the content is or will remain appropriate.

Every effort has been made to trace all copyright holders, but if any have been inadvertently overlooked the publisher will be pleased to include any necessary credits in any subsequent reprint or edition.

The translation of this work was supported by a grant from the Goethe-Institut which is funded by the German Ministry of Foreign Affairs.

For further information on Polity, visit our website: www.politybooks.com

Contents

Acknowledgements

This book has undergone a number of revisions, all of which were the object of intensive discussions. Natan Sznaider, Edgar Grande and Christoph Lau, in particular, read all of it at every stage of the 'birth process' and they all took part in intensive discussions about it with me. Their criticisms, proposed additions and suggestions for further reading were not the least important incentives spurring me on to further revisions. At an early stage, Navid Kermani took the trouble to discuss my fundamental thesis with me. The same goes for Wolfgang Bonß and Sven Hillenkamp. A public debate with Arnold Angenendt and of course his book *Toleranz und Gewalt: Das Christentum zwischen Bibel und Schwert* [Tolerance and Violence: Christianity between the Bible and the Sword] have had a major influence on my argument. Once again, my lifelong discussions with Elisabeth Beck-Gernsheim have played an essential part in helping me formulate my ideas. They all deserve my warmest thanks, without of course being responsible for my exaggerations and omissions.

In times like these, when the very existence of the social sciences and the humanities is under threat as seldom before, it is of vital importance to testify that without the creative discussions that took place in the framework of the research group investigating the nature of 'reflexive modernization', this adventurous excursion into the fascinating byways of the volcanic landscapes of religion would never have been possible. And the efforts of that research group were made possible in their turn only through the generous financial assistance of the Deutsche Forschungsgemeinschaft. For that reason my heartfelt thanks are due to the DFG and to all those who helped to make this labour of co-operative sociological curiosity a reality.

1

The Diary of a 'God of One's Own'

Etty Hillesum: An Unsociological Introduction

Is it possible to begin a book with a confession of failure? Yes, it is possible and, in this instance, essential, even though the irony implicit in the question is unmistakable, since the question contains its own answer. Nor is it an expression of arrogance (as some readers may perhaps surmise); it is not a frivolous game with one's own limitations and blind spots. No doubt, a certain metaphysical ingenuousness is needed to coin the glib phrase a 'God of one's own' and to 'expound' it (whatever that might mean). In principle, however, the sphere of religion relates to that of sociology like fire to the water that puts it out.

As a sociologist with a firm belief in the redemptive power of sociological enlightenment, I have the idiom of secularism in my blood. The premise of secularism – more specifically, the idea that with the advance of modernization, religion will automatically disappear – cannot simply be expunged from sociological thinking, not even if that prognosis were to be refuted by history. It is for this reason that the contents of religious beliefs, with their – relatively – autonomous force and reality, their visions of a different humanity and their power to make whole worlds tremble, are so rarely exposed in their full ambivalence to the gaze of sociology. Sociologists are more concerned to demonstrate that even though rain-dancing Indians produce no rain with their dance, they successfully 'interact', because their dance has the 'function' of contributing towards the 'integration' of the group. However, such an approach tells us absolutely nothing about the whys and the wherefores of the cultural productivity and destructiveness of religious belief.

In sociology such lacunae are regarded not as defects, but as proof of scientific integrity. The discipline concerns itself with only one half of such basic religious distinctions as that between creator and creation, eternity and time, the next world and this one. Even if sociologists do not deny the depth and power of religious feelings, they refuse to accept that religious phenomena must be understood and explained in religious terms. Instead, they establish a *'methodological secularism'*, according to which religious phenomena are primarily seen as having social causes and functions. And that is as it should be: it satisfies the sceptical scientific mind.

However, such a view is in conformity with the process of secularization. It makes visible its own leading idea: the de-mystification of the religious sphere. And it renders invisible and incomprehensible something that increasingly determines reality, namely the re-mystification of reality by religion. Hence it is not necessary to be religious but merely to think consistently in sociological terms to be subject to doubts about whether the a-religious or anti-religious tendency of sociological scepticism is best suited to decoding not just the religious significance of a 'God of one's own', but its social and political power as well. Thus the present book sets out on what is doubtless a vain quest for an alliance of fire and water – in the service of both: that is to say, of sociology's claims to knowledge and perhaps also of religion's own self-understanding.

Etty Hillesum

In her diary Etty Hillesum, a Jewish woman from the Nether-lands, left a record of the 'God of her own' she had sought and found. Her handwritten diary entries start in March 1941 and end in October 1943. At the beginning of her diary the young woman leads the life of an ordinary citizen, although her very existence is threatened by the racist delusions of National Social-ism. As her outward life became increasingly confined, Etty Hillesum progressively turned her gaze inwards. She read Rilke,

Dostoevsky, Pushkin, St Augustine and, again and again, the Bible. Slowly and almost imperceptibly, the conversation with herself turned into a conversation with God. Etty Hillesum even developed a special style for speaking to God. She talks to God as if talking to herself. She speaks to Him directly without a trace of self-consciousness. Self-discovery and the discovery of God, finding herself and finding God, inventing herself and inventing God – all merge naturally into one. Her 'own' God is not the God of the synagogues or the churches or the 'believers', as distinct from the 'unbelievers'. 'Her' God knows nothing of heresy, the Crusades, and the unspeakable cruelties of the Inquisition, Reformation and Counter-Reformation, or of the mass murders of religiously motivated terrorism. Her God is free from theology and dogma; He is blind to history and, perhaps for that very reason, merciful and helpless. She says, 'When I pray, I never pray for myself, but always for others, or else I carry on a crazy or childlike or deadly serious dialogue with whatever is profoundest in me and which for simplicity's sake I call God' (Hillesum 1981: 165).

What is needed is the viewpoint of a sociology of religion that does justice to this subjective dimension of the religious – even if establishing such a yardstick makes failure unavoidable. Historians have discovered religious biographies and autobiographies and other works of testimony that have proved to be documents of extraordinary revelatory power, and so it may well be meaningful to allow one such work of testimony to speak for itself and then to interpret it.

11 July 1942, Saturday morning, 11 o'clock. We can really only speak of the ultimate and the deepest things of life if the words well up inside us as simply and naturally as water from a spring. And if God does not help me to go on, I shall have to help God. The whole surface of the earth is gradually turning into one vast prison camp from which few escape. It is a phase we have to get through. The Jews here are telling one another some weird stories: that in Germany people are being buried alive or exterminated by poison gas. What is the point of passing such stories on, even if they turn out to have some truth in them?

... I know that I shall cope with whatever happens, all by myself and that my heart will not be paralysed by the bitterness of it all, but that even the moments of deepest grief and black despair will leave fruitful traces in me and will finally make me stronger. I do not deceive myself about the actual situation and have even given up any pretence that I'm trying to help other people. I shall always strive to help God as best I can, and if I succeed in that, well, I shall be able to help others as well. But it would be wrong to have any heroic illusions about that either.

I wonder what I would really do if I held the summons to be deported to Germany in my hands and had to leave in a week's time. Just imagine that the summons came tomorrow, what would I do then? To begin with, I wouldn't tell a soul; I would retreat to the quietest corner of the house and try to gather all my physical and psychological energies together. I would have my hair cut short and I would throw my lipstick away. I would try to finish reading the Rilke letters that same week. I would have a pair of trousers and a jacket made out of the heavy coat material I have left over. . . . I would take the Bible with me as well as the two slim volumes of *Letters to a Young Poet* – and *The Book of Hours*,[1] surely there would be room for them in a corner of my rucksack? I would not take any photos of my loved ones but shall keep the images of their faces and gestures in the most secret corners of my mind, so that they will always be with me. . . . And even if I do not come out alive, how I die will say something about who I really am. It's no longer a question of keeping out of a particular situation, come what may, but rather with how I would conduct myself in any given situation and then go on living. . . .

Sunday morning prayer. Dear God, these are terrible times. Last night was the first time I lay there sleeplessly in the dark with burning eyes, as scene after scene of human suffering passed before me. I promise You one thing, God, just one small thing: I shall not let my fears for the morrow weigh heavy on today, but that does take some practice. Each day is sufficient unto itself. I shall help You not to abandon me, God, but I cannot vouch for it in advance. One thing alone is becoming ever clearer to me: You cannot help us, but we have to help You, and only in that way will we end up helping ourselves. The only thing that matters is to safeguard a piece of You in us, God. Perhaps we can help You to enter into the tormented hearts of other people. Dear God, You do not seem able to influence circumstances very much; they are just all part of the life we have. I do not hold You responsible. In the time to come You will call us to account. And almost every heartbeat tells me that You cannot help us, but that we must help You and defend

[1] [Two books by Rainer Maria Rilke (Trans).]

Your dwelling place in our innermost being to the last. It is true that there are people, there really are people, who at the very last moment want to rescue their vacuum cleaner and their silverware, instead of safeguarding You, dear God. And there are people who want only to rescue their own bodies, although these are nothing more than a shelter for a thousand fears and bitter feelings. And they say, 'I shan't let them get me into their clutches. But they forget that we are in no one's clutches if we are in Your arms. I am gradually starting to calm down again, God, thanks to this conversation with You. I shall soon have many conversations with You in the hope of preventing You from abandoning me. You will probably also have some lean times with me, God, times in which my faith fails to nourish You, but believe me, I shall always labour for You and remain faithful to You and I shall not drive You from my heart.

Dear God, I feel I have sufficient strength to endure great, heroic sufferings; what frightens me are the thousand little everyday cares that sometimes attack us like some noxious vermin. Well then, I'll just scratch myself a little in my despair and tell myself every day: I have taken care of today, the protective walls of a hospitable home still surround me like a familiar, well-worn item of clothing. I still have enough to eat for today and the bed with white sheets and warm blankets awaits me at night. So don't let me waste even a spark of energy worrying about my own petty material cares. Let me make use of every minute of the day and enjoy it, let me make it a fruitful day, a sturdy stone in the foundations on which to support the wretched, anxious days of the future.

The jasmine behind the house is quite bedraggled from the rain and the storms of recent days, the white blossoms are floating in the muddy black puddles on the low garage roof. But somewhere inside me the jasmine goes on blooming, as lush and delicate as ever. And its perfume wafts around the house in which You dwell within me, dear God. As You see, I take good care of You. I bring You not just my tears and my fears on this grey, stormy Sunday morning; I even bring You sweet-scented jasmine. I shall bring You all the flowers I find on my path, and there will be many of them. You shall be as comfortable as possible in my care. To give just one example, if I were to be shut up in some cell or other and a little cloud were to float past the barred window, I would bring You that cloud, dear God, at any rate, I would as long as I still had the strength. I cannot guarantee anything, but my intentions are the very best, as You can see. And now I shall surrender to this day. I shall meet many people today, and the many evil rumours and threats will press in on me like so many enemy soldiers storming an impregnable fortress. . . .

I should like one day to be the chronicler of our fate. I must forge a new language for these events and store them within me for when I no longer have the opportunity to write anything down. My feelings will be dulled, but I shall spring back to life; I shall fall over and pick myself up again. Much later on, I shall perhaps succeed in finding a quiet space that belongs only to me and there I shall remain, even if it takes years, until life springs up in me again and the words come to me to enable me to bear witness to the things to which witness has to be borne. Four o'clock in the afternoon: the day has turned out quite differently from what I expected. . . .

The misery is truly great and yet in the evenings, when the day has faded away behind me, I often run around beside the barbed wire with a spring in my step, and I find my heart overflowing – I can't help it, that is simply the way it is, I just cannot contain myself: there is something so great and splendid about life. Later on, we shall have to build a world all over again and we shall have to produce a small portion of love and kindness from within ourselves to counter every new crime and every new act of cruelty. We may indeed suffer, but we must not crack up. And if we survive this age intact, intact in body and soul, above all in soul, without bitterness, without hatred, then, once the war is over, we shall have the right to have our say. Perhaps I am an ambitious woman. I should like to have my say, however small. . . . One would like to be a plaster on many wounds. (Ibid.: 154, 155, 159–61, 178, 224)

Perhaps we are moved by the utter childlike earnestness of this individual, intimate, dialogical voice because Etty Hillesum expresses and embodies things that appear entirely incompatible. Instead of hatred for the persecutors, trust in her own God. She, even she, faces destruction, she suspects it; we know it. Nevertheless, she writes, 'And if we survive this age intact, intact in body and soul, above all in soul, without bitterness, without hatred, then, once the war is over, we shall have the right to have our say. Perhaps I am an ambitious woman. I should like to have my say, however small.'

Completely helpless in the face of catastrophe, she notes with the victim's lack of guile, but repudiating her role as victim, 'One would like to be a plaster on many wounds.' Caught up in an utterly hopeless situation, she denies that the victims' situation is hopeless and restores their dignity of action. '. . . we shall have to produce a small portion of love and kindness from within our-selves to counter every new crime and every new act of cruelty. We may indeed suffer, but we must not crack up' (ibid.: 224).

Etty Hillesum was Jewish but she grew up in a family in which Jewishness played no role at all. It was as a Jewess that she was deported to a concentration camp and killed, but she did not accept Jewish identity. Nor, however, did she convert to Christian-ity. Etty Hillesum experienced and practised a radical version of a God of her own choosing. No synagogue, no church, no reli-gious community. Was Etty Hillesum a non-Jew in her lifetime and a Jew in her death?

Even when imprisoned in the camp, Etty was present without belonging. The metaphor she uses to describe her situation is 'shipwreck'. Drowning people jostle each other to grab hold of a piece of driftwood in the endless expanse of the ocean.

> And then it is everyone for themselves, push the others away and let them drown. All that is so unworthy and I don't care for pushing anyway. I suppose I am the kind of person who would rather drift along in the ocean on my back, with my eyes raised towards heaven, and then gradually go under in humble resigna-tion. (Ibid.: 169–70)

This condition of 'not belonging' is, as Natan Sznaider writes, what turned the Jews into Europe's cosmopolitans, but also into the defenceless victims of the Nazis. 'European Jews were simul-taneously assimilated, orthodox, Jewish and non-Jewish' (Sznaider 2008: 96). And it was precisely Etty Hillesum's not belonging that collided with the ontological malevolence of the anti-Semitic men-tality and the resolve of the anti-Semitic state to eradicate these transnational Jewish cultures and societies at the heart of Germany and Europe.

What is the message that Etty Hillesum's diary can convey to us today? Is the good Jewess the non-Jewess who, in a kind of exaggerated eagerness to love her enemy, forgave her German mass murderers for acts that were unforgivable? 'I should like to enter all the camps of Europe, to be present on every front. I have no wish to be in so-called safety, I want to be present, and I want to create a little brotherhood between so-called enemies everywhere where I am' (Hillesum 1981: 213). Etty Hillesum does not just utter these deeply controversial words about 'creating a brotherhood between so-called enemies'; she embodies them right down to their ultimate logical consequences – without her being in a position to know 'what' was happening and 'what' she was forgiving. Is it these words that make Etty Hillesum's voice in her diary so moving for many readers and so problematic for others?

'There is no poet in me; there is only a small part of God in me that could grow into a poet' (ibid.: 214). The calm statements in her diary, which set out to ascertain the sources of her own life 'in a world that has been savagely turned upside down', go in search of readers, kindle life, startle, disturb and bring joy. Almost involuntarily or incidentally, Etty Hillesum succeeds in making a universal truth visible through her own introspection and her reflections on herself. 'Style is God.' This saying of Gottfried Benn's acquires a literal force in her writing. The style cultivated by Etty Hillesum in her diaries does not act as a substitute for God (as Benn meant to say). It is nearer the mark to say that Etty Hillesum speaks to God in her diary as if to herself. Her style creates the impression of the reader's direct participation in a prayer that is conducted as a dialogue in the mute presence of a helpless God. 'When I pray, I never pray for myself, always for others.' These 'others' include her tormentors, the 'gloomy young military policeman' who said to her on one of the transport nights, 'On a night like this I lose five pounds' (ibid.: 224); but also the mother who said to her child, 'And if you don't eat up your pudding, you will have to go on the transport without your Mummy' (ibid.: 225). 'I feel,' Etty Hillesum writes, 'as if by paying close attention I can bring out the best and deepest in people, they open themselves to me, every person is a story in himself, one that life itself tells me' (ibid.: 216).

And that precisely is the secret of her diary style. Readers do not feel that they are merely listeners; through reading they are drawn as narrators into Etty Hillesum's dialogue with herself. They narrate their lives to themselves, and therefore to Etty Hillesum, and also to God. Thus, the very inwardness of the diary contrives to generate something of a public sphere. In the process, all traces of a striving for literary effects are erased. Etty Hillesum succeeds in a marvellous way in creating a work of both authenticity and transgression. The element of transgression is her language, this immediacy of transcendence. These unpretentious sentences, the flow of dialogue with herself and with God, make it possible to immerse one's own life in the space of the other – lessons in style in which the inner and the outer become one.

A God of one's own is not an omnipotent God. He is a God who has become impotent and homeless in an apocalyptic age. He is a God who, if He is not to perish, stands in need of the human beings who have repudiated Him. Why did God create man? Because He wanted to be acknowledged – this view is expressed in the Qur'an but is not confined to it. Perhaps we should add: because humanity in its helplessness must rescue God in His helplessness and preserve Him within itself.

Blessed are those who are resigned to their fate, who have forgotten the possibility of being other. 'Happiness strikes where all is hopeless' (Kermani 2005: 76). 'There must be something else since the mind would be unable to despair of the horror, were it not for the fact that it cherishes the idea of a different colour whose scattered traces remain present in the negative totality, as Adorno maintains' (ibid.: 74). People suffer not because they have lost hope, but because they are unable to give up hoping. It is the people who hope who are tortured.

For all its simplicity, Etty Hillesum's diary is a document which expresses a cry of despair and a monstrous accusation – not least because, as far as we can judge from the external facts, her life ended in utter desolation. According to a Red Cross report, Etty Hillesum was murdered in Auschwitz on 30 November 1943. Her trust in a good God died with her. 'If a God has created this world,' Schopenhauer writes, 'I should not like to be Him: its misery would break my heart.'[2]

Etty Hillesum's diary is the imaginary site at which the horror of human history unfolds. Those who experience an apocalyptic terror will reject a positive dialectics of history of whatever kind and will defend their refusal to acknowledge that life has meaning. Etty Hillesum, however, neither complains nor accuses. Not even her executioners. She discovers solace and dignity (not safety!) in the intimacy of her relationship with her own helpless God in which God Himself becomes the questioner who has no answers.

---

[2] Arthur Schopenhauer, *Handschriftlicher Nachlass*, vol. iii, p. 57 (quotation taken from Kermani 2005: 190).

I neither can, nor would I wish to, write a theology of a God of one's own. Such a theology would have to place in the centre of its concerns this connection between knowledge of the human self and knowledge about the presence of God in one's own life, as well as the connection between the love of another – the 'religious other', the 'national other', the 'neighbour', the 'enemy' – and the love of God, and the connection between the helpless self and the helpless God of one's own choosing. What this shows is that the basis of religion is that both things – the God of one's own and a life of one's own – are unfathomable mysteries. Only the tragic has a lasting reality.

> When I walk along the streets Your world gives me much to think about, though it can't really be called thinking. It is more like the attempt to apprehend it with an entirely new sense. I sometimes imagine myself surveying the present age as if it were an historical epoch whose beginning and end I can see and which I can 'assign' to its proper place in history as a whole. And this is why I am so grateful that I am not in the least embittered or full of hate, but that I feel a great tranquillity, which is not the same thing as indifference. I feel that I can even understand the present situation to a certain extent, strange though that may sound! . . . The most depressing thing is that hardly any of the people I work with have managed to broaden their mental horizon. Nor do they really suffer. They hate and their optimism blinds them to the reality of their own situation. They constantly intrigue and are led by their ambitions to defend their own little positions. The whole thing is a giant pigsty and there are moments when I feel discouraged and just lay my head down on the typewriter and feel like saying, I can't take any more of this. But life goes on and I keep learning more and more about people. (Hillesum 1981: 170–1)

How can she possibly fail to meet hatred with hatred, violence with violence, aggression with aggression? In her quest for the 'great simplicity' and for 'deeper humanity' in her diaries, what makes Etty Hillesum shine out is undoubtedly connected with her own character, with her particular qualities. But the reality is that Etty Hillesum's dignity derives from a higher source, one she shares with all human beings. In everything she says and does we see something of humankind as a whole. It is the connection between her particular existence and the *universal* individual, the *universal* God of one's own, that struggles to express itself in her diaries. What is admirable and even sacred is the human race, which finds expression with her voice and her experience. This exemplary religious individualism refutes every suspicion of an ego cult because it achieves self-transcendence.

Dear Etty, you could not have had any inkling of what you had done when you and many like you placed your life in the hands of a God of your own choosing. A 'God of one's own' can only be made practicable, liveable, hope-able, conceivable, when He becomes something of 'one's own'; in other words, when God, the world and humanity cease to be thought of as a unity, and when 'religious belief' is banished from the public sphere and turned in on itself. This separation, which marks the distinction between religion and religiosity, is something you have carried out in quite a radical fashion; you have taken God into your own hands. Previously people were either Catholics or Protestants or Jews (or atheists or heretics). They were born into an 'official' religion, made their choices according to the demands of that religion, conceived children and brought them up in the spirit of the religion they were born into. They went to war with weapons blessed by the church, even though there were Catholics, Protestants or Jews fighting on the side of the enemy. In a world morally devastated by the madness of terrorism, you chose to ask for something more, over and above the collective religiosity that constantly preached conformity. You acted just as if one could assume responsibility for one's own life, including its religious dimension. A highly risky idea, fraught with consequences! You accepted the idea of the ego (in the meaning it has in Fichte and Sartre), in its full, merciless freedom together with the responsibility it entails and a God of one's own. This was to give rise to a minor infinity which would make hope, love and life possible even in the midst of the destruction of humankind. This idea overturns the order of faith that has survived for millennia through every vicissitude. The individual who doubts and decides becomes the church, the guardian of God and faith – while in contrast the church itself becomes a heresy.

Every religion has been conversant with the dialogue between the pious and 'their' God (Kermani 2005). And in the same way, the cosmic journey of the soul in search of God is a persistent refrain in world literature. We may think of Dante's *Divine Comedy*, Attar's *Book of Adversity*, Milton's *Paradise Lost*, Goethe's *Faust* Part Two, Thomas Mann's depiction of Joseph's ascension to heaven or Gerhart Hauptmann's *Great Dream*. The gaze of the historian of literature or religion perceives here an entire tapestry, a kind of meta-comedy, albeit one full of bogey-men, of the journeys of people's souls yearning for God, as they roam through different epochs, languages, imaginations and religions. Even so, the narrative of a God of one's own has broken the ecclesiastical spell and liberated people from dogmas, liturgies and exegeses, while constituting a practical form of dialogue with a humanized fellow-God who is both individualized and standardized. This mundane form of dialogue is based on mutuality and has perhaps even been democratized, while remaining ultimately mysterious. Whereas, previously, religion preached insuperable opposition to the worldly and this opposition was held to be sacrosanct, it is now pressed into service as an all-inclusive phenomenon. There is no longer a religious code which enables us to peer behind all the mirrors of one's own God. And needless to say, we inevitably find ourselves confronting the question: What is specifically 'one's own' about the 'God of one's own'? Is the 'God of one's own' a God at all, or simply the idolization of whatever happens to be one's own? What characterizes the God of one's own above all is the many things He is not: He is not a label, not proof of one's underdog status, not party to any double morality, and, above all, not an absolute who has always stood for one thing. The God of one's own is as capable of being divided up and reassembled as the individual him- or herself; He is the guarantor of the independence of both the individual and of God.

Dear Etty, the fact is that your unaffected dealings with your own God frequently involved you in a kind of love-relationship. Indeed, as a reader, I am sometimes uncertain whether you are talking to your human or divine lover. And you sometimes become entangled in the *paradox of freedom* in love.[3] Just as we wish to take possession of the freedom of the person we love, so too do we wish to take possession of the freedom of our own God. Needless to say, this cannot be achieved by the exercise of power; such hubris is unthinkable. In the case of 'our own' God, a person who desires to be loved does not seek to subjugate God, to shape Him

---

[3] Which Jean-Paul Sartre (2003) outlined in the case of the earthly religion of love (see also Beck and Beck-Gernsheim 1995).

in accordance with human notions of being loved. He or she does not yearn for a Godlike love-automaton. Even if this were practicable and appropriate, it would mean no more than treating one's own personal God as a mechanical aid to living that could be wheeled out for every conceivable purpose – an ultimately humiliating relationship for both parties. It follows that the person who loves does not wish to possess the beloved God as one owns an object. He or she goes in search of a special kind of ownership. He or she desires to own God's freedom as a form of freedom.

Of course, if we think of God's freedom as something other than a love-machine that fulfils all wishes, and instead take it seriously, this opens the door to divine indifference, rejection and ignorance. Why should God love humanity if he is supposed to be as free as those who love Him? Can we make a home for our 'own' God and protect Him from a world that is about to destroy itself by allowing Him the freedom of non-love, or, even more radically, of hatred? Perhaps human beings are all-too human in their dealings with their own God! They wish to be loved by this godly freedom and at the same time to demand that this freedom as such should cease to exist. They want God's freedom to decide of its own free will to become love – not merely at the start of the adventure but at every moment. We wish to chain our personal God to our own desires, traumas, hysterias, fears and hopes, and at the same time, we want to keep these chains in our own hands. In that case, how are we to escape the temptation of debasing our own God, changing Him into a tame, cuddly God?

I could extend this discussion over many pages. But here is something that you will not have thought possible, Etty. Your story of a God of your own has become utterly commonplace, banal and trivial. It has been devalued by endless repetition. No distinction is made any longer between God and idols. We move in a world of multi-faith quotations whose source and meaning we do not know. Only rarely do we detect the faint breath of the alien past with which we used to decorate the interior of 'our own God'. I would single out only a catalogue destined for the New Age market – for the God of our own choosing has become venal. In this catalogue we discover advertisements which praise the power of crystals, offer to teach you how to embrace birch trees in order to release spiritual energies, or undertake to reveal where you have to go and which forms you need to fill in if you wish to be reborn. Needless to say, all these voyages into the unknown depths of the soul have their price. And it comes as no surprise to learn that just as there are erotic fairs, there are also esoteric fairs which promise to gratify every religious need – as long as you are prepared to take at face value and pay in ready cash for the products of the growing world industry serving para-religious needs and promising heaven on earth.

A life of one's own, a room of one's own, a God of one's own

A God of one's own might well be the template for a life or a space of one's own. In *A Room of One's Own* (1929), Virginia Woolf writes: 'But, you may say, we asked you to speak about women and fiction – what has that to do with a room of one's own?' (Woolf 1984: 5). And she replies: 'All I could do was to offer you an opinion on one minor point – a woman must have money and a room of her own if she is to write fiction. . . .' A woman who can shut the door behind her has the opportunity to break with convention. A lock on the door means the freedom to develop one's own ideas.

The struggle for a 'life of one's own' and a 'room of one's own' involves more than the spatial organization of everyday life. It involves control and subversion, the shaking off of internal and external constraints. A room of one's own means independence, in other words, (prohibited) reading matter, laziness, masturbation, boredom, self-questioning, testing one's own qualities in privacy, and the ability to launch oneself on spiritual odysseys in search of a 'God of one's own'. It is here and in this way that the incalculable nature of social life begins. What is at stake is the ability to create and secure an *inner* space as the premise of a life of one's own.

Anyone who discovers his or her own life and goes in search of the reasons for it and the mysteries underlying it falls into a bottomless pit. More precisely, that life appears as the intersection of two infinite lines, one internal and the other external. The *individual* is precisely not indivisible – as Nietzsche insisted – but rather is divisible, a *dividuum*. As an intermediate condition in the course of an infinite divisibility, he or she cannot serve as a unit. It is quite unclear whether an individual has, or should have, one life or several, one identity or many.

This kind of multiplicity and alterity in one's own life arises with the fragmentation of modernity. This is also the source of the compulsion to give an account of oneself and others in all sorts of situations, plausible and implausible. The reflexive ego is the *detective in oneself*; more precisely, the eternal detective, who cannot resist investigating and reporting on himself. He opens files and prepares answers. These answers amount to an official master key (more recently with psychological and sociological underpinnings). Confronted with the inquisitorial compulsion with which the ego accompanies the ego every step of the way, interrogating its every motive and anticipating its every action, collecting and collating its traces and prospects, religiosity, organized church faith, finds itself forced constantly to justify itself.

To put the matter differently and more fundamentally: If it is true that a life of one's own is another name for the *contingent* and *reflexive* nature of that life, what form of individually internalized, practical and natural religiosity and spirituality remains open? Two options present themselves here. The first appeals to the *intractable*, unbending nature of any given religion, both historically and individually, and hence accepts the closed system of church, God and individual. This option denies the reality of religious plurality, repudiates modernity, denies individualization and, in the light of the irrevocable historical pressure in favour of individual religious commitment and choice, takes refuge in dogmas of faith that are incompatible with individualized experiences and ambivalent feelings. The decision to believe (or not to believe) that is required of individuals faced with the plurality, comparability and availability of religions, heresies and forms of atheism, expects – as Peter L. Berger provocatively puts it – an attitude of self-deception on the part of individualized individuals. This is Sartre's *mauvaise foi*: in other words, the denial of one's ability to choose and one's own responsibility.

This option fails to acknowledge the religious origins of individualization in Christianity. Individualization and the manifold confusions this leads to on every side is misinterpreted as an individual process to be ascribed to individual excesses – the frothy hunger for experience, inflated expectations, manic egoism and the declining readiness to see things through, to fit in and to make sacrifices. But that is erroneous. For in reality the religious forms assumed by the 'God of one's own choosing' symbolize the *victory* of church doctrines according to which the subjective freedom of belief and conscience is indispensable.

In contrast, the second option recognizes the empirical and historical fact that the social forms of a new religiosity, namely the religiosity of the 'God of one's own', correspond to the social forms of a space of one's own and a life of one's own. In the European context of an individualized modernity there is no longer any religious faith that has failed to pass through the eye of the needle of the reflexivity of one's own life, experience and self-knowledge (exceptions here merely confirm the rule). Individuals uses their religious experiences to construct their individual religious shelter, their 'sacred canopy'.[4] Individuals make decisions about their faith, and no longer merely or primarily defer to their origins and/or the religious organization they were born into. This does not spell the end of religion, however, but only signifies the entry into the self-contradictory narrative of 'secular religiosity' which it is our task to decode. We can begin with a few examples by way of illustration.

Religious individualization and committed churchgoing are not mutually exclusive but may well reinforce each other. In the tentative search for the connections between a reflective religious belief and a personal relationship with God, individualization may force us to choose, and thus to compare, migrate or to flirt with heresy, atheism or conversion. Religious individualism is another term for doubt, the brother of faith whose narratives thread their way through the history of religion from St Augustine's *Confessions* – always relevant and now once again highly topical – down to Mother Theresa's confession that she was almost driven to despair by God's silence. Individualism is a *contingent* process, and for that reason it is *highly ambivalent* in its consequences; and this is to be explained not by the conceptual fuzziness of theory but by the complex nature of the real world.

Individualization does not preclude the unquestioning belief that is innocent of all knowledge of the abyss. Equally, however,

---

[4] To cite the famous formula of Peter Berger (1969), to whose book I am also indebted for the following idea.

it may lead just as readily to the committed defence of the old Latin Mass, which sees itself as the vanguard of the church, as to its critique. We shall have to assume that a conventional relation to religion is atypical for the different forms assumed by a subjectively desired, 'individualized' church membership. What we find instead is an unreflective, traditional religiousness combined with an instrumental pragmatism in people's recourse to churchgoing at times of crisis, illness and death, etc., 'above all among the great mass of people who remain at a certain distance from the church, who are reluctant to leave it altogether but who are also unwilling to commit themselves fully' (Pollack 1996: 83).

Thus at the start of the twenty-first century we come back to the question raised by Ernst Troeltsch a hundred years ago, but this time in a new, more radical form: To what extent will a Christianity that has undergone an inner renewal be able to open its mind to the individualization specific to the modern age so as to gain a new religious vitality? One theme of fundamental importance for such a question would centrally concern the departure of 'Gods of one's own choosing' from churches in Europe and the United States, as well as many other parts of the world caught up in such changes. Would such departures persist or would a 'more flexible church' (Troeltsch 1913)[5] be able to create a new, higher synthesis of subjective piety and institutional organization that might reverse this trend?

Needless to say, as Etty Hillesum's diary convincingly shows, the conflicts triggered by symbolic distinctions and the monopolistic claims to supremacy that hold sway in the universe of priestly religions are of no importance in the world of individualized faith

---

[5] Interestingly, Troeltsch regards individualization as a general process that changes the social foundations both of 'the social constitution of nations' and 'of the churches'.

> Christ's disciples face great challenges and the approach of grave crises. These crises may perhaps affect nations in general, but they certainly affect the churches. Our view is that we should hold things together as far as possible. We need to equip ourselves with the religious confession of a personally upright personality who acts from a vital inner impulse, while on the other hand, we must develop a genuine desire to cultivate the community of the corpus mysticum Christi with which we feel united in love. (Troeltsch 1913: 133; quoted from Graf 2004: 178; see also Joas 2007b: 22ff.)

movements. In contrast, the institutionalized religions have two faces. Faith, the very thing that is supposed to guarantee a common humanity that rises above all national and ethnic divisions, opens up religious chasms between one individual and another, and, more specifically, between believers and non-believers. This casts doubt on the ability of the religions to bring about peace.

> The road to peace is a lengthy process, it lasts to this day. The religious creeds have not left it behind; it is a task that still confronts them. The Peace of Westphalia offers important lessons in this respect. At that time, the Christian denominations were forced to inquire into the roots of their capacity for peace. The truth today is the same as it always has been: whoever desires to establish peace must himself be peaceable. (Kamphaus 2007: 7)

Even the plausible riposte of the West – the rule of law as the solution to the violent proclivities of religion – is effective only in the framework of the nation-state. It fails to grasp the specific reality, namely the universal religious and social nature of the dynamics of conflict. For the test of liberty of conscience is whether it is extended to include the liberty of those who hold different beliefs, not least their right to give up all beliefs and even to hold beliefs in contempt. Thus the world has a chance of surviving only if the many faiths that believe in only one God succeed in civilizing themselves, if they abjure the use of violence as an aid to missionary activities, and if they are prepared to commit themselves to supporting the principle of mutual tolerance between religions.

But is not such a hope nothing short of ludicrous?

2

The Return of the Gods and the Crisis of European Modernity

A Sociological Introduction

The topic of a God of one's own introduced in the previous chapter cannot be treated in a vacuum. For it is simply one of a large number of threads in an almost impenetrable tangle of religious trends and counter-trends whose substance and meaning are based on a bewildering mixture of conceptual clarifications, empirical findings and theoretical postures. This introductory sociological chapter sets out to consider the individualization of religion in its relation to the religious revival of the beginning of the twenty-first century and to the looming crisis both in the European monopoly of secular modernity and in the European understanding of it.

Disagreements between the religions and the civilizing of world society

Farewell to secularization?

The return of the religions at the beginning of the twenty-first century breaks with the conventional wisdom that has prevailed

for the past two hundred years up to the 1970s.[1] The Enlightenment liberated humanity from God and enabled it to achieve
autonomy in every sphere of activity. Religious belief is atavistic,
a product of bad conscience. Europeans look down with contempt
on all those who are still religious or have become religious once
again. It is an essential part of the image of modern, enlightened
Europeans that they have overcome pre-modern superstition.
Europe is the key to secularization.

The further and faster the modernization process has advanced,
the more obvious the disempowerment of the gods has become
– in other words, what we have witnessed with growing clarity is
the victory of scientific and technical rationality and the demoli-
tion of the structures underpinning the plausibility of religious
belief. Over a time-span of two hundred years religion appeared
to be a second-order, non-fundamental phenomenon which progressively faded away or lost ground as its causes were eliminated.
Once a highly visible poverty has been overcome, education has
become universal, social inequality has been dismantled and political oppression is a thing of the past, religion will acquire the
status of a personal hobby. Insofar as religion still exists, it does
so as a private concern. Religious faith survives as an option;
it has binding power over the personal conscience of believers
but has lost its role in the formation of individual or collective
identity.

The secularization theory was heir to the Enlightenment critique of religion as articulated in Europe by Feuerbach and Marx,
Nietzsche and Freud.[2] In this way, the secularist genealogy was

---

[1] In what follows I summarize the results of the critique and revision of the
theory of secularization. See Asad 2006; Beckford 2003; Beckford and Levasseur 1986; Berger 1969, 1979; Bourdieu 1987; Bruce 2006; Casanova 2006a,
2006b, 2007; Davie 1994, 2000, 2006; Göle 2006; Habermas 2007a, 2007b;
Heelas 2006; Hervieu-Léger 1990, 2006; Jakelič 2006; McLeod 2000; Martin
1978, 2005; Norris and Inglehart 2006; Riesebrodt 2000, 2007; Roy 2006.
[2] In contrast, the American Enlightenment contained no anti-religious strand.
Even the separation of church and state, which was written into the First
Amendment of the Constitution, is just as concerned to protect the free exercise
of religious belief from state intervention as it is to protect the state from the
encroachments of religion. Nor should it be forgotten that the American experience really does constitute an exception. No other modern society has a population in whom belief is so strong, but which also clings to the separation of
church and state. Its political rhetoric is always messianic but the legitimation

constructed as the triumphal emancipation of rationality and liberty from the worldly aggrandizements and bigotry of the religions. And every 'progressive' social revolution and movement in Europe and the United States, from the French Revolution to the ecological revolution in the present day (in which 'just' solutions to the expected climatic catastrophes are being sought worldwide), has been, and still is driven by secularized actors who are fighting for salvation in this world.

Secularization theory is based on two assumptions: first, that modernization as it emerged in the European context (Max Weber called it 'occidental rationality' a century ago) is a *universal* process which leads to similar developments all over the world; and, second, secularization is *inseparable* from modernization and is as irresistible. From the very outset, this version of secularization theory has been a core element of otherwise very different theories of modernization (those of Durkheim, Comte and Marx, etc.). The decline of religion in the course of the 'disenchantment of the world' is, according to Max Weber, one of the unintended consequences of the Protestant Reformation and is a constitutive feature of the general development of modernity.

The collapse of secularization theory is, therefore, of far greater significance than, for example, the collapse of the Soviet Union and the Eastern bloc. After all, it does not 'just' affect individual geopolitical empires; it threatens the entire edifice of fundamental assumptions and basic institutions and hence ultimately the future of European modernity. Secularization is (or was?) a constitutive premise of both democracy and modernity. It is surely to the credit of Jürgen Habermas (2007b, 2008) that he should have raised this taboo-laden question. What then is the meaning of a 'post-secular' modernity in Europe? In the final analysis, its meaning lies in the desire to uncouple modernity and Westernization and to withdraw from the West its monopoly of modernity.

---

of its institutions is never under threat. This became clear even in the presidential election of 2008. Paradoxically, the religious messianism of the Bush Administration quite unintentionally unleashed something that had been inconceivable even a short time previously: a counter-wave of liberalization (which had long been a term of abuse in American politics). This is an exception. And it remains so, despite the fact that the separation of church and state is a feature of both Japan and India.

What evidence has the sociology of religion accumulated since the 1970s that might contribute to the fall of secularization theory, or indeed has already done so? Amidst the widespread talk of the 'return' of religion, it remains unclear to what extent we are talking about a change in the real world or a change of attitude (or indeed both). Four questions and lines of argument will be elaborated here.

1. Is secularization a European special path?
2. The paradox of secularization.
3. The essence of the religious revival in Europe is the decoupling of (institutional) religion and (subjective) faith.
4. The authority principle governing the revival of religion is the sovereign self.

Secularization – a European special path? If we take the frequency of churchgoing as an index of secularization, then the decline in the regular practice of religion in some countries in Western Europe since the end of the First World War has assumed truly catastrophic proportions, whereas elsewhere this is a more recent development.

> In only three European countries (Ireland, Poland and Switzerland) does a majority of the population regularly go to church. In the majority of European countries it is under 20 per cent and in eastern Germany and Scandinavia the numbers that go are in single figures. Conversely, in Poland, Ireland, Switzerland and Portugal, fewer than 10 per cent never go to church, while in France, Great Britain, the Netherlands and eastern Germany – on a rising scale – this is true of over 50 per cent. (Casanova 2007: 326)

However, although in Western Europe (albeit with considerable variations) the Christian churches are emptying at an almost spooky rate (so providing evidence in support of secularization theory), the opposite picture emerges at a global level, where outside Europe we see the revitalization of religious belief, especially of Christianity. In fact, at present we are witnessing one of the strongest phases in the expansion of Christianity in its entire history.

Astonishingly, many commentators (Samuel Huntington, for example) observe the demographic trend only in connection with the global development of Islam, but not with that of Christianity. And yet many of the fastest-growing nations are either entirely or strongly Christian in orientation. We need think only of Brazil, Uganda or the Philippines, where the population has almost doubled since 1974. Some of these countries will see their population at least double again by 2050, and this will result in major changes in the ranking of the countries of the world according to population. But equally, demography is not the only factor in the rapid expansion of Christianity throughout the world. Contrary to the expectations of the critics of colonialism, who regarded Christianity as a Western implant which had no future in an alien environment, Christianity only began its rapid expansion in Africa after the end of colonial rule, partly through mass conversions. Estimates show that at the present time roughly 23,000 people are added to the total Christian population every day in Africa – by birth, but also more than a sixth as the result of conversion. Between 1965 and 2001, the proportion of Christians in the African population as a whole increased from 25 to 46 per cent. Statistics of religious affiliation are perhaps not highly reliable, but the trend, at least, seems beyond dispute. In Asia, too, Christianity has some astounding successes to its credit, most spectacularly in South Korea. . . . In Latin America the triumphal progress of the Pentecostal movement and the Protestant sects is evidently more than a passing phenomenon. These trends evidently play a major role, especially for women, who look to them for a 'reformation of machismo'. (Joas 2007a: 983)

Thus Christianity as such is by no means on its last legs. It is merely that European Christianity is confronted with a rapid decline in church attendance in some of its national bastions, including Germany. What secularization theory has to say is, if framed in general terms, false. Looked at regionally, it amounts to the assertion that Christianity is in the process of being *de-Europeanized*. Christianity is thriving outside Europe; European Christianity is fading away (even though there are fresh shoots here too – more on this point later on).

This finding points us to an epistemological insight: anyone who fails to make the switch from a national point of view to a cosmopolitan one fails to grasp the real situation. The religious sphere and the actors and possibilities of action in it are not identical with those of the national sphere. 'If a world religion is on offer, ethnic, national or regional supports must be renounced. . . . It is essential to address everyone who is recognizable as a human being. . . . World religions are an important, perhaps the most important contribution to the formation of a system of religion. They may be said to anticipate the world society' (Luhmann 2000: 267, 157). If religious movements and religious changes become supranational events, then we need a cross-border, cosmopolitan gaze in order to *see* that developments within national boundaries are merely pieces in the jigsaw puzzle of global religious movements.

An important finding of the cosmopolitan gaze is

> the fact that orthodox and conservative branches of existing religious communities are everywhere gaining ground. This is as true of Hinduism and Buddhism as of the three monotheistic religions. What is striking above all is the regional expansion of these established religions in Africa and the countries of East and South-East Asia. One factor in such missionary success is evidently the mobility of the forms of organization. The multicultural universal church of Roman Catholicism is better equipped to exploit the trend towards globalization than the nationally based Protestant churches, which turn out to be the great losers. Most dynamic of all are the decentralized networks of Islam (especially in Sub-Saharan Africa) and the evangelical churches (above all, in Latin America). Their distinguishing feature is the ecstatic religiosity that is ignited by individual charismatic figures. It is the fastest-growing religious movements, such as the Pentecostalists and the radical Muslims, that are best described as 'fundamentalist'. Their cults combine spiritualism and imminent expectations with rigid moral codes and a literal interpretation of the Bible. (Habermas 2007b: 2–3; see also Martin 2002, 2005)

The paradox of secularization. In the relevant literature, secularization is equated with the disempowerment and the loss of significance of religion and religious organizations. This means that no one asks whether or not the opposite is true, namely whether secularization can and must be regarded as a *great gain* for religion.[3] To achieve this change of perspective, this 'gestalt switch', it is essential to understand the *paradox of secularization.*

[3] I owe this idea to a conversation with Ulrich Wengenroth.

Let us consider the European debate. Following the Wars of Religion in the early modern era, the collapse of the temporal power of the church was partly lamented and partly hailed as a triumph of the secular rationality of science and the terrestrial foundation of political rule, two key actors in the modernization process that had been freed from the spell of superstition and the power-lust of the papacy. But may we not make the same claim for the Christian religion itself? Hasn't Christianity itself been freed from superstition and the heavy burden of legitimizing its own temporal power? Isn't the *emancipation* of religion the beneficiary of the separation of religion and science as well as religion and the state, the very thing that appeared to many Fathers of the Church as the reason for the alienation and decline of religion? For, once emancipated, freed from the ballast of tasks it cannot carry out, religion can devote itself to its true mission of spirituality. Despite the lamentations that have continued to accompany the victory of modernity down to the present, should we therefore not regard the enforced process of secularization as a gift of God, a gift, moreover, that in the final analysis helped to prepare the way for religious revival in the twenty-first century, that spiritual re-awakening that has suddenly come to public notice and has been received with such a combination of astonishment, admiration and dismay?

Religion is both empowered and disempowered by secularization. Driven from its throne and expelled from its place at the centre of society, religion has two successes to its credit (successes denied to the preachers and actors in the drama of Christian salvation). First, it has succeeded in passing the responsibility for rational knowledge to science and/or the state. It now falls to science to proclaim its terrestrial discoveries as transcendent truth. And it is left to politics to sanctify the earthly transcendence of the sovereignty of the political commonwealth in the shape of the 'nation' and the 'state'.

Second, and as a consequence of the first point, religion is forced to be *religion and nothing else*; its duty, in other words, is to foster, cultivate, practise, celebrate and reflect the indestructible spirituality of the human condition, human beings' need for and consciousness of transcendence, and to help to bring about its triumph in the public arena. Having passed through the fire of secularization, religion is fully aware of its own limits, that is to say, of the need to impose limits on itself. It is obviously not possible to ascertain and proclaim the laws governing heaven and earth by applying the methods available to religion! Conversely, the idea of a 'heaven here on earth', that is to say, the idea that a society might be able to organize itself in such a way as to be at peace with itself, is an expression of the arrogance of secularism and is doomed to failure. The church no longer claims to be the expert on everything, but only on spirituality and religiosity. Both science and the state, in contrast, are forced to squirm in the trap created by the claim that they are universal experts.

In other words, the enforced secularization of religion has paved the way for the revitalization of religiosity and spirituality in the twenty-first century. The risk this poses for the churches is that the movements and the competition based on people's 'own personal gods' will empty them and they will end up as profane institutions.

The key to the 'revitalization' of religiosity in Europe is the decoupling of (institutional) religion and (subjective) faith. Quite early on, as early as the 1960s, sociologists of religion recognized that church attendance was not the be-all and end-all of religious practice, and certainly not the only expression of faith and religious membership. They began to look for indicators that would reveal what lay behind formal church membership and what goes on outside the church and yet merits the epithet 'religious'. In Italy, France and Belgium, in realms where religious practices were least expected, observers registered the occurrence of such phenomena as pilgrimages, healing rituals and local saints' cults.

Paradoxically, phenomena such as these were found to have an unexpected attractiveness and an ability to renew themselves even during the

> modernization wave of the 'Golden Sixties'. Subsequent studies of new forms of religious festival have impressively confirmed the validity of these pioneering observations. They found that at such festivals, collective religious memories in the form of 'holy places' and 'moments of ecstasy' could achieve an impact on a global European plane. It was not until the beginning of the 1970s, however, that these reflections began to undermine the dogmas of secularization that had dominated the research assumptions of the sociology of religion. (Hervieu-Léger 2004: 138–9)

When people opened their eyes to what was happening between nations and between religions, the so-called 'New Religious Movements' suddenly became visible. Thomas Luckmann named them *'invisible'* or *'implicit'* religions' (1967). Since then it has become almost commonplace to point out that such concepts were invoked in order to talk about a new spiritual culture that transcended the frontiers of nations and religions and borrowed its religious beliefs and practices at will from the religious and spiritual traditions of both east and west, which then, enriched by the changing fashions of various psychological schools, were cobbled together to form versions of 'Gods of their own'. These movements emphasize the individual quest for perfection and personal development which accompanies the 'enrichment of the soul'.

There are two noteworthy features about these changes. First, the epithet 'new' in 'New Religious Movements' points yet again to a Eurocentric approach. For to non-Western eyes, and especially the eyes of the pantheistic religious traditions of Asia, this 'postmodern' religiosity turns out to be a familiar story. Individualistic mysticism is well known as an option in all the great religious traditions, but was regarded there as a 'deviation' or else was the preserve of elites and virtuoso exponents of religious belief (in the Hindu, Buddhist or Taoist traditions).[4]

---

[4] Just how far the paradoxes of a God of one's own were from being confined to Judaism or Christianity is made clear by Navid Kermani in his discussion of *The Book of Adversity* by the Muslim poet Farīd ud-Dīn Attar, who lived in Nishapur, a town in the north-east of what is today Iran, at the end of the twelfth and the beginning of the thirteenth century.

> Probably because the God he depicts is unreliable, we find many of his verses affecting because of his attitude, which strikes the modern reader as enlightened or existentialist. He constantly emphasizes the individual's responsibility, and the psychological dimension of the creative process finds clearer expression here than in any other classical work of Persian literature. One entire chapter is devoted to an attack on fanaticism, and there are dozens of passages in which he makes the case for compassion, forbearance, brotherly love and such newly fashionable phenomena as religious pluralism, which, far from being merely tolerated, is praised as being better than riches. For a poet of the twelfth and thirteenth centuries, it is quite remarkable, perhaps even unique, to see how resolutely he stresses that the individual's responsibility is to experience personally the true nature of the Creator and to follow *His* ordinances not blindly but from his own free will. In Attar's eyes, imitation – *taqlid* – is almost as damning a word of abuse as dogmatism – *ta'assob*. The offspring of asses have simply not been created in order to follow the path of Sharia, he says; if they do follow that path we would know that they are blindly following their mother. Because the religious law was not

What is novel here, and a mark of the cosmopolitan constellation, is the simultaneous presence and availability of all (world) religions and cultural and spiritual symbolic worlds, from the 'most primitive' to the 'most modern', separated for the most part from their temporal and spatial context, and open to every conceivable appropriation and misappropriation throughout the world, including terrorist ones. Thus the processes of the individualization and cosmopolitization of religious faiths come together and merge in the concept of implicit or invisible religion (on this point see pp. 63ff. below).

Second, research in the sociology of religion shows that the religious revival movements outside the churches recruit their members not from among non-modernized social milieus, as might be supposed, but from highly modernized backgrounds that have been fully integrated into cultural and economic modernity.

On the basis of the existing empirical studies, Beckford and Levasseur (1986) conclude that in both Europe and the United States the supporters of the New Religious Movements are drawn from the ranks of young adults between the ages of 21 and 40 who have completed their education and frequently have a university qualification. They come from families that enjoyed an above-average degree of material comfort and economic security. In general, they have good career prospects as far as both income and professional advancement are concerned

> They belong among the more privileged both economically and culturally and their experience is constantly broadened by foreign travel. In short, their chances in life are above average and they

given to man as part of nature, no compulsion can take from him the need to choose to obey it. Such attitudes and in general his individual style of writing, of his way of looking at things and his convictions make him appear as a harbinger of modernity. The fact that these could have been so explicit and repeated so frequently in a text of the twelfth and thirteenth centuries points to the pervasiveness of the Sufi appropriation of the humanism that had emerged two centuries earlier under the Buyid dynasty in Baghdad. Attar evidently believed that this humanism was under threat since otherwise he would surely not have defended it with such anger. His fears were confirmed with the Mongol invasion, which razed the cities of the Islamic Orient to the ground and destroyed their cultures. Islamic culture has never really recovered from this catastrophe. Attar lived in the dying era of his own life-world. (Kermani 2008: 63) are unrepresentative of others in their age-group. Their social profile is clearly differentiated, according to Beckford, from that of recruits to the older wave of sectarian movements. And their membership of the cultured intelligentsia may well have been not the least important factor in helping their religious motives and adventures to find an echo in the public mind. (Hervieu-Léger 1999: 141–2, citing Beckford and Levasseur 1986; see also Barker 1989)

The authority principle underlying the revival of faith is the sovereign self. Secularization does not mean the demise of religion and faith, but instead the development and massive dissemination of a religiosity that is based increasingly on individualization. This process is part of a larger trend to revive faith in a society in which religious influences overlap and interpenetrate and whose fundamental preconditions include the artificially created uncertainty of a modernization that modifies its own premises (for 'reflexive modernization', see pp. 66ff. below).

This phenomenon can even be seen where many people would suppose it is least likely to be found, namely among American Jews, a fact revealed by Steven M. Cohen and Arnold M. Eisen.

American Jews at century's end . . . have come to view their Jewishness in a very different way than either their parents or they themselves did only two or three decades ago. Today's Jews, like their peers in other religious traditions, have turned inward in their search for meaning. They have moved away from the organizations, institutions, and causes that used to anchor identity and shape behavior. . . . The principal authority for contemporary American Jews . . . has become the sovereign self. Each person now performs the labor of fashioning his or her own self, pulling together elements from the various Jewish or non-Jewish repertoires, rather than stepping into an 'inescapable framework' of identity. . . . American Jews speak of their lives, and of their Jewish beliefs and commitments, as a journey of ongoing questioning and development. They avoid the language of arrival. There are no final answers, no irrevocable commitments. . . . The 'first language' that our subjects speak is by and large one of profound individualism. . . . Community – though a buzzword in our interviews, a felt need, even a real hunger for some – is a 'second language,' subordinate to the first. . . . The more committed and active among our sample told us repeatedly that they decide week by week, year by

year, which rituals they will observe and how they will observe
them. . . . The 'sacred canopy' (Peter Berger's famous term) no
longer overarches existence, and so the demand to choose and re-
choose identity (which Berger called the 'heretical imperative') is
inescapable. Nowhere have these processes been more evident than
among Jews. (Cohen and Eisen 2000: 2, 7)

The findings and interpretations of this study amount to a neither/
nor. They neither confirm the modern narrative of Enlightenment
and secularization which proclaims or predicts the decline of
religion, nor do they confirm expectations of a pre-existing, collective Jewish tradition and identity that are largely intact. The
voices that make themselves heard in this study attempt to link
their own individuality with their Jewishness by making a selection from old and new practices and texts, and by looking for
combinations that satisfy their own ideas of authenticity. To cite
the study's authors once again: 'Almost all our subjects, including
the most Jewishly active among them, knowingly and unknow-
ingly betrayed enduring ambivalence towards the organizations,
institutions, commitments and norms which constitute Jewish life:
families of origin, synagogues, federations, God' (ibid.: 9).

Pluralization strengthened by the growth of non-Christian religions

Talk of the 'return' of the religions has a further layer of meaning.
In daily life, but also in every sphere of society and politics, the
pluralization of the religions has come to replace the linear process
of secularization. This is one of the products of the great waves
of migration following the Second World War, since the course
of that migration was marked by the emergence of 'European
Muslims', an oxymoron for the Western European, secularized
Christian conception of itself. This process has been a defining
feature even in the major European states, where, despite the
growth of atheism, the populations are still marked by Christianity. Many millions of Muslims have been added to the population,
as can be seen from the birth statistics; the share of Muslims in
the growth of religiosity has been rising fast.

To pick out one key indicator, in Germany alone more than
160 mosques are currently being built or are at the planning stage

– a matter in which the general public, at local and national level, has taken the liveliest interest (to express the situation euphemistically). In a country such as Germany, where the outward appearance and indeed the glory of its cities and towns are strongly marked by their Christian churches, these changes have enormous symbolic significance because they are accompanied by the dramatic dismantling of the church-centred structure. In his sober report *The Future of the Church and Church Buildings in the Coming Decades*, Jürgen Lenssen, the canon of Würzburg, has provided an exemplary account of the catastrophic situation in his own diocese:

> On the one hand, we observe a progressive secularization process, with the consequence that there has been a sharp decline in church-going in the younger and middle-aged age groups and an almost complete absence of children. The reduction in the size of the congregation to about 10 per cent is by no means confined to a few localities, and every death causes a gap that can scarcely be filled any more because increasingly even the elderly are staying away from church. On the other hand, we see – though principally in the towns – the growth of a diffuse religiosity remote from Christianity of every kind. The clergy has a hitherto unprecedented preponderance of members over 60. Of the roughly 400 active priests (including retired ones), numbers will decline to around 250 over the next five years, and we are reckoning with a total of about 150 for the period after 2020. The fact that in 2008 only one deacon will be promoted to the rank of priest is clear evidence of the way the wind is blowing. The roughly 600 parishes will be combined into 180 parish associations, even though in the long run we shall not have enough priests able and willing to service even them. This means that weekly Sunday masses will no longer be guaranteed. . . . (Lenssen 2007: 2–3)

The fine phrase 'religious pluralization' understates the seriousness of the situation. In the public mind, the claim of second- and third-generation migrants to be, or to be on the way to becoming, 'German Muslims' or 'Muslim Europeans' constitutes a platform for a *fundamentally possible alternative life*. This platform amounts to a challenge to the basic assumptions of the Christian/atheist populations of the European nations and it naturally triggers anxieties. In the European mind, as we have noted, there is a causal connection between secularization and modernity. In the light of Turkey's aspiration to membership of the European Union, Western Europeans find themselves confronted by the confusing reality of an opposite causality: the more 'modern', or at least the more 'democratic', Turkish politics becomes, the more Muslim and the less secular it becomes. Turkey's claim to be simultaneously Muslim, modern and European throws European cultural essentialism into utter confusion.

What, for example, is the meaning of the much vaunted and much called-for '*institutional* integration of Muslims in Germany', in a country, in other words, in which the separation of church and state is still maintained, however artifically? Does it mean that Germany will soon see the emergence of an artificial state Islam (complete with Church tax and Radio Council) to place alongside an artificial state Christianity and an equally artificial state Judaism (Central Committee of Jews in Germany)? To put it another way, will German Muslims be subjected to a process of 'organizational assimilation' that is quite alien to their religion? Or, conversely, will the Christian churches soon meet up again on the other side of a prescribed freedom from church taxes (as in the United States) and have to re-orientate themselves accordingly?[5]

Viewed from this perspective, the heterogeneous nature of the grand coalition of conflicting interests that feeds Islamophobia in

---

[5] A similar question must be put in regard to secularism (*laïcité*) – the strict separation of church and state – in France. To non-religious persons this may seem to be the perfectly sensible arrangement. Viewed historically, however, secularism is the product of a struggle between atheist civil servants and the Catholic Church. '*Laïcité*' is not just anti-Muslim, it is also anti-Catholic. It has been generally forgotten that Catholics abandoned the state education system early on in the twentieth century. Now that Muslim immigrants experience this concept as hostile to them, the French state acts as if laicity were a fair deal. It is a deal, but with very high costs. There is now a giant system of private Catholic schools. Is it really sensible to compel Muslims to build up a similar system, abandoning the public schools? (On this question, see Appiah 2005.) [In Germany churches receive about 70 per cent of their funds from the proceeds of a church tax amounting to around 9 per cent of income tax paid, which is deducted by employers from their employees' wage packets. It is possible to gain exemption by claiming that one does not belong to a religious community. For their part, since the state charges for collection, small religious organizations may prefer to opt out of the system and collect money directly from members of the community. (Trans.)]

Europe is perhaps less surprising. The voices from the growing camp of xenophobes who are opposed to immigrants in general, the conservative defenders of Christian culture and civilization, the champions of a secular fundamentalism, as well as the Jeremiahs warning us about networks of Islamist terrorists – all these blend into a unified anti-Muslim discourse that pervades the European continent.

This discourse fails to recognize that the 'return' of religion in Europe does not mean a 'return' of traditional Islam, and that these forms of religious renaissance have put down *new* roots in the new situation they find themselves in *within* Europe. They are based on a *separation* between the Muslim religion and the culture of origin. The new Muslim self-image, which is expressed, for example, by young women wearing headscarves, and likewise the religious fundamentalism among Muslims in the West do not result from importing features of the original territorially based Muslim culture into the West. Rather, European Islam presupposes a 'deculturation of Islam' (Roy 2006: 129).

> Second and third generations tend to prefer the language of the guest country over that of their parents' home country, and they tend to speak better French than Arabic (when they speak Arabic at all), . . . and even, but far more slowly, German than Turkish [if indeed they speak correct Turkish and correct High German]. . . . Fast food is more popular than traditional cuisine. Moreover, fundamentalism is itself a tool of deculturation. . . . Contemporary fundamentalism, therefore, entails a disconnect of religious markers from cultural content. For instance, '*halal*' does not refer only to a traditional cuisine but describes any cuisine; hence, the flourishing of *halal* fast-food restaurants among born-again Muslims in the West, but few Moroccan or Turkish traditional restaurants. This disconnect means that the issue is not a clash of cultures between West and East, but the recasting of faith into what is seen as a 'pure' religion based on isolated religious markers. (Ibid.: 129)

As a number of empirical studies vividly show, what we are witnessing is the emergence in France, Germany and elsewhere of individualized forms of Muslim religiosity. The Muslim religion is being released from its territorially defined, national (North African, Turkish, Pakistani/Bangladeshi) social norms and constraints and transformed into a religiosity based on the decisions of individuals. Like American Jews (see pp. 29–30 above), European Muslims are gradually separating themselves from holy places, authorities and religious organizations and turning to a new spirituality characterized by a process of searching, selecting and combining that is carried out under the aegis of individual faith. Thus the individualization of religious practice is fast becoming a dominant feature of Muslim religiosity in Europe, one which makes possible the establishment of a cross-border community that is de-territorialized and preoccupied with the construction of an 'imaginary Ummah' (Beck-Gernsheim 2007; Schiffauer 2001; Tietze 2001, 2002).

What characterizes this Islamic religiosity is the fact that it

> cannot be traced back to socialization in a family originating in the Muslim world. On the contrary, it is the product of an emancipation of the individual from his family and their economic and social background. . . . This means that we can scarcely speak any longer of a 'Muslim existence' as a stable condition. Instead, we are dealing with Muslim experiences arising from an ongoing process of adapting the elements of the religious tradition to meet the challenges of constantly changing social circumstances. (Tietze 2002: 230)

What is striking is the very different situation and level of satisfaction of Muslims in America and Europe. A recent study (Pally 2007) found that 'European Muslims are noticeably poorer than the general population, they feel frustrated about their economic prospects and are socially isolated', whereas the majority of American Muslims declare that they feel at home in the USA because they can be both human beings and Muslims without having to hide or to assimilate.

This is the great difference between Europe and America. In Europe, and especially Germany, Muslims have to become 'integrated', only to discover that even if they satisfy all the relevant criteria, scarcely any economic and political doors are open to them. The United States, in contrast, was established on the principles of religious pluralism. The diversity of the religious confessions does not come as a shock but is felt to be part of everyday normality: for example, in the fact that the same job can be filled by members of very different religious communities. In the USA, people can display their religious allegiance in public while preserving their distinctive appearance *and* they can seize their opportunities in society and the economy *without* having to assimilate.

> Prejudices tend to disappear as participation rises. For a very long time no one was interested in disrupting a pragmatism based on the motto of live and let live. One consequence of this tacit agreement is what sounds like the paradox of a 'familiarity with otherness'. Since immigrants take part in America's economic and political life, Americans have grown accustomed to people of different kinds and have learned to distinguish between those that might harm the country and those that do no harm and may indeed bring benefits.
>
> By contrast, Europe is warier in its dealings with the adherents of different religions, requires a greater degree of assimilation, and provides a less permeable economy and political system. That means a lower participation rate and hence the host nation's lesser degree of familiarity with the otherness of others. As far as the immigrants are concerned, there is greater resentment towards their hosts and their new country, and a greater degree of resignation about involvement in politics and the economy. Acts of violence are possible and immigrants may well decide under certain circumstances to retain symbolic distinctions (see the headscarf controversy) – an ironic development in a society that finds it harder to accept such symbols because such distinguishing features are disturbing signs of otherness. (Ibid.)

In other words, in the final analysis America does not accept the distinction between native and foreigners. This is because the United States is a country open to immigrants and is thus unable to maintain that sort of distinction because all US citizens are both natives and foreigners. In Germany and Europe, in contrast, foreigners are automatically classified as non-natives even if they speak the host country's language perfectly and have a passport for that country. It is only when you divide people who are originally locals and incomers into 'opposing teams' that you encounter the 'problem of integration', which then becomes insoluble because the distinction between natives and foreigners is constantly reinforced and renewed by such things as names and appearance.

The problem of Islam in Europe is twofold. On the one hand, how far will it be possible to *decouple* the link between Islam and terrorism which is current at the present time? In other words, will it be possible to follow the American example and regard Islam in Europe as part of a cosmopolitan Europe (including, incidentally, in its foreign relations to such Islamic countries as Egypt and Indonesia)? Granting the Turkish application to join the EU is the litmus test here. On the other hand, the recognition of Islam means also the recognition of an *Islamic modernity*, both in European history in its activities in the shape of the 'Islamic Enlightenment' (Johann Gottfried Herder) and also in the struggle to connect Islam and modernity in Europe and beyond it, in the present and the future. If we consider the future of the Islamic world against the background of the concept of the 'axial age' (Jaspers, Eisenstadt), the recognition of religiously determined modernities may even be a matter of life and death. After all, the way we view the future of the religions depends on what we think of the fate of religiously determined multiple modernities in general.

A final point. In the post-communist, East European countries, we can perceive a further variant of the self-contradictory revival of the religions and the way in which they clash with secularist expectations in Western Europe. As we can see from the available data, it is undoubtedly true that following the collapse of the Soviet Union and its communist satellite states, there was a stark decline in the open acceptance of the church and the various religious practices for which data could be collected. Indeed, the figures are almost comparable with those documenting the West European trend towards secularization. At the same time, however, we have seen the emergence of a new, deeply grounded, collective Christian identity based on the fusing of religion and nation.

> In order to understand that collectivistic Christianities are a significant religious force operating in Europe, and in order to understand what these Christianities may do for the European Union, one needs to appreciate their key aspect: *belonging*. This belonging is specific, historically embedded, and – something that collectivistic Christianities share with Islam – public. Even if this belonging does not coincide with believing, as social scientists triumphantly declare, it has a different character than in Western European Christianity: it is rarely private and it is rarely de-institutionalized. (Jakelič 2006: 137)

The mass mediatization of religion: The phenomenon of Pope Benedict XVI

When we speak of the revival of religion in Europe we must also focus our attention on the following contradiction and attempt to decipher its meaning. On the one hand, there is a cataclysmic decline in the power of religion – fewer and fewer people go to church. On the other hand, there is simultaneously what amounts to an explosive expansion in church power, thanks to the interest aroused by a *mass-mediatization of the papacy* that literally transcends all frontiers.

Billions of people throughout the globe watched the progress of the semi-public death of Pope John Paul II. People all over the world watched spellbound the images of the Pope and listened to the voice emerging from his fragile body, proclaiming in the hours of his death that he, the dying Pope, felt joy at the prospect of meeting God. The universal search for the meaning of life and death received a straightforward, personal answer.

In other words, on the one hand, the churches in Central and Western Europe, both Protestant and Catholic, are in a terrible state, regardless of which indicators we use (loss of worshippers, age profile, financial situation, difficulty of finding a new generation of clergy, etc.). On the other hand, we have the 'Benedict phenomenon'.

With their powerful symbolism, the election and enthronement of Pope Benedict XVI respond to human yearnings: the liturgy develops tremendous force. It is the simple signs – bread, wine, light, colour, a shared meal – that unleash this magnetic force. As interpretations of our existence, they have grown up, acquired their shape and become dense with meaning over thousands of years. They are images that require no explanation to grip us with mystical power. The Pope's sermons are simple tales, not complicated theories. A man went forth from Nazareth two thousand years ago, told stories, and performed symbolic actions. This experience is handed down from generation to generation. This simplifying personalization can be conveyed much more directly than any scripture-based creed. The millions who respond to his sermon are the proof of this. (Weidenfeld 2005: 5)

This 'cosmopolitan event' fills no churches, nor does it put a stop to the decline in church membership. But it is a 'cosmopolitan event' that includes cultural others – religious and non-religious, baptized and non-baptized, heretics, atheists, fundamentalists, and so forth – not through coercion, but voluntarily, on the basis of a need for spirituality. And it points to the path that has long since been taken – by God in the age of His technical reproducibility (to adapt a phrase of Walter Benjamin's). The universal church, staged in an accessible way in the mass media, mobilizes the entire culture of subjective concerns. 'If the emotional effusions of religion are suspended like dense swathes of mist over a stone-cold society, there must be serious reasons for this. Evidently we live at a turning point in religious history' (ibid.). Catholicism celebrates a culture of the eye. Its globalization through the mass media makes possible a worldwide presence, participation without the formal membership that might bind together the free-floating waves of religiosity for at least a second at a time. In the process we see re-emerging the same questions that Benjamin had asked in his day. For example, there is the question of aura. To what extent does the atomized consumption served up by the mass media destroy the aura of the liturgy as it is normally experienced in the ritualized interaction of the faithful? Or is what we are witnessing a cultural critical reflex that simply refuses to see the worldwide inclusion of others?

Another example revealing the 'potential' of mass-mediatized, i.e. globalized, religious emotions can be found in the so-called 'cartoon controversy'. A provincial newspaper in Denmark published some cartoons caricaturing the Prophet Muhammad. After a certain time-lag, this triggered furious protests in the Gaza Strip, Libya, Saudi Arabia, Egypt, the Yemen, Pakistan, Syria, and even in Russia. This was followed by a worldwide debate about secularism, freedom, art, the dignity of religious others, religious fanaticism, tolerance, and so forth. All of this testifies to the *inflammatory* nature of religious conflicts in a global society, their texture thickened by the mass media. The real world of politics and society may continue to insist on its frontiers. That becomes very clear when we consider the mass deaths of refugees attempting to reach the EU by sea. In the mediatized worlds of mass communications, by contrast, social neighbourhoods have become separated from territorial ones. This experience of a universal neighbourhood without frontiers becomes the source of both hatred and violence (the cartoon debate), on the one hand, and cosmopolitan compassion (the mass-mediatized papacy), on the other.[6]

Multiple modernities, multiple forms of secularization

To sum up, we must answer the question: must we conclude that secularization theory (however we understand it) has utterly misinterpreted the place of religion in the ongoing modernization process? Many writers go so far as to bury secularization rather than religion (Stark and Finke 2000). However, between the death of religion and its antithesis, the death of the secular, there is a third broad alternative, one that has become increasingly influential among sociologists of religion. This is the question of a *non-linear* theory of modernization and secularization, which focuses on the multiple developmental pathways, phases and forms in their dependence on their historical contexts (e.g. Norris and Inglehart 2006).

Just as there are 'multiple modernities', so too there are 'multiple secularizations' (Martin 2005). Secularization theory is not completely false; it assumes different forms in different contexts – it means one thing in Western Europe and another in Eastern Europe, one thing in Latin America and another in Asia, Africa and in Turkey or Iran. In the United States and Africa it enters the thinking of elites, but not that of the mass of the population. Even within the United States, as in Western Europe, there are multiple secularizations rather than just one.

But what is the relation of secularization to individualization? Whereas secularization theory states the more modernization, the less religion, the thesis of religious individualization proceeds from the opposite assumption: that with increasing modernization, religions do not disappear but change their appearance. It is true that ties to organized religious communities are being loosened, just as the authority of the Fathers of the Church on existential questions is being weakened. But this should not be taken to mean that religious experiences and issues are of

[6] Other examples are the death of Princess Diana and the catastrophe of the tsunami in South-East Asia.

declining importance for individuals. 'On the contrary – the decline of *established religious institutions* goes hand in hand with a rise in *individual religiosity*' (Pollack and Pickel 2008: 604). In other words, individualization theory differentiates between (organized) religion and (individualized) faith in order to distinguish itself from secularization theory (see also pp. 48ff. below).

Detlef Pollack and Gert Pickel have subjected the religious individualization thesis to empirical quantitative tests, admittedly only with reference to Germany (both East and West). They reached the conclusion that the growth of individual, non-church religiosity does not compensate for the dramatic decline of institutionalized religion. 'Religious individualization is only a component of the predominant secularization process' (ibid.: 603; for a critique, see Wohlrab-Sahr and Krüggeler 2000). Interesting though this study is, its authors do not explain that when they speak of religion they mean the Christian churches that predominate in Germany. The growing numbers of German Muslims and Muslim Germans are simply excluded from the way they conceived their study. Yet in Germany of all places the return of religion to the public realm is being enacted against a background in which mosques are being built while churches are being closed. A similar situation obtains in other European countries. In Central Europe the thought of Islam unleashes cataclysmic visions that have given rise to a real wave of Islamophobia. For that reason it makes little sense to describe the trend towards secularization in Germany and Europe, let alone to extrapolate from it, while excluding the situation of Muslims both in Germany and in Europe more generally. This can be seen from various demographic data such as the birth rates for Christians and Muslims. In this context, it would have been interesting to know what effect it would have had on statements about secularization and individualization if the authors of the study had focused their attention on what German society as a whole (but evidently also some sociologists of religion) think of as the unusual combination of a German passport and the Muslim religion.

Be that as it may, given that we now live in a religiously mobilized world society, we must ask what potentials for conflict arise from Europe's pluralistically secularized societies, and what are the forces that drive them?

New forms of coexistence and conflict among the world religions: How are conflicts between world religions to be civilized?

What is the novel element in the religious dimension of the human condition at the beginning of the twenty-first century? One striking feature is the '*cosmopolitan constellation*', that is to say, the contact between the world religions and the New Religious Movements and their mutual interpenetration. The territorial exclusivity of religious *imagined communities* is coming to an end, and even where it still exists, the voices of the different religions collide with one another in a global society where communication knows no bounds.

We may also put it this way: in the new communicative thickness of the world, the *non-comparability* of religions based in national territories is coming to an end. That fact – a shared present and universal proximity – supplies the contemporary context of all religious belief systems and symbolic systems in which individualization becomes possible and necessary, and even acquires its meaning. And individualization here includes the choice of de-individualized religious attachment in the context of global religious plurality. This state of affairs is reflected in the growth of transnational forms of life in which comparisons between the world-pictures of the various religions and discussions of their relevance in everyday life act as an existential stimulus. Kiran Desai (2007) describes such a scene where religions are compared with each other in her novel *The Inheritance of Loss*:

> Sai eavesdropped . . . on Noni talking to the librarian about *Crime and Punishment*: 'Half awed I was by the writing, but half I was bewildered,' said Noni, 'by these Christian ideas of confession and forgiveness – they place the burden of the crime on the victim! If nothing can undo the misdeed, then why should sin be undone?'
>
> The whole system seemed to favor, in fact, the criminal over the righteous. You could behave badly, say you were sorry, you would get extra fun and be reinstated in the same position as the one who had done nothing, who now had both to suffer the crime and the difficulty of forgiving, with no goodies in addition at all. And, of course, you would feel freer than ever to sin if you were aware of such a safety net: sorry, sorry, oh so sorry.

Like soft birds flying you could let the words free.

The librarian, who was the sister-in-law of the doctor they all went to in Kalimpong, said: 'We Hindus have a better system. You get what you deserve and you cannot escape your deeds. And at least our gods look like gods, no? Like Raja Rani. Not like this Buddha, Jesus – beggar types.'

Noni: 'But we, too, have wriggled out! Not in this lifetime, we say, in others, perhaps. . . .'

Added Sai: 'Worst are those who think the poor should starve because it's their own misdeeds in past lives that are causing problems for them. . . .'

The fact was that one was left empty-handed. There was no system to soothe the unfairness of things; justice was without scope; it might snag the stealer of chickens, but great evasive crimes would have to be dismissed because, if identified and netted, they would bring down the entire structure of so-called civilization. (Desai 2007: 200)

This 'age of comparisons', as Nietzsche called it, can be characterized by three components: (1) the cosmopolitan constellation: this creates new forms and images – *imagined communities* – a global sociality determined by religion, and (2) unleashes the shock discovery that the European or Western model of the modern nation-state is not universal, in consequence of which (3) the question of how to civilize conflicts among the world religions has to be confronted.

'Imagined communities' of a religiously determined global sociality

The contribution of religion to the images of society in the first modernity, that of the nation-state, consists, on the one hand, of the fusing of nation and religion as we see it expressed in 'secular nationalism' or in the national 'civil religions'. No doubt, these still are, as they always have been, prominent vectors of religiously coloured collective identities. But in globalization we see the formation of a new, religiously determined, global sociality in which increased significance is attached to transnational, religious *imagined communities* which complement, and enter into competition and conflict with, the institutionalized forms of national societies and national institutions.

This reminds us of Samuel Huntington's thesis of a 'clash of civilizations'. Huntington's inference is premature. He conceives of the 'civilizations' determined by the world religions as *territorial units*, on the analogy with nation-states and imperial superpowers, and this leads him to predict future global conflicts along religious lines. The reverse is true. At the beginning of the twenty-first century, it is the *dissolution* of this territorial unity of religion, nation and society that is the source both of the opportunities open to the world religions and of the threats facing them. Globalization offers the ancient world religions – but not only them – the opportunity to break free from the territorial constraints of the nation-state and to discover the transnational, transethnic dimension grounded in their history but submerged by the nation-state, and to give that dimension new life. At the same time, however, this produces a new threat because globalization presupposes and also encourages the de-territorialization of all cultural systems. In other words it dissolves the essential bonds of tradition, peoples and territories that have defined the world-religious civilizations (that Huntington has in mind) in the past.

The shock of discovering that the European or Western model of modernity is not universal

With the encounter of the world religions with the New Religious Movements and their interpenetration, we see a breakdown of the universalist claims of the two great European cultures: the Christian faith and secular rationality. This applies also to the universalist claims of other religions, that of Muslim universalism, for example, the 'Ummah'. Thus it is not just differences between the religions that have such huge potential for conflict, but the imploding of contextually shaped universalisms and hence too of social and moral certainties forced together in the global space.

The consequences can be seen in the social conflicts emerging on a global scale: there is little agreement about such matters as the standardization of attitudes towards sex, the value of individual liberty and autonomy (as opposed to the value placed on the community), the rights of animals or the natural environment, to say nothing of the urgency of the terrorist threat. Even the threats posed by the man-made climate catastrophe or the question of the value of human life are still controversial issues for the great religions. Anyone who feared the emergence of a secular monoculture can breathe freely once more. The opposite threat is more alarming: that with the demise of secular universalism the foundations of rationality might be destroyed, since if that were so, it would undermine all efforts to civilize the potentials for conflict among the world religions in a global society. The threat that is ultimately conjured up by the death of secular hope is the rebirth of religious warriors and religious wars – only now these wars would be fought out in the suicidal age of nuclear weapons and gene technology! This was a threat that had been overcome, so we all imagined, by the advances of secularized modernity.

How to civilize conflicts among the world religions

At the start of the twenty-first century, the potential for conflict and violence among the world religions has ceased to be a matter of merely national importance. It is now a universal problem, one for which up to now no institutional solutions have been discovered. Today, in the late phase of modernity, we are no longer concerned with the question that was of burning interest in the early modern period: how can we prevent wars of religion within Christianity (Catholicism and Protestantism)? The question that counts today is: how are we to civilize the global potential for conflict between the monotheistic world religions? By placing God in quarantine, the constitutional nation-state may have come up with a suggestive idea, but because it is a nation-state and not a global state, it lacks a real answer.

This can be demonstrated by comparing the class conflicts at the start of the first modernity of industrial capitalism and the global religious conflicts at the inception of the second, globalized modernity. As is well known, Karl Marx subordinated nation to class. His social theory made it clear that the greatest problem facing the future of nation-states would arise from class conflicts that transcended national frontiers. An international workers' movement was beginning to appear on the political horizon and this opened up the prospect of a world revolution. Marx's ideas triggered panic in the nation-state. Its response was to treat the class problem that had grown out of the upheavals caused by industrialization as a problem *within* the nation-state. In this way, transnational class dynamics were transformed into numerous separate national 'social questions', and, following this, the integration of the proletariat into the different nation-states rose to the top of the political agenda. This task had such high priority that distinct concepts such as socialism, the welfare state or, on the plane of academic studies, the sociology of class all sought solutions on the tacit assumption that the framework of the nation-state was to be accepted. The success of this stratagem was such that national integration and solidarity were both treated as the presupposition of class order and at the same time became unrecognizable.[7]

The global religious conflicts at the start of the twenty-first century, by contrast, frustrate from the outset any piecemeal solution to 'social problems' by confining them to the context of national churches or nation-states. This is the point at which the kindred utopias of national communism, social democracy and the welfare state let us down, since their prospects appear increasingly hopeless. This means that there are no state agencies to curb global religious conflicts and there is no historical film script to ensure that the sacrifices and costs of civilization can be transformed into opportunities for all on the basis of a consensus. But since external authorities are unavailable at the level of the global state, and indeed are undesirable, we must pose the question with which we introduced this study: how, given the new thick texture of the world, will it be possible to achieve the *self*-civilizing of contradictory religious certitudes operating on a world scale, the *self*-civilizing of monotheistic global conflicts? Two answers will be rehearsed in this book. This civilizing process can be achieved (a) through the irony of the unforeseen consequences of the individualization of religion; (b) by means of a new type of tolerance whose goal is not truth but peace.

The irony of the unforeseen consequences of the individualization of religion

This approach can be elucidated with reference to Max Weber's *The Protestant Ethic and the Spirit of Capitalism* 1974[1905]. We

[7]Today, in the light of accelerating global inequalities, national frontiers have ceased to do what they once promised, namely to ensure that understanding and solidarity came to a full stop at the garden gate of the nation. Now a further danger threatens. This is that the hope that the national welfare state would civilize the global exclusion of the poor and 'superfluous' is about to disintegrate.

may recall how in the early modern age the 'spirit' of capitalism emerged as an unintended consequence of the affirmation of religious individualism. Similarly, we may inquire at the start of the twenty-first century whether the 'cosmopolitan' spirit of global society can conceivably arise from the radical affirmation of the individualization of faith – likewise as its unintended consequence. And what significance must we attribute in this process to the cosmopolitan, religious, 'imagined communities' already mentioned?

The question of the type of tolerance whose goal is not truth but peace

Secularists may hope that the fires burning in the religions, and hence also in religious conflicts, will be extinguished by the advance of modernization. But if these hopes for the globalizing religions and the New Religious Movements are disappointed, will that not mean their liberation once and for from all the constraints that make a civilized coexistence possible? The task, then, would be to elaborate a framework of norms and (procedural) rules that would contain the conditions for the world religions to live and work together, even if that framework neither can nor should survive for ever or be valid for every context. This raises in principle the question of the type of toleration 'whose goal is not truth but peace' (Gray 2007: 208).

Those who regard truth as the supreme goal of tolerance do indeed aspire to consensus and harmony. But they simultaneously condemn and even damn all those who refuse to bow to this 'truth'. In contrast, those who see that consensus and harmony are neither realistic as goals nor are they even all that desirable find themselves confronting a problem: how is 'cosmopolitan tolerance' to be achieved, beyond all universalisms? And what contributions to it can be expected from the world-religious movements and their adherents? This process of self-civilization on the part of the world religions does not amount to political action but it is highly significant from the point of view of global politics. 'It is the only Holy War which religion may and indeed must call for, the inner struggle with whatever stands in the path of peace' (Kamphaus 2007: 7).

3

Tolerance and Violence
The Two Faces of the Religions

The broad-brush picture of the religious landscapes we painted in the previous chapter resembles the one drawn by Michel de Certeau and Jean-Marie Domenach (1974). As in a late Kandinsky painting, it looks as though the components of the European religious universe had 'departed from their proper course with each component following its own pathway, drifting off and then finding itself tied into a different use, just as if the words of a sentence had been scattered over the page, only to be recombined into a different set of meanings' (Certeau and Domenach 1974: 126; quoted by Hervieu-Léger 2004: 147). This means (1) that we cannot avoid raising the whole issue of the definition of religion in this chapter. What is meant by religion if the frontier with non-religion has become blurred and the object of quarrels about definition? This is the foundation on which (2) the sociological theory of religion that informs this book is presented: 'Individualization and cosmopolitization: religion in the context of reflexive modernization.'

What does 'religion' mean?

Every analysis of religion, whether it be undertaken from a historical, sociological, political or theological perspective, must be informed by two principles. On the one hand, it must distinguish clearly between the analysis and the practice of religion; on the other, it must strive for an understanding of the meaning of religion for believers and non-believers in different societies and in the world community. A critical sociology of religion cannot concern itself with the evaluation of specific beliefs and practices (even though fundamentalist atheisms have recently taken to making precisely such judgements). Its task must be to uncover the dual nature of the meanings and functions (manifest or latent) of the religions for people's individual social and political existences.

Religion, religious

The difficulties facing current definitions of religion are many and various. I wish to single out only two. In the first place, a definition of religion must be broad enough to go beyond the historical religions and include the diverse new spiritual and religious movements that can boast of growing numbers of 'believers' both inside and outside religion itself. Second, a definition of religion must take account of religious differentiation: in other words, it must make it possible to focus attention on the similarities and differences between religions and within them. Traditions have not been fixed once and for all; they are not monolithic. What we find, rather, is a complex of intertwined and contrasting symbols, myths and rituals that change over longer or shorter time-spans, either for external reasons, i.e. their need to adjust to changing circumstances, or for reasons internal to themselves. If our studies fail to shed light on this complexity and diversity within and between seemingly fixed 'religions', we shall all too easily overlook the fact that people who regard themselves as belonging to different religious traditions often have more in common with one another than with their fellow 'brothers and sisters in faith', with whom they naturally assume an identity of views. In periods of latent or open individualization, this point gains an enhanced significance both inside and outside the churches. Through a comparative analysis of oneself and others, believers may well discover beliefs in themselves whose presence they criticize in others. In an age characterized by an intensified miscegenation and polarization of both religious and political beliefs, this is an important insight whose significance goes well beyond that of academic concerns with definitions.

In the meantime, it has become almost a truism to point out that the concept of religion itself has a *Eurocentric bias* (Haußig 1999). That is to say, as the product of the Western mind, it is projected onto the religious life and experience of other, 'alien' cultures and continents. The very question 'what is religion?' presupposes an understanding of communities clearly distinguishable from religion and to which one either does or does not belong. This finding is strengthened by reflecting on the choice of words: *religion* is treated as a *noun*, which implies a clearly demarcated social set of symbols and practices that constitute an either/or. You have only the choice of believing or not believing them, and, as a member of a faith community, you cannot belong to another such community at the same time.

This background understanding of 'religion' is doubtless *monotheistic*, i.e. it is based on the premise that each person can choose one God and one God alone, and must exclude all others. Such exclusivity, however, was not just alien to the religious views of the ancient world; it is also inapplicable to non-monotheistic religious traditions in Africa, Asia and Latin America today. Above all, it blocks the path to an understanding of what we saw (in Chapter 2, above) as the key question about the extent to which the age of individualization is also the age of do-it-yourself religions.

For this reason it is essential and also meaningful to maintain a distinction between *religion* and *religious*, between religion as noun and as adjective (Esposito, Fasching and Lewis 2006: 5–6; Simmel 1922). As a noun, 'religion' organizes the religious field according to an either/or logic. The adjective 'religious', by contrast, organizes it according to a 'both/and' logic. To be religious does not presuppose membership (or non-membership for that matter) of a specific group or organization; it signifies a specific *attitude* towards the existential questions of humanity in the world. The noun 'religion' starts from the image of one of the separate spheres of action with clearly defined boundaries (economics, science, politics and even religion itself). The adjective 'religious' takes account of the amorphousness and absence of boundaries of the religious sphere, and hence enables the *syncretist alternative* to the monotheistic noun 'religion' to enter our purview.

Religion is globalization from the outset

If we attempt to identify the fundamental difficulty in providing a (sociological) definition of religion, we encounter the naïve question: '*What, religion, is your attitude to the alien nature of the world, to the actual and possible frontiers between us and others?*'

I have tried to develop the theme of the 'original globalization' of religion in a conversation with Johannes Willms:

> Let us try to follow out the implications of this question in connection with the Catholic Church. A similar argument can be made for the other world religions, but let's play it through with the church. The Catholic Church has been a *global player* from its beginnings. Unlike political parties or unions, it didn't need nation-state capitalism to come into existence and it doesn't face the problems they do in overleaping its boundaries. They have all internalized their methodological nationalism. This is not true of Catholicism. According to its fundamental message, the Christian faith is not bound to ethnic and national differences, or even to the distinction between man and woman. Instead, it is predicated on Christian brotherhood and hence an image of mankind, a humanity that transcends all borders and that therefore possesses a fundamentally cosmopolitan structure.
>
> Before I start sounding like a convert, I have to point out that this foundational cosmopolitanism has been based on a grave defect ever since the beginning, which is that to be recognized as a brother or sister, you have to be of the faith, you have to be a Christian. Equality prevailed only on the assumption of a generally accepted sameness. Not the other or the stranger, but only the similar person was accepted into the transnational fraternity, even though we know that brothers have some pretty long-running difficulties with their sisters. In other words, you had to be baptized, i.e. belong, in order to belong. Otherwise, you might easily risk getting killed. This is why when we speak of the church being a 'global player' in times gone by, the first things that come to many people's minds are the wars of religion, the violent intolerance of dissenters and the wake of worldwide devastation that followed the imperialist drive to convert other people.
>
> So the Christian concept of humanity has left an ambivalent legacy. It is a transethnic and transnational system of faith that is also precisely not a recognition of the other in his otherness.

But even so, there is a long institutional experience of existing as part of a global, multiethnic world society. It was out of that history that the church developed its form of organization. It transcends states and borders, and disregards (at least in principle) everything that nation-states regard as central, such as borders and the principle of excluding other nationalities, skin colours, and political persuasions. The church still preserves in its collective memory the idea that humanity is not determined by these oppositions, but by their overcoming. (Beck and Willms 2004: 207–8)

Globalization, then, is not the product of powerful economic, political and mass-media developments at the start of the twenty-first century; it is no belated, external, optional characteristic. Globalization, more accurately the question of the *multiple, contradictory frontier-regime* of religion, has been part of the essence, or, less pompously, of the definition of religion from the very beginning.[1] I therefore propose to make this insight the connecting thread in the search for a solution to the problem of finding a definition of religion. As shall become evident later on, this points to a specific aspect of 'reflexive modernization', my heuristic approach. In accordance with that approach, a key task facing the sociologist of religion is to explore religious interpretations of the salvation of the individual's soul (or the soul of humankind as a whole) both in this world and in the next with a view to discovering how profound transformations of both individuals and societies can be achieved by a huge effort of the imagination; by discovering, in short, how *to abolish boundaries between people and cultures and simultaneously to construct new ones*. The religions thus find themselves suspended between tolerance and violence, and it is this fundamental ambivalence that now moves into the centre of attention.

---

[1] For this reason we must distinguish here (although we can only touch on this) between the 'original globalization' (which is part of the core definition of some religions) and the role of religions in 'the global age' (Albrow 1996). It is in the latter case that the 'frontier politics' of religion has to be invoked in a modern world in which frontiers have been eliminated by a globalized economy and globalized communication technologies.

Key features of religion: Erase boundaries, overcome boundaries, establish boundaries

How does religion or religiosity deal with the otherness of others? Where social distinctions exist, religion establishes one absolute criterion: *faith* – all other distinctions seem insubstantial in comparison. The New Testament asserts: 'We are all equal in the sight of God.' This equality, this elimination of the boundaries between people, groups, societies and cultures, is the social foundation of the (Christian) religions. The consequence is that just as distinctions between the political and the social are obliterated, so too, and with the same absoluteness, a new fundamental distinction and sense of hierarchy is introduced into the world – the distinction between believers and non-believers. 'Non-believers', according to the logic of this duality, are denied the status of human beings. Religions can build bridges between human beings where hierarchies and frontiers exist; at the same time, they open up new, religion-based chasms between human beings where none existed previously. This ambivalence of tolerance and violence can be understood more precisely as the combination of three theoretical components. World religions *overcome social hierarchies* and frontiers between nations and ethnicities. They are able to do so where they give birth to a *religious universalism* which rises above all national and social barriers. This may be achieved at the cost of replacing ethnic, national and class barriers with *barriers between believers and heretics* or unbelievers.

Overcoming pre-existing hierarchies and boundaries. The monotheistic religions come to terms with the otherness of other religions in ways that differ fundamentally from the model of vertical differentiation. In that model the attempt is made to transform social otherness into a hierarchical relation of superiority and inferiority. The principle of hierarchy, the exclusion and devaluation of others, has led to the formation of highly differentiated systems of social classes and castes. The same principle was also used to define relations with other societies. What is characteristic here is the way in which 'others' are denied the status of equality of kind and rank and are categorized as subordinate or inferior. In extreme cases they are treated as 'barbarians' without rights of their own. The same thing cannot be said of societies based on religion; these abolish distinctions that everyday, sociological realism shares and regards as (more or less) immutable. How can that be possible?

Religious universalism. Religious universalism represents the counter-principle to the hierarchical subordination of others. Both as an image of humanity and as a mission, universal Christianity elevates frontier-transcending to the status of a programme. According to Scripture, believers are liberated by their faith from all earthly powers and inequalities. Their 'society' is based on the Kingdom of Heaven, which transcends all worldly concerns, not least all individual nation-states, all class distinctions of rich and poor, men and women, young and old. It is in this spirit that St Paul states: 'There is neither Jew nor Greek, slave nor free, male nor female' (Galatians 3, 28). Worldly distinctions pale beside the one and only point of view: the eternal salvation of the individual and his or her soul. According to the Tübingen theologian Ottfried Höffe, 'With this statement the New Testament achieves a significant approach to the concept of human rights because the covenant with God is open to every human being and thus divests itself of every ethnocentric limitation.' That was universality on the basis of a faith community and it led both to 'anti-popular tendencies' and an 'anti-family' ethos. Sociologically, this meant that the original cells of religious faith, such as people and family, were subordinated or even dissolved. Thus Christianity 'no longer had room' for the large family units of antiquity with their religious, political, economic and sometimes aristocratic elements. Indeed, 'with the victory of Christianity the family as a cultural entity actually disappeared'. The New Testament explicitly fixes its gaze on the constant threats involving foreigners and violence and issues a challenge that is diametrically opposed to normal behaviour: 'Love your enemies' (Angenendt 2007: 193).

The political significance of this religious universalism has become visible, for example, in the US presidential elections. Barack Obama, the black candidate for the presidency, told his enthusiastic listeners: 3 January is the day when 'America remembered what it means to hope', and he ended with the words: 'We are ready to believe again!' In the church that Obama regularly attends, the pastor, Dr Jeremiah Wright, an apostle of black liberation theology, delivers sermons on how 'the African diaspora' struggles under the yoke of the 'white supremacists' who run the

'American empire', and preaches in support of salvation, which is not far off:

> The good news that's coming is for all people! Not white people – all people. Not black people – all people. Not rich people – all people. Not poor people – all people. I know you'll hate this . . . not straight people – all people! Not gay people – all people. Not American people – all people. . . . Jesus came for Iraqis and Afghanis. Jesus was sent for Iranians and Ukrainians. All people! Jesus is God's gift to the brothers in jail and the sisters in jeopardy. The Lord left his royal courts on high to come for all those that you love, yes, but he also came for those folk you can't stand. (Raban 2008: 21)

When Wright says 'white racists', Obama talks about 'corporate lobbyists'; when Wright speaks of 'blacks', Obama says 'hard-working Americans', or 'Americans without healthcare' (ibid.). But the political promise that Obama represents follows the same pattern as Wright's sermon; it is the pattern of a secularized religious universalism that seeks to inspire the voters and re-awaken the American Dream with such words as 'hope' and 'change'.

The dualism of good and evil. The seed of religiously motivated violence lies in the universalism of the equality of believers which withholds from non-believers what it promises to believers: dignity for fellow human beings and equality in a world of strangers. The humanitarian 'we' of believers is based on identification with God *and* on the demonizing of the enemies of God, who, as St Paul and Luther put it, are the 'agents of Satan' (Pagels 1995: 180). The existence or non-existence of humanity depends on a ruinous game in which all existence hinges on the individual decision in favour of belief, all non-existence on the decision not to believe. Whoever declares him- or herself in favour of belief will be saved. Whoever neither will nor can believe will be damned – in this world and the next. The distinction between 'we' and the 'others' becomes emotionally charged by the cosmic struggle between the 'powers of good' that have to overcome the 'powers of evil' if the world is to be saved. In this way, the absolute nature of the one-and-only monotheistic God creates an entire world of 'others' who have to be combated. Brutes and subhumans of every type – labels such as heretics, heathen, apostates, idolaters, renegades, etc., abound (see Angenendt 2007; Assmann 2003, 2007) – they are the flip side, the dark side, and the violent side with whose assistance universal Christianity conjures up a transethnic humanity.

By committing themselves to universalism, the world religions create a hierarchy of superiority and inferiority which results in a radical otherness. This occurs because it is rooted in the dualism of believers and unbelievers, not as a pre-existing fact but to be understood as the consequence of a choice, ascribable to individuals.[2] This means the distinction between 'we' and 'others' fuses with the distinction between Good and Evil.

> What fascinates us about Satan is the way he expresses qualities that go beyond what we ordinarily recognize as human. Satan evokes more than the greed, envy, lust, and anger we identify with our own worst impulses, and more than what we call brutality. . . . Thousands of years of tradition have characterized Satan instead as a spirit. Originally, he was one of God's angels, but a fallen one. Now he stands in open rebellion against God, and in his frustrated rage, he mirrors aspects of our own confrontations with otherness. (Pagels 1995: xvii)

Judgements based on the distinction between good and evil are radical insofar as we feel ourselves called upon to construct a relationship of inclusion with *or* exclusion from others. Anyone who labels people and groups and cultures or religions 'good' or 'evil' opens up new chasms in global civil society and creates unbridgeable gulfs, thereby changing human beings into monsters. Evil is construed as an absence, as the manifestation of God's absence. It points to actions and thoughts that are inconceivable, beyond the possibility of any justification. Indeed, evil even transcends the concept of crime since crimes can be imagined; they can be cast in legal forms and hence 'normalized'. To talk of evil is to question the humanity of others.

That is the concern that is becoming pervasive: the fear that as the flip side of the failure of secularization, we are threatened by a new dark age.

[2] This does not just hold good for the age of individualization, as might be supposed. For, *in principle*, if not also *de facto*, it is not the individual's origin that constitutes the community of Christians, but his or her freely taken decision to believe in God (see Chapter 4).

Three examples: Colonialism, mixed marriages, Catholic cosmopolitanism

Colonialism. In colonialism the dark side of Christian universalism has become a reality. Colonialism is in actual fact as old as civilization; it is an integral part of the history of almost all religions and civilizations, in the East as in the West. But of course, modern Western colonialism came closer to the goal of global dominance envisaged by universal Christianity than any other colonial movement. Unimaginable violence and cruelty were able to legitimize themselves by enlisting the aid of the concept of unbelievers who needed to be converted for the sake of their souls. All opposition, and especially the religious world-view, values and rituals of the colonized, was destroyed by the amalgam of conquest and missionary work. With Columbus the role of domination in the dialectic of believers and unbelievers emerges undisguised. He defended the principle that 'those who are not already Christians can only be slaves' (cited in Angenendt 2007: 468). There is a paradoxical combination consisting of a formally free decision to accept baptism, (the threat of) force and the 'missionary school', which together are supposed to set in motion an individual and social modernization process.

> In the 'Requirimiento', a law passed in 1513, this programme was given juridical form. It was read out to the Indios and in this way the conquest was represented as theologically legitimate, as a 'just war'. An abbreviated catechism describing the history of the creation of the world and salvation at the hands of Jesus Christ was followed by a lecture on the authority of St Peter, to whom all power, lordship and jurisdiction in the world had been confided, as well as further guidance about the authority of the Pope, who had donated certain lands in America to the King of Spain, lands whose inhabitants were now his vassals. (Angenendt 2007: 467)

The brazen cynicism sugared with benevolence with which the natives are called upon to exercise a 'free' choice in favour of Catholicism can scarcely be surpassed.

> Wherefore, as best we can, we ask and require that you consider what we have said to you, and that you take the time that shall be

necessary to understand and deliberate upon it, and that you acknowledge the Church as the ruler and superior of the whole world, and in her name, the High Priest, known as the Pope, as the Lord and Master of this island and this continent by virtue of the above-mentioned donation, and whether you are willing to agree that the monks assembled here should explain what has been said and proclaim it. If you act in accordance with this, you will act rightly and will fulfil your duty; in that case His Majesty and I shall treat you with love and kindness and shall let your wives and children free and shall not press them into service. . . . In that event, we shall not compel you to become Christians. . . . But if you do not do this, and maliciously make delay in it, I certify to you that, with the help of God, we shall powerfully enter into your country, and shall make war against you in all ways and manners that we can . . . we shall take you, and your wives, and your children, and shall make slaves of them, and as such shall sell and dispose of them as their highnesses may command. (Reinhardt 1985: 64; quoted in Angenendt 2007: 467–8)

'Be on your guard against mixed marriages!' The imperialist vision by which the world is constructed – the inclusion of the 'good', the exclusion of the 'evil' (a vision reciprocated by and on behalf of the religious others concerned) – can be seen very clearly in the case of the 'mixed-marriage wars' between Catholic and Protestant men of God and their followers in Germany (but also in other countries) in the nineteenth and twentieth centuries. '[In the nineteenth century] mixed marriage was the principal source of conflict between Catholicism and Protestantism; it was *the* bone of contention in a Germany marked by profound religious divisions' (Bendikowski 2002: 215). This disagreement is particularly illuminating because it shows how equals were turned into enemies by the militantly confrontational stance adopted by the different denominations. Catholic and Protestant communities mutually attacked and excluded one another as unbelievers and, in defiance of the growing equality of the nation, ensured that hatred and contempt were constantly reinforced by inflammatory speeches and actions. The tolerance of others at the national level appeared to be a 'threat' and had to be combated by the institutionalized intolerance of religious others. And this conflict went deeply into questions of marriage and the bringing up of children.

In particular, both Catholics and Protestants regarded the notion of allowing the other denomination any control over children's education as the betrayal of one's own religion.

> Whoever possesses not just the name of a Protestant Christian, but also the Protestant faith, for whose sake thousands once died a martyr's death, knows what this faith is worth. . . . Whoever abandons his children to the Catholic Church from indifference or for the sake of some worldly good gravely sins not only against their souls, but also ceases to be a Protestant Christian himself; he can no longer permit God's Word to dwell in his house; nor can he and his worship his God and Saviour in the spirit and in truth. (*Evangelisches Gemeindeblatt für Rheinland und Westfalen*, No. 18, 3 May 1885: 167; cited by Bendikowski 2002: 228–9)

> The core of such stories contained the burden of the message 'Be on your guard against mixed marriages!', the title of a prize-winning pamphlet written by the Silesian parson Adolf Fauth and published by the Protestant press association in Silesia. By 1885 it had already appeared in a second edition. In it the man of God warned young people against taking a fatal step: 'Experience teaches us again and again that mixed marriages do not lead to a quiet life but are the source of endless strife. Such action hurls the torch of dissension into the midst of peace-loving families. Such marriages have sown dissension in communities in which Catholics and Protestants have lived together in harmony for many a long year. . . . I tell you on the basis of years' experience: if you enter upon a mixed marriage you must prepare yourself for a life full of trouble and strife, even if you are the most irenic man in the world. . . . I have often been told frankly by both men and women, Protestants and Catholics: "If we had to decide on this again, we would never agree to enter into a mixed marriage! We knew not what we did." Hence take note, dear Protestant Christian: "Be on your guard against mixed marriages!" '. (Cited by Bendikowski 2002: 230)

Mixed marriages frequently led to court cases in which the law was asked to offer plaintiffs protection from 'religious violation' (ibid.: 231). The upshot was that both sides – Catholics as well as Protestants – were constantly striving to erect and maintain a regime of religious apartheid. This brought a kind of unity to the hostile churches: 'Hence we are in agreement in our repudiation and combating of mixed marriages' (ibid.: 235).

Not until 1968 do we find Uta Ranke-Heinemann referring to 'so-called mixed marriages'. This is followed in the 1970s by the expression 'interdenominational marriage', and since the 1980s people have begun to talk in the best ecumenical manner of 'marriages linking the denominations' (ibid.: 216). We see here how through the progress of secularization an age-old invisible and seemingly immutable 'Iron Curtain' has gradually been eroded.

The denominational fundamentalism that is unable to see and acknowledge the Christian in the 'unbeliever' is increasingly rejected by active believers.

> The need for Christian churches to define themselves against one another encounters diminishing support across the board. It may be supposed that such attitudes can bank less and less on the approval of believers. Daniel Deckers has hit the nail on the head when he speaks of a 'reversal of the burden of proof' in the context of ecumenical cooperation: people have more explaining to do when cooperation is absent than when it is present. (Joas 2007a: 983)

Catholic cosmopolitanism. It is difficult to identify the elements of a cosmopolitan religiosity that are effective *in practice* – particularly after a consideration of colonialism and mixed marriage (and setting all confessions of faith and promises to one side). We have the formula *urbi et orbi* – 'church of the nations', 'church of strangers'. In Wilhelminian Germany, Catholics had to put up with being abused as 'traitors to their country', a badge of honour in reality because it expressed their distance from and in part even their resistance to the ethnic nationalism that subsequently became mass-murderous state racism. Be that as it may, at least some Catholics fought the idea of 'Hitler as Reformer' (a slogan proclaimed by Protestant worshippers of the nation in contrast to a Catholicism that was regarded as disloyal to the nation and subservient to the Pope).

Christian communities of different denominations have not been backward in demonstrating their committed cosmopolitanism, and they have taken on the task of standing up for the rights of people who have been stripped of all their rights – that is to say, so-called 'illegal immigrants'. Such actions are in the tradition of the church as an asylum, but it has also long been part of the practice of Christian groups and communities. For example, they offer help to the migrants coming from Mexico who have to overcome the high security of the US frontier but also the desert conditions alongside the frontier where many would-be incomers are at risk of dying of thirst. These Christian groups have systematically set up and continue to maintain drinking-water facilities – in the face of state persecution and frequently the hostility of nationalistically minded Christians.

If we ask which organizations in Germany stand for appropriate or enlightened attitudes on such key questions as migration and multiculturalism, rather than look to the major parties, the SPD or the CDU/CSU, to say nothing of the trade unions, we will have much better luck with charity organizations like Caritas and many of the clergy, both Catholic and Protestant. Gertrud Höwelmeier, who has produced an ethnographic study *Nuns at the Airport: Cosmopolitans in Transethnic Religious Organizations*, summarizes her findings as follows:

Even though the Catholic Church had a 'global' outlook in its origins, it can be said to have undergone a further change in its public role in the world following the resolutions of the Second Vatican Council. The Catholic Church became more politically conscious, above all in its forthright commitment to the expansion of global civil society. This opening to the world was not without its effect on the faithful, on priests and not least on the religious orders, in particular those of religious women. The majority of these organizations date back to the nineteenth century and their mission was principally to help the poor in Europe and the United States. At that period and up to the Second Vatican Council, their outlook cannot properly be called 'cosmopolitan'. A cosmopolitan outlook among Catholic nuns began to emerge after the Second Vatican Council, when the Catholic Church began to globalize itself in a novel way, above all by encouraging people from non-Western nations to become involved in the Catholic Church. Missionary zeal and conversion to Catholicism ceased to be the chief interest. Tolerance towards other faiths, on the other hand, now moved to the top of the agenda. From the 1960s on, women from Africa, Latin America and Asia joined congregations in Western countries, converting them into genuine transnational communities. Sisters began to transform Christian humanism from welfare for the poor into active aid to the world in general. The kind of cosmopolitanism they represented implied a new awareness of problems of class and caste within and between nation-states, the growth of poverty in the world, but also the need to deal with cultural distinctions on equal terms, including the difficulty of combining unity and diversity, as well as the sensitivity to racism. . . . Whoever recognizes 'cosmofeminism' as an integral part of the debate on cosmopolitanism enlarges the prospects for global justice and human dignity. (Höwelmeier 2006: 9)

How is a separation of powers to be effected in the realm of the absolute?

In his book *Die mosaische Unterscheidung oder der Preis des Monotheismus* ['The Mosaic Distinction or the Price of Monotheism], Jan Assmann blames monotheism for the fundamental ambivalence of the world religions. The religious downgrading of the other and the use of force in religion starts with the 'Mosaic Distinction': in other words, the 'distinction between true and false in religion' (Assmann 2003: 12). This claim of revealed truth to absolute validity is what brings into being the evil that has to be combated, namely the unbelievers who have made their decision against the 'truth'. According to Assmann, this applies in the first instance to Judaism, but is subsequently extended to include Christianity and Islam. Together with its propensity for religious violence, the ambivalence of monotheism also has individualization as one of its consequences: man 'develops and becomes an autonomous or theonomous individual in partnership with the One God, who is outside the world but who turns His face towards it' (ibid.: 62; see also Angenendt 2007: 89 on this point).

The world divides into the community of believers in which boundaries are abolished and to which humanity is ascribed, and the community of unbelievers to whom humanity is denied. A latent state of war exists between these two groups, which is waged with more or less peaceful means because overcoming unbelief is a necessary component of faith. In his conversation with Jürgen Habermas, Cardinal Ratzinger, the present Pope Benedict XVI, formulates the question prompted by this situation:

Is then religion a healing and saving force? Or is it not rather an archaic and dangerous force that builds up false universalisms, thereby leading to intolerance and acts of terrorism? Must not religion, therefore, be placed under the guardianship of reason, and its boundaries carefully marked off? This, of course, prompts yet another question: Who can do this? And how does one do it? But the general question remains: Ought we to consider the gradual abolition of religion, the overcoming of religion, to be necessary progress on the part of mankind, so that it may find the path to freedom and to universal tolerance? Or is this view mistaken? (Habermas 2006: 64–5)

The answer given by the present book is as follows. If we pick up the distinction between 'religion' and 'religious', do the paradoxes of the border regime hold good for 'religion' but not for 'religious'? Can the monotheistic either/or, with its potential for violence, be neutralized, subverted or blunted by a syncretistic tolerance of both/and? *Might* the contact between the religions and their mutual interpenetration dilute their potential for violence in this way? The God of one's own choosing – and this is my contention – has ceased to be the one-and-only God who holds the key to salvation by assuming control over history and empowering its agents to practise intolerance and the use of force. The principle of religious hybridity helps to bring into focus the *humane principle of a subjective polytheism* that must not be confused with the polytheism of antiquity, nor with the facility with which missionary Christianity, for example, has proved able to integrate local religious traditions and rituals. Such individualized forms of a hybrid religiosity that transcends the boundaries of particular religions benefit not least because they act as a kind of resistance to the institutional insistence upon absolute conformity by its members.

The fluid forms of belief in 'a God of one's own' might (to take up and vary a formula of Odo Marquard's) result in a subjectively desired and realized separation of powers 'within the realm of the absolute' that opposes the claims to exclusivity of the monotheistic religions (Marquard 1995: 90–116; cited by Angenedt 2007: 88). The example of Japan makes clear that this *syncretistic tolerance* has spread out imperceptibly through the space of a free-floating religiosity (where if it has been noticed at all it has been met, in Europe at least, with a greater or lesser degree of contempt). But in addition it has also permeated institutional forms, where it functions perfectly naturally. People in Japan have no difficulty at all in visiting a Shinto shrine at specific times of the year, marrying in accordance with Christian rites and being buried by a Buddhist monk. The fact that this surprises us is the product of our monotheistic horizon of a monogamous God ('Thou shalt have no other Gods before me!'). This is quite alien not just to the religious eclecticism prevalent in Japan, but also to East Asia in general. Peter Berger, the sociologist of religion, reports that according to the Japanese philosopher Nakamura, 'the West has been responsible for two basic mistakes. One is monotheism – there's only one God – and the other is Aristotle's principle of contradiction – something is either A or non-A. In Asia every intelligent person will tell you that he knows full well that there are many gods and that things can be both A and non-A' (Berger and Mathewes 2006: 154).

Individualization and cosmopolitization: Religion in the framework of reflexive modernization

What does the fundamental ambivalence of religion consist in? The entire humanity of the religions secretes a totalitarian temptation. In a world bereft of orientation, they all contain a promise of meaning that grips the entire human being and his or her relation to the world. Such a promise of meaning is even capable of wrenching individuals out of the orbit of their origins. The universalism of the religions gives birth both to fraternal feelings that transcend class and nation *and* also to deadly enmity. Religion can civilize people or turn them into barbarians. This explains why modern humanity is tormented by the idea that religious people might be utterly serious about their faith.

Nowhere in sociology has the interaction between religion and the otherness of others been systematically researched. On the one hand, the monotheistic religions anticipate the cross-border ethics of the world society – and thus liberate potentials for violence that are hard to contain. This dialectic between a boundless humanity and a religiously inspired building of barricades has been much in evidence since the start of the twenty-first century. It does indeed figure prominently in *historical* analyses and debates on religion (such as those by Jan Assmann, Elaine Pagels, Friedrich Wilhelm Graf and Arnold Angenendt) or it can be perceived as a background problem in religious diagnoses of the contemporary world and empirical stock-takings (see Chapter 2). But as far as theoretical approaches to the sociology of religion are concerned, this dialectic figures only cursorily (Berger 1979; Luckmann 1967) or not at all (Luhmann 2000).[3]

In their discussions of religion, important philosophical, historical and sociological voices find themselves in agreement in their assessment of an ambivalent 'post-secular society' (Habermas 2008; Joas 2007a). However, this means that we cannot avoid the follow-up question about whether and how to develop a theoretical frame of reference that would take account of this 'religious signature of the age', implicated as it is in a modernization process some of whose key categories are constantly changing. By deploying the theory of reflexive modernization, I can bring together the basic features of a diagnosis of the age from the standpoint of the sociology of religion. One such feature is individualization, whose relevance to religion or religiosity was examined early on by Peter Berger and Thomas Luckmann, and then again more recently by Danièle Hervieu-Léger, Paul Heelas et al., Ronald Inglehart and W. C. Roof.[4] The concept of the *'cosmopolitization of the religions'* that I intend to develop further here is introduced for the first time in this book. My intention is to distinguish it empirically from globalization in general and normatively from the concept of religious universalism.

After a brief description defining the nature of the problem, my approach will be (1) to give an account of the components of the theory of reflexive modernization, and (2) to explain the concepts of cosmopolitization and (3) individualization with reference to religion. I shall follow this up (4) with a discussion of the relation of cosmopolitization to individualization, and conclude (5) by summarizing the argument of this book in ten theses.

On the issue of conceptual clarification, it would be prudent to define more narrowly the claims made in this study. Only one rule

---

[3] In Shmuel Eisenstadt's approach to *multiple modernities*, the problems of *religious* border regimes figure only at the margins; in contrast, the dialectics of opening up and constructing boundaries have been a key topic of research in the theory of reflexive modernization (Beck and Lau 2005).

[4] To be sure, only in the framework of the sociology of religion and not against the background of a general theory of individualization, a topic I have been concerned with for more than two decades and intend to clarify further in this book.

obtains in the present age's sociology of religion, namely that there is *no* rule with which to explain the development of religion in a global framework. While the language of the religions pushes us in the direction of universal validity, it is of crucial importance to resist this and to tie everything back into its particular context. This book cannot possibly analyse the entire field that is opened up by my definition. The fact is that when I speak of religion in this book, what is meant for the most part is Christianity. It is not possible here to include all the (world) religions in a study of the 'cosmopolitan vision' and to consider their various interactions under the headings of individualization and cosmopolitization. In actual fact, my analysis is based on an *asymmetry*: as the intersection of the contradictory dynamics of the different religions, the European context stands at the focus of attention. This includes the internal divisions within Christianity, but also the presence and the competing nature of the European and non-European versions of the Muslim religion and religiosity. By contrast, however, the Asiatic hybrid religions are largely ignored here. And this remains the case even though they would be an absolutely indispensable complement, as well as a possible corrective, to the sociology of a 'God of one's own' that is supposed to stand at the centre of this book.[5]

[5] This fact in itself makes it clear that the book is a failure if it is measured by the standard it has set itself, namely to develop a cosmopolitan change of vision and to apply it to the key topic of religion. This is compounded by the spectacular gaps in the present writer's knowledge (along with many other factors, such as the plan to produce no more than the outline of an argument). But what may appear as an individual problem also has a dimension that is generally applicable. In the presence of frontiers that are porous – in other words, that have ceased to function as frontiers – I have uttered the magic formula of a cosmopolitan existence: I am concerned with the preservation of individuals as well as entire societies faced by the influx of aliens. The demand of the cosmopolitan vision (or of methodological cosmopolitanism) that we should incorporate the points of view of religious and cultural others into our own way of seeing makes excessive demands on even the most accommodating, particularly when we bear in mind that other people will have limited experience and will have passed through the education systems of different nation-states based on different traditions. Considered in this way, the cosmopolitan vision that is being called for is simply another term for a painfully acquired ignorance (which admittedly can also be transformed into curiosity). This could be changed only if we were to succeed in developing a new cosmopolitan methodology for the social sciences and the humanities, and also to open up the contents and foundations of

The theory of reflexive modernization

Jürgen Habermas has summed up certain aspects of the theory of reflexive modernization as follows:

> Normally, members of a lifeworld draw solidarity from inherited values and norms, and form established and standardized communicative patterns. In the course of the rationalization of the lifeworld, however, this ascriptive background consensus shrinks, or shatters. It has to be replaced by the interpretative accomplishments of communication participants themselves. . . . In the sphere of the lifeworld, 'rationalization' does not plug the wellsprings of solidarity; rather, it discovers new ones as the old ones run dry. This productive force of communication is also significant for the challenge of 'reflexive modernization'. This theory places post-industrial developments in a specific light – the collapse of social differentiations along traditional class- and gender-based lines, the loosening up of standardized mass production and mass consumption, the disruption of stable commercial and security systems, the increasing flexibility of large-scale organizations, labour markets, party affiliations, etc. Post-industrial societies have expended all the reserves that had fuelled 'simple' industrialization – pre-existing natural resources as well as the cultural and social capital

our education systems and reform them in an appropriate spirit. At the same time, the lightning speed with which the ethnic and religious lifeworlds of the younger 'European generation' become pluralized plays a crucial role. If young people attend school in classes where over twenty languages are spoken, when they grow up they will find themselves facing both constraints and opportunities for the exchange of ideas that transcend religious and ethnic boundaries. In Germany, for example, it may come to be regarded as a matter of course that there will be German Muslims, German Jews, German Buddhists and perhaps even German Hindus and German Sikhs, who are capable of building bridges to other cultures and faiths, and will do so with a naturalness that is unprecedented in history because they will be equally at home in both traditions. In such circumstances, it will also be possible to lay the foundations in the lifeworld for a cosmopolitan change of perspective. In that case, it will be the *transnationalization* of everyday life (profession, television and internet), whose cross-border potential is frequently overlooked or decried, that might form the multinational and multireligious roots of an approach to cosmopolitan understanding. It remains to be seen whether the (world) religions will build on their transnational faith and contribute to this development or whether they will lapse once more into nationalist rhetoric (see pp. 182–4).

of pre-modern social formations. At the same time, post-industrial societies encounter the consequences of social reproduction, which appear in the form of systemically generated risks that can no longer be externalized, i.e. shifted onto foreign societies or cultures, to other social sectors, or to future generations. Hence modern societies collide with their own limits in a double sense: they become 'reflexive' insofar as they perceive this situation as such and react to it. Because they are less and less able to reach back to traditions, or external resources like nature, they must increasingly reproduce on their own all the conditions for their continuing existence. The modernization of 'halfway' modern societies that Ulrich Beck refers to succeeds only 'reflexively', insofar as these societies are obliged to fall back on their own resources to deal with the problems arising from social modernization. (Habermas 2001: 154–5)

Accordingly, we can set out the theory of reflexive modernization in three complex arguments – the theorem of the (world) risk society, the theorem of intensified individualization and the theorem of multidimensional globalization. All three argue along the same lines and their arguments mutually reinforce one another. 'Risk society', 'individualization' and 'globalization' (or 'cosmopolitization') are the radicalized forms of a modernization dynamic that was turned on itself at the opening of the twenty-first century and dissolved simple modernization in the process. This simple modernization followed a logic of ordering and acting that drew sharp distinctions between categories of human beings and religions, things and activities, and made clear distinctions between spheres of action and forms of life that facilitated the unambiguous ascription of competences and responsibilities. This *logic of non-ambiguity* – we might speak figuratively of the first modernity as the *Newtonian phase* of social, religious and political theory – is now being replaced by a logic of *ambiguity* – we might speak of a Heisenberg phase in which the realms of the social, religious and political are governed by something like an Uncertainty Principle. Needless to say, classical sociological theory was also plagued by crises and dysfunctionalities, but these were exceptions.

The idea that with their *victory* the foundations of the modern world become porous, so to speak, fragmented or that their meaning could be reversed is alien to classical sociological theory but also to more modern theories. As I have shown, what we have to explore is precisely the law governing the pluralization of religion with its tendency to abolish old boundaries and redraw new ones. The institutionalized dualities and coordinates of 'national' and 'international', 'we' and 'others', are dissolved and recast. In the same way, the theorem of *'unintended consequences'* that underpins the spread of a new hybrid religiosity in the monotheistic European milieu has been known to classical theory ever since David Hume and Adam Smith (see Beck, Holzer and Kieserling 2001). But in the second modernity, the 'invisible hand' leads neither to compromise nor to revolution. The logic of non-ambiguity – the either/or model of society, religion or politics – is being replaced by the logic of ambiguity – the both/and model of society, religion and politics (on this point, see Beck, Bonß and Lau 2001; Beck and Lau 2005; Beck and Grande 2004: 50–1).

The distinction between cosmopolitization and globalization

'Cosmopolitization' refers to the *erosion of clear boundaries* separating the markets, states, civilizations, cultures and not least the lifeworlds of different peoples and religions, as well as the resulting worldwide situation of an *involuntary confrontation with alien others*. The boundaries have of course not disappeared, but they have become blurred and porous, letting through streams of information, capital and risk, and even people, though to a lesser extent (tourists can pass, migrants cannot). Needless to say, it would be utterly mistaken to equate cosmopolitization with the idea that nowadays everyone is automatically a cosmopolitan. The opposite is more likely to be true: a worldwide trend towards the rediscovery of national identity. But we can perceive a new challenge and a new need (even in everyday life) for a *hermeneutics of the stranger* in order to live and work in a world in which violent tensions and divisions and unpredictable confusions have become the norm and novel threats are inextricably interwoven with opportunities for change.

Isn't 'cosmopolitization' just a new word for what everyone refers to as 'globalization'? My answer is: No. Globalization is something that takes place 'out there'. Cosmopolitization, by contrast, happens 'within', in the realms of the nation, the local and even one's own biography and identity. Globalization is based on the 'onion model' of the world in which the local and the national form the inner layers and the international and the global are the outer skin of the onion. The point of the concept of the cosmopolitan is to abolish the duality of global and local, national and international, and to merge them with one another in new forms to be analysed empirically. In other words cosmopolitization encapsulates the specific process of blurring boundaries, abolishing boundaries, erecting boundaries characteristic of (world) religions from their origins on (see above).

This makes clear that spatially and thematically the concept of cosmopolitization and the phenomena it embraces are *not fixed*. The concept is *not* tied to the 'cosmos' or the 'globe'; it definitely does not include 'everything'. On the contrary, the principle of cosmopolitization is to be found or practised in connection with *specific themes* – in connection with given boundaries in every sphere and at every level of social and political action; in transnational organizations, transnational families and neighbourhoods, in the form of the 'cosmopolitan criminal', the 'cosmopolitan worker', and not least in the management of boundaries between the different religions. Whether and to what extent we can speak of the 'cosmopolitan', and in what forms, is an empirical question that has to be looked into separately and investigated in the relevant contexts and thematic realms. The underlying premise for such research is of course the distinction between cosmopolitanism and universalism.

The distinction between cosmopolitanism and universalism as exemplified by the religions. I made a distinction above (pp. 52–4) between three *non-cosmopolitan* ways of dealing with ethnic and religious otherness: the essentialism of the 'natural' social hierarchy, religious universalism and the dualism of good and evil. My aim was to pinpoint the fundamental ambivalence involved in transgressing old boundaries and erecting new ones in the course of dealing with other religions. This left open the question of the nature of the distinction between religious universalism and religious cosmopolitanism.

Christian universalism is based on a single, decisive point of view: the eternal salvation of the human being and his or her soul, a point of view before which all other social boundaries and distinctions pale into insignificance. In the famous controversy of Valladolid over four hundred years ago, the Dominican priest Bartolomé de Las Casas defended the rights of the native Indians. He argued that they bore a surprising resemblance to Europeans. They satisfied the ideals of the Christian religion, which recognized no distinctions of skin-colour and origin. The Indians were very friendly and modest; they abided by the norms of human intercourse, family values and their traditions; and in this respect they were better prepared than many other nations of the world to listen to the voice of God and to put His wisdom into practice.

In short, Las Casas made the case for Christian universalism. Hence he vehemently attacked a hierarchical world-view based on distinctions of class, caste, nationality and ethnicity. The principle opposing the hierarchic subordination and inferiority of others calls for the dissolution of such distinctions. Yet – as we have seen – this universalist approach to religious otherness has a Janus face in principle. This can already be seen in the Dominican priest's arguments: What determines our attitude towards others is not their alterity but their *similarity*. Beneath the universalizing gaze, all forms of human life are assembled within a single order of civilization. This has the consequence that cultural differences are either cancelled out or else devalued and ultimately excluded. In this sense the universalizing gaze acts as a hegemonial principle that grants admittance to the voice of others only as one of sameness, as self-confirmation, self-reflection, monologue. If we imagine an African universalism along these lines, the true white man would have a black soul.

Thus religious universalism implies the promise that existing hierarchies will be overcome. In this sense it is characterized by its *structural tolerance*. But by simultaneously demonizing unbelievers, it opens up new abysses between the religions and creates potentials for violence that can be contained only with difficulty. To this extent, religious universalism, like every other, is characterized by its *structural intolerance*.

Religious cosmopolitanism may be distinguished from such templates by the fact that the recognition of *religious otherness becomes a guiding maxim* in its way of thinking, its actions and its social existence. Cultural and religious differences are neither hierarchically organized nor dissolved, but accepted for what they are and indeed positively affirmed. Religious cosmopolitanism accepts what is excluded by attitudes that insist on hierarchical distinction and universal sameness. That is to say, it perceives religious others as both particular *and* universal, as different *and* equally valid.

The alien faith, the faith of the stranger, is not felt to be threatening, destructive or fragmenting. Rather, it is felt to be enriching and the judgement passed on it is correspondingly positive. It is my curiosity about myself and about alterity that makes others so irreplaceable in my eyes. What is involved is an egoism of cosmopolitan religiosity: those who integrate the religious perspectives and traditions of others into their own religious experience learn more about themselves *and* about others. This is the explanation of the fascination exerted by the idea of a God of one's own choosing, and hence of the decoupling of religion and religiosity.

Summing up, we can say that, whereas religious universalism distinguishes between believers and unbelievers (where the latter category includes a random collection of individuals, such as Protestants and atheists, heathen and heretics, Hindus and Buddhists, all in the same pot), religious cosmopolitanism distinguishes among non-believers, the broad spectrum of believers in other faiths. It regards them, however, not as a threat to its own religious monopoly on truth, but as an enrichment in a quite personal sense, and ultimately even as part of the normal state of affairs. More specifically, the recognition of the faith of others means also the recognition of various religiously defined representatives of modernity, which, as a glance at the Muslim world tells us, might well be a matter of life and death.

With the emergence of religious cosmopolitanism, a general principle of tolerance asserts itself: How do religious communities come to terms with one another and with the growth of the idea of a 'God of one's own'? The resistance to this development can scarcely be overestimated. 'As early as *Daybreak,* Nietzsche had denounced the "gentle moralizing" of well-meaning humanity as the "euthanasia of Christianity". . . . In 1886, in *Beyond Good and Evil*, his prelude to a philosophy of the future, he had observed that "while it is true that the religious instinct has grown powerfully, it is theistic satisfaction that it regards with the greatest distrust" ' (Kallscheuer 2006: 78).

Admittedly, a similar description of the cosmopolitan constellation can also be found in the writings of Pope Benedict XVI:

First, we have the formation of a global community in which the individual political, economic, and cultural powers become increasingly dependent on one another, touching and intersecting each other in their various existential spheres. *Second*, we have the development of human possibilities, of the power to make and to destroy, that poses the question of legal and ethical controls on power in a way that goes far beyond anything to which we have yet been accustomed. This lends greater urgency to the question of how cultures that encounter one another can find ethical bases to guide their relationship along the right path, thus permitting them to build up a common structure that tames power and imposes a legally responsible order on the exercise of power. . . .

If we are to discuss the basic questions of human existence today, the intercultural dimension seems to me absolutely essential – for such a discussion cannot be carried on exclusively either within the Christian realm or within the Western rational tradition. Both of these regard themselves as universal, and they may perhaps be universal *de jure*. *De facto*, however, they are obliged to acknowledge that they are accepted only by parts of mankind, and that they are comprehensible only in parts of mankind. (Cardinal Ratzinger in Habermas 2006: 55, 73)

For this reason the cosmopolitan constellation needs a kind of grassroots culture in which the religions are the object of mutual recognition – transcending all the mutually exclusive universalisms. This is – if we may be allowed the expression – hellishly difficult.

There are beliefs whose incompatibility cannot simply be disguised by euphemisms, however subtle. We are not infrequently infuriated by peculiarities of other people's thought and behaviour, the more so the closer they are to us. Only people to whom everything is a matter of indifference will become neither angry nor indignant. To live more or less in harmony with people whose peculiarities we find repugnant calls not for indifference but for strength of character. It calls for tolerance. For tolerance is a virtue that encourages us to grit our teeth and put up with people with different convictions or kinds of behaviour without cringing or being overwhelmed by them. Tolerance begins where we find it painful to put up with something. In this sense we may think of fundamentalism as a flight from pain. This brings it close, oddly enough, to the inability of the postmodern society it loathes to endure suffering. That precisely is the price of tolerance. . . . Today, we are confronted by the task of practising this attitude of forbearance, of putting up with alterity and strangeness, and treating it as a political virtue. Without it neither religious peace nor juridical harmony can survive. . . . Religious intolerance doesn't just interfere with religious peace; it destroys one of the chief foundations underpinning human society as such. (Kamphaus 2007: 7)

Can we identify any signs of a cosmopolitan theology? As Francis Schüssler Fiorenza writes in his essay 'Karl Rahner: A Theologian for a Cosmopolitan Twenty-First Century' (2006), the key to Rahner's religious vision is to be found in a triple interconnection that underlies his theology:

The interrelation between the knowledge of the human self and the knowledge of God; the interconnection between the love of neighbour and the love of God; and the interconnection between love and knowledge. . . . This triple interconnection is often overlooked in any interpretation of Rahner's theology in terms of an abstract Enlightenment concept of autonomy or self-interest. But it has implications for the understanding of human dignity and rights to the extent that Rahner underscores the religious: it provides an openness in understanding dignity and human rights for cosmopolitan dialogue and posits at the same time a transcendent religious basis. Freedom is related to the responsibility for the other and entails an obedience to God's will. . . .

Today, the emergence of postmodern philosophical and religious reflections and postcolonial criticism of the modern West leads to a new set of issues. These issues challenge the modern West insofar as they question the values not only of modernity, but also of the West. The challenges are that we as Christians face a world that is increasingly globalized and cosmopolitan, a world that is increasingly aware of the tension between . . . the increased striving for justice and the growing exploitation and injustice. . . . Rahner's theology has a complexity and multifacetedness that offers a superior theological vision. (Fiorenza 2006: 132, 134)

The distinction between descriptive and normative religious cosmopolitanism. A descriptive cosmopolitanism aims to gain a new (social and intellectual) perspective on the contradictory phenomena of the dissolution of boundaries, pluralization and the construction of new boundaries in the field of religion. Normative cosmopolitanism struggles to focus attention both in thought and in practice on the universal principle of tolerance (in contradistinction to universalism, hierarchical differentiation and particularism).

The two do not necessarily coincide. The growth of religious cosmopolitanism within the experiential space and scope for action of the nation-state does not necessarily mean that the agents of religion adopt a cosmopolitan perspective – we see that in fact the opposite is true to an alarming degree. However, the tensions and contradictions between growing religious transnationalism and re-nationalization, between fundamentalism and cosmopolitanism, *cannot possibly be analysed* within the limits of a national purview. What is needed is a sociological and humanities-based standpoint as well as a corresponding conceptual framework that would make it possible to observe the dialectics of the dissolving of religious boundaries and the erecting of new barricades between religions from a vantage point beyond national and religious differences. And there is a certain irony in the fact that this growing cosmopolitanism of the religious sphere turns out to be the unwanted and unforeseen consequence of actions that are not intended to be 'cosmopolitan' in the normative sense of the word.

Cosmopolitan society. The new contours of contemporary society that are crystallizing as the 'unintended consequences' of globalized and radicalized modernization processes can be diagnosed as a 'second modernity'. Its novel features include: the intermingling of people and populations throughout the globe; growing inequalities in the global space; the emergence of new, supranational organizations in the realms of the economy (multinational businesses), politics (non-state agencies such as the IMF, the World Bank, the WTO, the International Court of Justice), civil society (campaigning social organizations such as Amnesty International, Greenpeace, feminist networks, Attac); new, normative concepts such as human rights; new types and profiles of global risk (climate change; global financial crises; Aids); new forms of war; globally organized crime and terrorism; as well as new forms of coexistence, of conflict and cooperation between world religions. The reality of frontiers that are porous, in other words, that have ceased to function as frontiers, points to the magic formula of a cosmopolitan existence: it is the proving-ground of the self and of entire societies in the face of the onslaught of the foreign. It implies a process of 'internal globalization' within local and national lifeworlds and institutions. It alters the conditions of social identity construction that now no longer have to be shaped by negative, confrontational dichotomies of 'us' and 'them'. It becomes very clear in our dealings with religious others that cosmopolitization operates not in an undefined abstract or global space, in the external macrosphere, somewhere over people's heads, but deeply within human beings, in their relations to God, the world and themselves. This is what gives the conflicts of religious cosmopolitization – the growth of fundamentalisms but also the search for a God of one's own choosing – their depth of focus.

The awareness of this change lags behind objective reality because people still have a 'national point of view' which leads them to believe that nation-states are the most important 'containers' within which human life unfolds. Even the dominant personal identity is defined by membership of a specific nation-state, as distinct from other nation-states. This is of course obsolete. Nation-states do indeed continue to exist as they have done in the past; but they behave less and less as self-contained entities with clear boundaries, as had been the case in the 'first modernity'.

In the same way, the majority of sociologists (as well as other social scientists) continue to apply the rules of 'methodological nationalism', since they still think of societies as natural units of data production and analysis within the territorial limits of the nation-state. They are the motorways of convention leading nowhere. Like the conceptual world of national economies, the conceptual world of nation-based sociologists coasts along in neutral, 'blinding itself empirically' to the facts.

This explains why the real, objective transformation of social conditions at the beginning of the twenty-first century is so poorly reflected in both social consciousness and sociological methodology. The national point of view must be replaced by a cosmopolitan vision and methodological nationalism by methodological cosmopolitanism. And the concrete realm of politics – in other words, national politics with its obsessive preoccupation with sovereignty and autonomy – must be transformed into a 'politics of politics', which will need to appropriate the problems of the cosmopolitan constellation through a series of self-transformations if it is going to be able to act successfully on the national plane (Beck 2005).

The society of the religions. Religions harbour an alternative understanding of society from which a sociology and political science trapped in a methodological nationalism could profitably learn. Can a sociology of God – of ideas about God, of religious rituals – succeed in clarifying our understanding of the 'ingredients' society requires in order to remain a society? Sociology's answer in the age of modernity is that society is held together, on the one hand, by ends–means rationality, interests, classes, the market, science and the corresponding organizations, on the one hand, and, on the other hand, by socially constructed 'nations' which distinguish themselves from other nations and which establish democratically legitimated nation-states and welfare states. The opposing view of society defines itself not merely through differences in regard to transcendence – either you believe in God or you do not. It claims instead: the essence of a religious society is that it establishes real, emotional, moral ties between individuals that extend beyond the social barriers of class, caste, gender and nation.[6]

We can consider the actual reality of religion from a sociological standpoint. In other words we can observe *that* and *how* religions join individuals, groups, organizations and societies together, keep and weld them together, how they distinguish them from one another and stir them up against one another. This *that* and *how* show that, as far as their conception of society is concerned, the world religions enter into the second modernity with a head start. Key distinctions introduced by the first modernity are superseded. It is an anomaly of history that the first modernity enclosed thought and action in national containers, and that this applies equally to social identity, the organs of political power and also the perspective of the sociologist (in both theory and research). In the context of the experience and the expectations of the world religions, there was always something presumptuous about this dualism of national and international that constitutes the totality of social and political activity. The same may be said of the fact that we prioritize nation-based class conflicts over global inequalities or that we accept the dominance of ethnic distinctions for the establishing of social identity and of politically relevant communi-

---

[6] John Milbank (2006) raises the central question of a social theory beyond 'secular rationality'.

ties. Religious citizens must decide whether their loyalty is to the state or their church. It is fitting that the supercilious credo of communitarianism that community can only be nation-based and not transnational – in other words, religious – proves to be a premise that is easily bypassed within the horizons of the world religions. Whereas the key actors of the first modernity – governments, political parties, trade unions, enfranchised citizens and populations – are the prisoners of their 'superstitious belief' in the nation-state, this superstition never attained the same absolutist, non-negotiable status in the social outlook of the religious creeds (despite the nationalization of God in Europe in the nineteenth century). Perhaps the world-religious elites and citizens are deficient in a number of mental blocks in this context. Traditionally they are in a certain sense 'more modern', more at home in the 'second modernity' than the key actors of modernization. They may then be relatively free of the ballast of the imperatives of the first modernity and have no need to jettison them. The self-confidence of the leading representatives of the first modernity has been badly shaken. Bemused, irritated and even shocked, they look on in wonder at the leaders of the world religions who have emerged from the 'museum of premodernity' and who draw their vitality precisely from their playful interaction with the boundaries to which they have been made subject. Paradoxically, it is their non-modern view of society that qualifies the religions for their role in the second modernity. Catholics, Muslims, Buddhists, etc., go through the revolving door behind the heroes and heathen of modernity and come out in front of them.

As long ago as his classic study *The Elementary Forms of Religious Life* (2001 [1912]), Émile Durkheim had argued that the sociology of religion can teach the sociology of modernization a crucial lesson, namely that, like the religions, modern societies produce and reproduce their reality and their interconnections *through rituals that create emotions*. These form the 'cement' that holds the members of the group or society together. This is reflected in the way in which religious rituals permeate everyday reality and stabilize it. Even in times of fundamental change and political crisis, the maintenance of rituals enables a kind of *transformation through integration*. Religious symbols, liturgies and ceremonies help to reinforce and give vitality to group solidarity and identity and sustain them through periods of personal and social crises of meaning. Religious rituals free human beings from the cares of ordinary life and open their hearts to the experiences and values of transcendence. This practical intermingling of this world and the next produces a kind of community and society that is not created by the rational awareness of common interests. This is because religion generates collective moral and emotional experiences that work counter to the centrifugal dynamic of individualization. Rituals 'naturalize' society: they produce and reproduce realities that are so self-evident that they are no longer consciously known. However, *for that very reason* they acquire social reality in the highest degree (as Garfinkel and others have impressed on us in the context of ethnomethodology with their so-called 'crisis experiments', which aim to neutralize this degree of 'naturalness', and to make us aware of it).

What empowers and legitimizes rituals? Is there a reality representing the omnipotence that believers ascribe to God? The fact is that 'society' is a power that is greater than all individuals; it can pass judgement on life and death. Everyone depends on society and our identity is intimately bound up with it. The image religion has of society is this: God is a symbol of society; society symbolizes God.

Similarly, when sociologists situate 'social conditions' in a realm beyond everyday consciousness, and maintain that these conditions determine our consciousness in all essentials (in a manner invisible to our minds), they proceed from the assumption that the existence of something outside ourselves, powerful and yet invisible, like 'God', like 'society', is no illusion. The idea of God as an analogy to society, and society as an analogy to God, is to be found in our inner life and our external existence, in our own eyes as well as in those of others. We are all part of society. The opposition of self and society is false. Descartes's *cogito ergo sum* can be replaced by the principle: *cogito ergo sumus: I think, therefore we are.* All consciousness of self presupposes others – recognition by others. What George Herbert Mead called the dialectic of the 'I and the me' can be given a religious interpretation as well as a secular one. The 'me' represents not just 'society' (the role of parents, teachers, members of one's age group, policemen and judges), but also the internalized God, the 'God of one's own choosing'. Since our world is constituted by social communication, this means that society exists both inside and outside us (however we care to define it). This is what makes religion so fundamental: religion expresses the essential facts of our human existence. What is articulated in religion is a structural similarity, an elective affinity between religious symbolism and life in society. It thus acquires exemplary reality. Since religion generates social bonds and determines what is 'good' and 'evil', and whatever an individual holds sacred if only for his or her own sake, the society of religion faces in two fundamentally opposed directions. It can turn egoists into altruists or tolerant human beings into fanatics who organize and practise suicide as a form of indiscriminate mass murder.

The individualization of religion

Individualization, too, is pre-national, national and post-national – pre-national because (in Christianity, at least) it has been moulded by the church and because the Christian churches (Protestant more than Catholic) have acted as the historical authorities on socialization and as the conservators of a confessional individualism that has been both trained and provoked. Those who prescribe Christian morality three times a day as an antidote to the 'rampant epidemic of individualism' promote the very individualism they set out to combat.

The formula 'the individualization of religion' articulates a very real contradiction. On the one hand, religion is the very *opposite* of individualization. It is attachment, memory, collective identity and ritual, and it is from these things that sociability is 'made', albeit in a secular, naturalized fashion. On the other hand, however, religion is the *source* of individualization: *Go and pray to the God of your choosing!* Religion is based on the decision of the individual to believe and thus ultimately on the assumption that the individual is free.

This means, then, that religion is both the opposite of individualization *and* its source. This antithesis leaves behind it a trail of blood that stains the entire history of Christianity. The first great insurance policy against the extinguishing of one's own life was the church's promise of *eternal* life. In the High Middle Ages a person's death was no more than a transformation into an *authentic* life, the life of all people in and with God. Death, as the occasion for proving oneself in God's eyes, was an invention that caused deep concern in people's minds throughout the centuries and *isolated* each person. Death meant having to give an account of oneself to God. This was the beginning of the original sin of individualism – which arose in response to the demands of the church.

This paradox has been at the centre of theological debates for centuries. The individual is nowadays held to be valuable and is conceived as autonomous in principle. He or she is fallible. Dressed up in theological garb, freedom appears as the human possibility of sin in the world. Such propositions already contain the seeds of heresy, schism, and the pluralization and privatization of religion. These seeds continue to conjure up the inner affinity of absolute truth and violence down to this day. For, where would the liberty of the individual find its grounding if not in the free decision to believe, a decision that the church institutionalizes – in other words, fosters, promises and encumbers with fetters? But what is left of the church if humanity takes in utter seriousness its freedom to believe? The idea that a Christian confession of faith is individual and free – that is to say, is not prescribed by one's origins, ethnicity, social position, sex or age – is the first step towards the secularization and individualization of religion, a step that nowadays finds a new focus in the multiple religious choices of a 'God of one's own'.

On this issue, too, church dogma remains strangely irresolute. On the one hand, the world and all the bustle of human beings are null and void. They are mere sound and fury in God's eyes. On the other hand, everything now depends upon the conduct of one's life: do we merit eternal life or eternal damnation? That is decided by our death. Death, then, is an examination, *the* examination which acts as a stepping stone to the career ladder leading to eternal life (roughly comparable to a university degree which opens the doors to a permanent, tenured position in the public service). The severity of the threatened punishment – Hell or Purgatory and/or hanging or burning at the stake in this life – is an attempt to compensate for the theological lapse implicit in allowing individuals the freedom to choose their faith. An individualized life comes into being but at the price of the threat of eternal damnation. This means that freedom, licence and the anarchy of an individualized society are simultaneously made possible and anathematized.

However, by the same token life is thrown back onto its own resources. Proving one's worth in one's profession is to prove oneself in God's eyes. As Max Weber shows in his study of Protestantism, modern humanity's ruthless conquest and demystification of the world – as well as tradition – derives its justification from this trial of humanity before God. To lead a self-centred, profit-seeking, 'rational' life becomes a divine commandment. This self-castration on the part of the church, this process by which theology digs its own grave, is spelled out step by step to its radical conclusion at every stage in the history of secularization and re-secularization.

This means that over the long term it is important to distinguish between *Individualization One* and *Individualization Two*. Individualization One refers to individualization *within* religion (e.g. Protestantism); Individualization Two means the individualization *of* religion (a 'God of one's own').[7] This raises the question: can religion (faith) exist without a community – for example, in the form of a 'virtual religion'? If we take the religiosity of a God of one's own choosing to its logical conclusion, does it imply the complete atomization of both society and religion? No, the religious practices associated with a 'God of one's own' presuppose the possibility of *choosing* a form of community or anticipate it as a future option; such practices function transnationally in networks and organizations appropriate for the purpose. Admittedly, it is precisely on the point of a realistic grasp of the weight of institutional forms that the question of how to institutionalize a 'God of one's own' shows itself to be problematic (Bruce 2006).

Individualization confronts the churches with a dilemma – that is Ronald Hitzler's claim. They can adopt two strategies with which to counter it:

On the one hand (and this is the route recommended by intellectuals close to the churches), they can focus on *their own* religious truth; they can revert (once again) to their role as guardians of the core beliefs of their particular religion. On the other hand, they can exploit the organizations at their disposal and emphasize their

[7] On this point, see 'Individualization One: The invention of a God of one's own: Martin Luther' (pp. 104–10) and also 'Individualization Two: The welfare state' (pp. 117–20).

professional expertise, built up over the centuries, in managing
questions of meaning and solving life problems.

Both strategies have consequences that the churches may find
unpalatable both institutionally and organizationally. They thus
find themselves in a *dilemma* when dealing with the trend towards
individualization and the problem of how to re-orientate themselves towards it. Taken to its logical conclusion, the first strategy
leads to a church with a very small number of adherents, in other
words to a kind of ghettoization of the churches. For with such a
policy a church is likely to prove attractive to relatively few people.
In consequence, it is likely to see a further erosion of its social
influence and economic power. The second strategy, that of providing the most 'open-minded' collection of more or less compatible
meanings and messages, will lead to a kind of church congress
meeting all the year round, in other words to a church for as many
people as possible. Whether such members can all be described as
'believers' is open to doubt. Such a strategy would mean the loss
of whatever had been regarded hitherto as its 'corporate identity'.
(Hitzler 1996: 272)

The relationship between cosmopolitization and individualization

What is the relationship between cosmopolitization and individualization as they affect the religions? Should we think of them as
lying adjacent to one another or as realms that need to be related
to one another and analysed? How are we best to specify their
mutual conditionality?

Cosmopolitization and individualization are two aspects of
reflexive modernization (see above). Both are (different) forms
of de-traditionalization. *Cosmopolitization opens up the outer
aspect of religious transformation, individualization the inner.*
Cosmopolitization presupposes stripping the religions of their
national and territorial foundations. This means that the religions
themselves become individualized since faith now becomes
optional and is tethered to the authority of the religious self. These
processes can be illustrated by reference to the Europeanization
of Islam (see pp. 30–6 above).

At the same time, I would like to propose the hypothesis that
individualization is the premise for the coexistence of the religions
– which appears as its unintended consequence. Unseen and unintended for the most part, a subjective separation of powers of the

'God of one's own' is slipped into the forms assumed by that God, and this may help to defuse the potential for violence inherent in the religions.

Of course, it is not enough simply to rely on this unintended consequence for our survival – that is to say, on the possibility that the opportunity for regulating conflicts will be seized. In other words, we have to use the global religious conflicts to develop rules that will enable us to transcend them. (This explains why I devote the last chapter of this book to the question of whether a universal church could conceivably function as a cosmopolitan actor on the world stage. Whether this idea of the unintended consequence will be capable of establishing a durable optimism, however vestigial, that might form the basis for step-by-step political activity is a question that will perhaps only be resolved if the thought experiment that this book is attempting to provoke actually comes into being.)

'World risk society' is just another term for the impossibility of excluding cultural others. It points to the thick texture of the world, where we all have to live in the new immediacy of the neighbourhood to which we have been assigned. Situated in the confined space from which there is no escape,

> the autodidactic tension rises. We perceive how the side-effects of our actions catch up with us faster and faster. Where fate used to rule, we now have feedback. Humankind has become a consciousness-raising group condemned to success, whose members put so much pressure on one another that they would probably be able to work out a halfway liveable code of behaviour as early as the current century. (Sloterdijk 2006: 5)

The divine irony of unintended consequences is opposed by the rivalry between the world religions for the power to sanctify the true way for humankind – the true Christianity, the true Muslim faith, the true Judaism, the true Hinduism, and so forth. It is opposed, in other words, by the struggle for the power to define concepts, to decide what we must accept as true and false, good and evil. Having entered into competition with one another throughout the entire world, each of the world religions regards itself not only as the only true religion but also as a moral movement that points the way for humankind as a whole.

We might well wish to ask whether such assertions do not embody the outlook of those who believe they can set the world to rights, an outlook in which it is cultural suicide to suppress the central truth of one's own cultural origins, which is that all human beings are furnished with inalienable rights and that in consequence democracy is the only form of government that guarantees human rights. In the present situation, in which everyone lives cheek by jowl with everyone else and is in direct contact with the fundamental sources of conflict, which thereby become omnipresent, this truth is in my view the key to survival. It is one part of the crucial reality: there are no impartial observers, impartial teachers and doctrines – unless they emerge from the crucible of the world religions' struggles for survival.

If the enforced proximity of old and new religions and religious movements blurs the boundaries between them and if the extreme fluidity of religious beliefs becomes manifest, then – in contrast to the fantasies of purity common to the ideologies of both West and East – we shall find ourselves reminded that religion must be understood as an 'impure', imbricated phenomenon. Nothing could be more wrong-headed than playing off 'the European heritage' against 'Islam'. Muhammad has been in Europe forever. Without Europe, antiquity and Judaism, Muhammad is inconceivable. Cultural imitations and borrowings, diasporic disseminations and syntheses, permeate history, culminating today in spiritual odysseys in which faith has become the means for self-realization. To what extent are we able to discern traces of a world-religious cosmopolitanism in this culturally much derided, subjectively active, multifaceted, 'do-it-yourself religiosity' that goes against the grain of mainstream religion? To what extent does the impurity of religious creeds represent an involuntary and easily overlooked step in the direction of a religious freedom from violence?

The active sense of the term 'step' is important here, since nothing could be more naïve than the supposition that Kant's 'eternal peace' might emerge spontaneously from the dialectic of unintended consequences. This is where the key difference from Max Weber is to be found. When Weber analysed the causal background to occidental capitalism and identified the 'spirit' of capitalism as an unintended consequence of Calvinist reform, capitalism *was already in existence* and its victory foreseeable.

But a *cosmopolitan agent* has no existence – in the realms of either religion or politics. This explains why cosmopolitization liberates countervailing movements that rediscover and amalgamate absolutist religious truths and ethnic identities, equip them militarily and politically with weapons systems of every kind, and even release the armed forces from political constraints, transforming them into terrorist organizations (as Mary Kaldor shows in her book *New and Old Wars* [1998]).

Ten core theses[8]

1. Religious belief spreads in proportion to the growth of insecurity triggered by radicalized modernization processes in every sphere of human social activity ('reflexive modernization'). In this sense, religiosity of this type is no mere vestige of a tradition that has become increasingly obsolete with the advance of modernity (as is assumed by theoreticians of the first modernity). On the contrary, it is the *product* of advanced modernizations that have started to question their own legitimacy.

Let us assume that the principle of religious freedom (the individual's right to choose between belief systems) is a fundamental principle of modernity; and, further, that this basic principle was realized as a halfway house in the first modernity of the nation-state. In that phase, it presented itself as a choice between the basic national institutions – for example, Catholicism and Protestantism. On these assumptions we can say that it is the *radicalization* of free religious choice that negates, undermines and generally weakens the institutionalized 'religious classes' and 'national churches' of the first modernity and opens up the opportunity for individual choices.

2. This does not spell the beginning of the end of religion. What we find is the renaissance of a new kind of subjective anarchy of belief which forms an increasingly poor fit with the dogmatic framework provided by the institutionalized religions. The unity between religion and religious, religion and belief, is shattered. Indeed, religion and belief come into conflict with each other.

---

[8] See, *inter alia*, Beck 1992, Part II; Beck and Beck-Gernsheim 2002; Berger 1979; Heelas et al. 2005; Hervieu-Léger 1999, 2006; Inglehart 1997; Luckmann 1967.

Western societies are characterized by an *institutionalized individualization* (in the shape of civil, social and political basic rights addressed to the individual), but also by the individualizing dynamics of the labour market. These societies have internalized the autonomy of the individual as a principle. This means that the individual human being becomes increasingly adept in creating faith narratives for himself – a 'God of his own' – adapted to his 'own' life and his 'own' experiential horizon.

In Europe much fuss is made about the risks – the imminent 'cultural catastrophes' – that are alleged to accompany this chaotic muddle and the clash between (institutionalized) *religion* and (individualized) *belief*. We should note two significant aspects:

On the one hand, this is by no means evidence of the end of modernity; what we are seeing, rather, is the *victory* of modernity. It is a radicalized (religious) freedom that now turns both against an inherited religion with its ties based on family, class, status-groups, ethnicity and milieu, and also against the pre-existing collectivity of religious group identities.

On the other hand, it is a fact that individuals form their competences as spiritual and religious 'do-it-yourselfers' (Ronald Hitzler) in their dealings with religious symbols that are almost always detached from the context that had previously guaranteed their legibility. To wax indignant about this merely confuses the issue. The individualization of belief simply has to be accepted as a reality. It is futile to mourn the passing of an age in which 'intact' religious milieus (families, classes, status-groups, nations) were socially distinct and clearly differentiated from one another and which accordingly made monotheistic group identities possible.

No doubt, the pragmatic stripping away of dogma gives rise to feelings of ambivalence. After all, it opens the floodgates to every trivialization of belief. Every wellness hotel decorates its premises with pearls of wisdom from Buddhist scriptures. Religious illiteracy spreads like a plague and atheists cannot even remember which God they *no longer* believe in.

3. The individualization of religion is comparable to the individualization of *social classes* (inequality, poverty) and the individualization of the *family* (parenthood, relations between the sexes, etc.). Only the interconnections between these different domains (which are mainly considered in isolation from each

other) constitute the *social* individualization that brings about profound changes in the aggregate situation, the quality of society as a whole. In all these key segments of social existence we see a new kind of inner diversity, contradictoriness and unpredictability. This has dissolved old institutional stereotypes, certainties and dominant ideas, and leads to the emergence of symbolic resources of varying quality. All are bound by the principles of individualization: the *dismantling of tradition,* the necessity and possibility of *individual decision-making,* and, as the presupposition of that, a (more or less limited) *horizon of options,* as well as the custom *of accounting for consequences.* 'Dismantling of tradition' means that collective religion is falling apart. In what way and into what elements? Into all the elements that were held together in religion: rites, the conduct of life, collective identity, morality, subjective faith. These components assert their autonomy and to a certain extent become organized independently of each other, so that each finds itself individually in demand and recombined with others.

4. An important consequence for all spheres of life and social activity (class, family and religion) can be seen in the break-up of institutionalized role models and the collapse of social realities. The religiosity of the second, globalized modernity divides into two worlds – the world of priestly religion and the world of individual faith. This is mirrored (at least as far as the Christian religions are concerned) by an *institutionalized double morality, double religiosity* and *double reality:* the institutionalized religions and the social practices of faith movements break away from each other and yet remain dependent upon one another in the shape of a very unbrotherly, tenacious and never-ending 'modernization dispute' about the true path of belief. Nowadays individuals write their own faith narratives with the aid of words and symbols which have abandoned their fixed 'orbit' in the institutionalized coordinates of sovereign world religions in which a particular tradition had held them fast for centuries.

5. This brings us to the paradox of the *second, religious modernity in the European context.* Declining church attendance and the revival of magical thinking and acting, the weakening of religious organizations and the strengthening of a fluid, post-church religiosity, make up the two sides of the same development. This can be seen in the fact that the claims made by the religions to

possess the true doctrine are questioned by their own faithful. For example, in a country-wide opinion poll on the religious beliefs of Catholics and Protestants in Switzerland, only 2 per cent of the respondents agreed with the statement that 'All religions should be respected but only mine is true.' This weakening of religious orthodoxy has taken on massive proportions among the young. According to an opinion poll in France in 1998, 6 per cent of those who responded and only 4 per cent of all 18- to 29-year-olds regard their own religion as the only true one (see Hervieu-Léger 2006).

The individualized faithful are turning their backs on the ancient church fathers and their dogmas – much as politically and morally concerned young people are abandoning the trade unions, the political parties and traditional associations. At every turn, opinion succumbs to the *fallacy* that declining membership and the increasing age of churchgoers must be the consequence of the apathy and indifference of the younger generation, even though it is evident that new forms of morality, politics and religiosity are in the process of emerging behind and between the established organizations and that sociology stands in need of new perspectives and a new conceptual apparatus with which to come to terms with them.

6. In general terms, the individualization of religion tends to be equated with the privatization of religion – in other words, with the banishing of religion from the public sphere. (This is the demystification thesis of the first modernity.) This is a mistake. Individualization may lead to the privatization of religion, but need not do so. It may also help to prepare the way for a new public role for faith. There are three different arenas for such a 'de-privatization' of an apparently private religiosity, i.e. of the religiosity of a 'God of one's own choosing': the state (including terrorist violence), political discourse (the public sphere) and, finally, a (global) civil society. We may illustrate this with reference to the individualism of human rights (an individualism that has always been highly controversial among the religions). In this sense, Amnesty International may be understood as a modern church dedicated to a God of its own making.

A caveat must be entered here. Since an individual faith in a 'God of one's own' lacks an authoritative reference point outside the individual, is it capable of challenging the status quo? Since the spark of every revolt lies within the human being, does this not mean that attitudes to circumstances may change, but not the circumstances themselves? Is it not likely that a collective habit of navel-gazing will go hand in hand with an inability to cooperate?

These questions about the political theology of a 'God of one's own' acquire relevance because a religious second modernity can succeed only by reaching what may be a difficult decision in favour of religion in the context of world-religious plurality. The individualization of religion and cosmopolitization represent a break both with basing religious belief on chance biographical facts and with the orthodoxy of the religious authorities' rights to a territorial monopoly. Taken together, they produce the paradox of a collective global setting in which individuals have to create their 'own' religious authenticity by choosing from among various competing religious options and biographical experiences or else by deciding to leave things as they are.

7. The individualization of faith also means raising the question of the *legitimacy* of faith. In this context 'individualization' refers to the integrity and personal commitment of the religious individual. In other words, it is the 'credibility of his or her quest' that confers personal authority, not any efforts to conform to pre-existing truths. This de-institutionalization and subjectivization of religious truth is frequently the product of church teachings themselves which regard the obligation to go in search of subjective truth as the mark of the success of their pedagogic efforts. In this way the individualization of belief is established as a new principle that can be formulated as follows: in religious matters there is no truth apart from the personal truth that one has acquired through one's own efforts. Since this principle applies to *both* sides, i.e. to both institutionalized religion and individualized belief, this implies that behind the façades with their apparent continuities there are profound shifts in the ascription and definition of religious 'truth'.

8. The individualization of belief is not synonymous with *standardization*. The de-traditionalizing of religious belief does not result in any truly individual proliferation of faith narratives, any more than de-traditionalizing love and sexuality leads

automatically to an individualized form of love and sexuality in a strict sense. This is true if for no other reason than the predominance of the commodity form in the available 'religious products' and the standardized way they are consumed. The individualization of belief, then, obeys the mechanisms of the symbolic economy of religion, which is increasingly penetrated by the laws of the marketplace. This culminates in the paradox that when looked at from outside, highly individualized faith cultures in which every man or woman ascribes to himself or herself the authenticity of a spiritual faith narrative function in a completely standardized manner. Hence we may say that the pattern of individualized faith is in actual fact the standard collective consciousness that I am unable to see for what it is because it thinks of itself as individual.

What is standardization? A good indicator – at least in the world of European Christianity – is the empirically demonstrable adherence to a 'minimum creed':

> This can be summed up as follows: 'God loves you, Jesus saves, and you can be healed.' Theological clarification of this 'creed' is not required and its practical effectiveness is meant to be experienced personally by each believer. This 'doctrinal reduction' is linked to the expansion within this movement of an emotional religiosity that explicitly preaches putting the intellectual mind on the back burner and promotes the value of emotional experience of the presence of the Spirit. This theological minimalism – which reduces the relation with transcendence to the mere emotionalized and personalized closeness experienced with the divine being – allows the efficient adaptation of the content of exhortation to the demands of modern individualism for self-fulfilment and personal realization. (Hervieu-Léger 2006: 64)

9. To what extent can the individualization of faith be based on the construct of a 'God of one's own'? What is the meaning of a God 'of one's own'? It should be noted that we are not dealing with a 'postmodern' concept. The 'God of one's own' is the pinnacle in a long process embedded in the Christian tradition itself. It is a tradition in the course of which the autonomy of the individual gradually comes to prevail *over* the collective definition of religiosity and the social. This process can be traced back to St Augustine and Descartes; others regard the great spiritual move-

ments of the seventeenth and eighteenth centuries and the invention of a 'caring' God – following the Reformation and the radical affirmation of a religious individualism – as the decisive steps.

The question remains of the extent to which a 'God of one's own' is a faith surrogate corresponding to the false promise of art-as-religion [*Kunstreligion*]. The idea of art-as-religion arose following the collapse of science-as-religion, which (to oversimplify) arose for its part in reaction to the collapse of religion proper. And in this context, art is seen for the most part as a parade ground on which the quasi-religious attitudes of a largely secularized society can be drilled. The experience of art is one which gives voice to a sacred aura in which the religious sensibility of a secularized world finds expression and asserts itself. This articulates a religious decisionism based on the paradox that the believer creates a 'God of his or her own' whose self-revelation holds out the promise of subjective certainty and redemption for a life 'of his or her own'. We are reminded here of the philosopher Fichte, who conceived of the self-postulating 'ego' as the source of all transcendent and immanent insights and certainties.

10. The horizon of possibilities opened up by this development encompasses various phases, including that of repudiating the privatization of religion and affirming its public role. That public role is treated in the present book in two ways. First, we ask how far religion plays the part of an *actor in the process of (cosmopolitan) modernization*. When states barricade themselves behind national walls, when global capital maximizes its profits, to what extent is it, or can it be made, possible for religions to join forces with transnational, civil movements to respond to global problems and put them on the world's agenda? Basing itself on the premises of secularization, sociology has turned the religions into the object of passive demystification at the hands of the irresistible process of modernization. Modernizing the religions and turning them into museum pieces seem to be two sides of the same coin. If the premise of secularization falters, this will open the door to a fresh sociological scrutiny of religions and religious movements in the twenty-first century, a scrutiny that will cease to think of them as victims, but will see them as the *agents* of an anti-modern modernization, one critical of modernization.

Second, the cosmopolitan vision of including religious others in one's own religiosity is illustrated in exemplary fashion by the

'Gandhi model' or the 'Martin Luther King model'. By learning to break with his religious origins, Hinduism in his case, by learning to see them through the eyes of his Western friends, and to assess them in the course of an exchange of views and discussion about Christian ideas (methodological conversion), Gandhi discovered the richness of Hinduism. This ultimately opened up the path of non-violent resistance in a way that created a role for religion in the eyes of a world public.

4

Heresy or the Invention of a 'God of One's Own'

The individualistic misunderstanding of individualization

The obfuscation that envelops the discussion of concepts such as the 'individual', 'individualism' and 'individualization' from the outset arises from the meanings that are seemingly inseparable from these words: in particular, the idea that individualism is the necessary consequence of individual and hence egoistic feelings and interests. Nothing can be further from the truth. It is this that I have termed the *individualistic misunderstanding of individualization*, and that I intend to refute and reduce *ad absurdum*. According to this grave and only seemingly self-evident error, the millions and thousands of millions of individual actions of human beings must be ascribed to their feverish egoism. Only when this error has been wholly eradicated will we be able to focus on the socio-historical architecture of individualization and view it as a historical form of subjectivity whose consequences and costs can be calculated.

In the remote past, individualism was a merely nominal value, an idea, an ideology. But more recently it has been consolidated and has crystallized into an *institutionalized morality* that powerfully and effectively establishes the foundations of what Eric Hobsbawm has called the twin revolutions of the nineteenth century: the revolution that led to the modern, democratic nation-state and the other revolution that produced what Max Weber called the 'spirit of capitalism', which emerged from the Protestant work ethic. Both – the democracy of the nation-state and entre-preneurial capitalism – are based on the principle of free individuals who represent their own enlightened self-interests, while simultaneously claiming the right to make their political views known (and of course their right to private property), and who defend these rights in the arenas of the democratic *polis*. Individualization, closely bound up with the ethos of Christianity and modernity, signifies the cultivation of the autonomous will of all human beings without distinction.

The subjectivist misunderstanding of individualization is based on the assumption that the individuals who revolve around themselves are also the authors of that revolving process. This interpretation fails to recognize that the utopia of one's own life, and, with it, the utopia of a God of one's own, is deeply etched into the institutional fabric of the Western world. To put it in a nutshell: *individualization* must be clearly distinguished from *egoism*. Whereas egoism is normally understood as a personal attitude or preference, individualization refers to a macro-historical, macro-sociological phenomenon that may – though not necessarily will – be reflected in changes in attitude. That is the *crux of the contingency* that comes into the world through individualization. How individuals come to terms with it is an open question.

Like Zygmunt Bauman and Anthony Giddens, I maintain that individualization is misunderstood if it is treated as a process that arises from conscious choice or individual preference. Individualization has in fact been imposed on individuals as a consequence of the long history of modern institutions. No one recognized this sooner or more clearly than Émile Durkheim, who showed over a century ago how the sacredness of religion was transferred to the sacredness of the individual: 'This is far indeed from that apotheosis of comfort and private interest, that egoistic cult of the self for which utilitarian individualism [or market liberalism] has partly been reproached.' In order to focus on institutional individualization, we must turn our attention

> from what concerns us personally, from all that relates to our empirical individuality, so as uniquely to seek that which our

human condition demands, that which we hold in common with all our fellow men. This ideal goes so far beyond the limit of utilitarian ends that it appears to those who aspire to it as marked with a religious character. The human person, whose definition appears as the touchstone, according to which good must be distinguished from evil, is considered as sacred, in what one might call the ritual sense of the word. It has something of that transcendental majesty which the churches of all times have given to their gods. It is conceived as being invested with that mysterious property which creates an empty space around holy objects, which keeps them away from profane contacts and which draws them away from ordinary life. And it is exactly this feature which induces the respect of which it is the object. Whoever makes an attempt on a man's life, on a man's liberty, on a man's honour, inspires us with a feeling of horror, in every way analogous to that which the believer experiences when he sees his idol profaned.

The institutionalized morality of individualization is therefore not simply 'a wise principle of economy. *It is a religion of which man is, at the same time, both believer and God'*.[1]

The historical subject form of individualization with which we shall have to deal, now and in the future,[2] is not the expression of human freedom of decision in the abstract, as Kant saw it. Kant identified individual motives as the source of evil: my actions are morally good only if the principle of my morality is capable of being universalized, if the maxims governing my actions do not derive from my social situation, my interests or my passions. Accordingly, an act is 'good' only if it is *uncoupled* from the subjectivity of the actor. Rousseau argues along similar lines. In his view only the *general* will, purified of all particular interests, may serve as the foundation of the social contract. Individualization, however, means more than this higher morality, which, on the one hand, takes its leave of the particular individual while, on the other, it remains attached to the universalized individual. Both individual individualism and the universalized moral individualism are replaced by an *institutionalized individualization*. This must be decoded as the product of religious struggles fought on

---

[1] 'L'individualisme et les intellectuels', in *Revue bleue*, vol. 10, 1898. Quoted here from Durkheim 1969: 21–2 (emphasis added).
[2] And throughout the world, if we accept John W. Meyer's empirical analyses of globalization and the diffusion of cultures, science and law, etc.

behalf of religious toleration, of civil, political and social basic rights, and, not least, of the universal human rights that are supposed to guarantee the freedoms of the universalized individual – a claim that is not invalidated by its constant violation in the real world. Considered from this point of view, individualization does not end up in anarchy – on the contrary, it represents the system of beliefs and values that can guarantee a moral unity that transcends boundaries, national defences.

> One often hears it said today that only a religion can bring about this harmony [that transcends boundaries]. This proposition, which modern prophets feel it necessary to utter in a mystical tone of voice, is really no more than a simple truism over which everyone can agree . . . Now, all the evidence points to the conclusion that *the only possible candidate is precisely this religion of humanity* whose rational expression is the individualistic morality. To what, after all, should collective sentiments be directed in future? . . . One is thus gradually proceeding towards a state of affairs, now almost attained, in which the members of a single social group will no longer have anything in common other than their humanity. (Durkheim 1969: 25–6, emphasis added)

Durkheim here anticipates the union of individualization and cosmopolitanism.

> This idea of the human person, given different emphases in accordance with the diversity of national temperaments, is therefore the sole idea that survives, immutable and impersonal, above the changing tides of particular opinions; and the sentiments which it awakens are the only ones to be found in almost all our hearts. . . . This is why man has become a god for man. . . . (Ibid.: 26)

The idea on which individualization is based, namely the belief that the individual is sacred, states that man has become a god for man. In this connection Habermas speaks of a 'salvaging translation':

> [Philosophy] has indeed transformed the original religious meaning . . . but without emptying it through a process of deflation and exhaustion. One such translation that salvages the substance of a term is the translation of the concept of 'man in the image of

God' into that of the identical dignity of all men that deserves
unconditional respect. This goes beyond the borders of one particular religious fellowship and makes the substance of Biblical
concepts accessible to a general public that also includes those who
have other faiths and those who have none. (Habermas 2006:
44–5)

And in the interior of the religion of the godlike individual, altars
are erected to a God of one's own. In the language of both
Durkheim and Habermas, we 'believe' in human rights because
in them man's likeness to God has acquired its secular-cum-sacred
form and has in part even been institutionalized in law.[3] Thus,
for example, Amnesty International may be said to represent a
modern church dedicated to a 'god of its own'. If today global
justice is on the agenda of cross-border civil societies, what we
are witnessing are secular priestly movements acting in the service
of the worldly religion of man's likeness to God (Kurasawa 2007).

Admittedly, 'heretical' questions inevitably thrust themselves to
the fore. If the individual's religion is based on man's likeness to
God, does he *not* deserve the dignity and rights of man as man?
When we recognize the dignity of persons who are religiously and
culturally other, is that human dignity no more than a secondary
phenomenon derived from the dignity of God, the unique creator
of the world? Does it follow from this that human rights are
merely a reflection of the glory of God? If God is the Christian
God (or the Jewish God or the Muslim God) who suffers no other
God beside Himself, then what is to become of the rights of
others? Would not the universal nature of human dignity and
human rights overtax each individual God and even force Him
into heresy? If we think of man's likeness to God as *specific to
specific religions* (and how else *should* we think of it), must we
not conclude, in the light of the limits imposed on God in the
monotheistic faiths, that human rights would have to be granted
to millions of people and denied to other millions? If all the
faiths conferred human rights only on their followers while
denying them to unbelievers, how could the universality of human
rights, their universal mutual recognition, ever come to prevail?

---

[3] On the relation of human rights to religions, see *inter alia* Hoffmann 1994;
Hoppe 2002; Höver 2001; Koch 1991; Nurser 2005.

Would not the world religions be forced to leap over their own monotheistic shadows?

Individualization is, as we have noted, an original Christian invention. From the very outset, Christianity addressed its gospel to the individual – beyond all questions of status, class, ethnicity and nation – and in that respect it is more modern than many of its opponents. And yet, paradoxically, these foundations of a political theology of a God of one's own were imposed on the Christian churches from outside. The Christian conception of the dignity and the rights of man was proclaimed 'in many respects in the teeth of the opposition of Christian churches and organizations', as has been emphasized by Wolfgang Huber, the chairman of the council of the Lutheran church. And this is true of Catholic and Protestant churches in equal measure:

> Papal doctrine regards ideas of human rights as 'unbridled doctrines of liberty' (Leo XIII) inspired by the Reformation and incompatible with both the natural law and the teachings of the Holy Office. The view prevailing in German Protestantism 'regarded human rights as an instance of individualism at work, which failed to appreciate the sinfulness of man and the necessity of a stable state power.... The dignity common to all men was never the determining factor in the ecclesiastical or political order in either the early church or the Middle Ages.' (Huber 1992: 591, 578; quoted by Angenendt 2007: 117)

In contrast to this, what we hear from Jean-Paul Sartre in *Being and Nothing* is that 'We are all Catholics.' Sartre's 'we' means 'we Europeans'. And what his words imply is that the emphasis on the individual bears the stamp of its origins in religion. At the same time, it shows that an individual's religion dissolves the outer shell of European religious identity by disseminating a spiritual individualism in its place. In so doing, it brings about a fundamental change in church institutions and the mechanisms for passing religious identity from one generation to the next. Admittedly, the journey to reach this goal had been lengthy, tortuous and improbable, full of contradictions and alternative byways that might have been taken. All this will now be sketched in with reference to the history of heresy, orthodoxy and tolerance (within Christianity).

Heresy and orthodoxy: Concerning the historical improbability of religious freedom

> Of all the great world religions past and present, Christianity has been by far the most intolerant. This statement may come as a shock, but it is nevertheless true. In spite of the fact that Jesus Christ, the Jewish founder of the Christian religion, is shown in the New Testament as a prophet and saviour who preached mutual love and non-violence to his followers, the Christian church was for a great part of its history an extremely intolerant institution. From its inception it was intolerant of other non-Christian religions, first Greco-Roman polytheism, then Judaism, from which it had to separate itself, and later on Islam. Early in its history, from the time of the apostles, it also became increasingly intolerant of heresy and heretics, those persons who, although worshippers of Christ, dissented from orthodox doctrine by maintaining and disseminating beliefs – about the nature of Christ, the Trinity, the priesthood, the church and other matters – that ecclesiastical authority condemned as false, and incurring the penalty of damnation. (Zagorin 2004: 1)

If today the truth and legitimacy of faith has been placed in the hearts, conscience and hands of the sanctified individual in the shape of a God of one's own choosing, the contrast to the orthodoxy of the Christian churches could scarcely be greater. And we would do well to be mindful of this fact in Europe, where xenophobic attitudes commonly castigate an extremely diverse religion like Islam for its intolerance and its religiously motivated violence and terrorism. Christianity may have undergone a conversion from an intolerance prosecuted with fire and sword to a limited form of toleration. It now finds itself facing the new challenge of global religious pluralism. Such a conversion could not simply be imposed from outside; it had also to involve an inner, substantive change. That being the case, this 'revolutionary conversion' can be construed as a change in Christianity's understanding of the truth of its faith (or its striving to achieve that understanding). I suggest that this as yet incomplete (counter-)revolution of Christian (in)tolerance should be regarded as derived from an original contradiction in Christianity and that it should be explored further in two directions. On the one hand, it may be seen as a dialectic between its 'fundamental principle' and its 'fundamental institutions'; and, on the other hand, we can examine it by means of the crucial cosmopolitan question: How do you, Christianity, (Judaism, Islam) regard your religious others – your *internal* religious others (heresy), your *ethnic* religious others (other languages, nations, histories, rulers and ruled), as well as *interdenominational* others (Hinduism, Buddhism, Judaism and Islam)?

On the dialectic of fundamental Christian principles and Christian institutions

One, perhaps even *the*, fundamental principle of the Christian religion is that of the freedom of the individual. It is symbolized by baptism: that is to say, the individual's free decision in favour of the imagined community of Christendom. The concept of the 'fundamental principle' goes together with a methodological notion: what is meant is *not* idealist principles that prevail in the historical process by virtue of their inner charisma (logic), but the *scope for potentials*, in other words collective, discursive constructs whose creation calls for not just pioneering insights but also material resources. The selection and validity of these constructs are grounded not least in the power relations of the historical context in which they share. In the case of baptism, we are dealing with a fundamental Christian principle with its own in-built *contradiction*. The sovereignty of *subjective choice*, the individual confession of faith on which everything else is based, includes the surrender of sovereign will, the integration of the individual into the *pre-existing hierarchy and orthodoxy of the religious community*. This principle enables us to make distinctions between the various religions (Catholics, Protestants, Buddhists, Muslims and New Religious Movements) by observing how they deal with this tension between the individualization and collectivization of belief – in other words, between inclusion or non-inclusion in a church. In an extreme case, the religiosity or spirituality of a 'God of one's own' would mean the proud awareness of being an utterly distinctive human being before God and in God's eyes, attached neither to a church nor to a community.[4]

---

[4] Which leads to the question: how far can this non-institutionalized individual religiosity be handed down in its extreme forms or, more simply, how far are these individualized monads of faith capable of cooperation (Bruce 2006)?

For this reason, it is desirable to introduce the distinction referred to in Chapter 3 above (p. 81) between Individualization One and Individualization Two. *Individualization One* reconstructs the struggles to achieve individualization arising *within* Christianity from the re-orientation of specific medieval 'potentials' embedded in the conflicts between individualization and collectivization (during the Reformation). Individualization Two reconstructs the genesis of a God of one's own *outside* Christianity, in particular in the context of *welfare-state* individualization after the Second World War in Europe ('post-religious individualization').

In its 'fundamental principle' (i.e. in its room for manoeuvre, which is always controversial and, as history shows, is only ever made a reality to a more or less limited degree), the Christian religion is not a religion of origins – that is to say, its boundaries do not coincide with ethnicities, nations, races, age groups, genders, rulers and ruled, or specific territories. It is a universalist religion (i.e. it recognizes the equality of believers while discriminating against non-believers) or else a cosmopolitan faith (i.e. a faith which recognizes the equality and difference of others).[5] In its origins it gave birth to the creator of individualism. Christian individualism does not lead to the glorification of the self. It consists in the general empowering of the believing individual, who, with the aid of Christian doctrine, establishes a commonality and community that transcends barriers. The driving force of this movement is not egotism, it is the *Imitatio Christi* which Christianity has preached for two thousand years, the sympathy for all human beings, compassion with their sufferings and tragedies, and the wish to combat them and assuage them. It represents a greater thirst for justice.

The supreme dogma of the Christian cult of the individual is the autonomy of individual experience, the individual conscience (which later even became known as 'reason'), and as its supreme rite, the tradition of free inquiry. Here we see the basic contradiction – or should we call it the irony? – of a Christian orthodoxy built on the individual confession of faith: the church hierarchy, including the Inquisition, becomes the breeding ground of a modern individualism which looks as if it might end up

---

[5] On the distinction between 'religious universalism' and 'religious cosmopolitanism', see pp. 69–73 above and pp. 175–7 below.

jeopardizing the authority and continued existence of the Christian churches, at least in Europe, or else forcing them into a redefinition of Christianity. Thus whoever attempts to represent the individualistic morality of modern society as a counter-principle to Christian morality, and to portray the latter as the antidote to the former, commits a capital error since he or she is attempting to replace the evil of individualism with the evil of the Christian morality of the individual.

The background of this movement towards individualism is the 'potential' of the fundamental principle. By insisting on the individual's faith as the essential prerequisite of piety, Christianity puts a dynamic in motion whose task is to set limits to this individuality in order to shore up the newly defined authority of the church, which feels threatened by it. The distinction between *church* and *individual faith* leads to the blurring of boundaries. This is because priority lies with the faith of individual Christians, which is always personal, specific and immediate, so that the authority of Christianity is based on the quicksand of individual piety. The fundamental problem of Christianity in the world lies in the difficulty of determining the boundaries of what is still 'Christian' and what no longer is, and who is to decide such questions.

In order to gain a conceptual handle on these 'Christian boundary politics' (see pp. 52–3 above), it seems sensible to distinguish between *first-order* and *second-order* questions. *First-order* questions are 'what-questions', concerning the nature of Christian faith; *second-order* questions are 'who-questions'. First-order questions deal with dogmas, rules and rites; they attempt to decide between 'true' Christianity and 'false'. They provide legitimate strategies with which to answer second-order questions about *who* is a Christian. What is at stake is the unity of Christianity, which is grounded neither in ethnicity, nationality or territoriality but instead operates globally, based on the choices made by believing individuals. These choices themselves presuppose plurality. Baptism's openness to the entire world leads initially to the linking of the 'who-question' with the 'what-question' and to providing an answer: the symbolic conflicts about the nature of belief serve to 'select out' the 'satanic and wicked' non-believers and, by abolishing social distinctions, to establish the unity and order of believers *urbi et orbi*.

In an apparent paradox, the fortifications of Christianity are not only, or not primarily, designed to defend the faith from attacks from without, from other faiths. The new fortifications are conceived as a defence against Christian others within, against Christian critics of Christianity who have articulated the contradictions between the basic principle of Christianity and the institutions of the church and contextualized them historically. The discourse of heretics and heresy among Catholic theologians and jurists labels the 'heretic' the enemy other who has no place in the community of believers. Jews and Muslims were and still are excluded as alien others and enemies of Jesus Christ. But a clear distinction was drawn between them and the wilful unbeliever, the heretic, because he is an apostate Christian who has betrayed his faith and has therefore excluded himself from the church (Pagels 1995: Chapter 6). Such a person was an excommunicate, forever damned, handed over to the secular arm for execution because the church itself shed no blood. He was guilty of divine *lèse-majesté*, of treason against God. He was held to be a 'putrid limb' that had to be 'cut off' in order to preserve the 'health of the body'. He was the wolf who preyed on the Christian souls of the lambs of God. Heresy is treated as a disease, and this is more than a mere metaphor. It contains the judgement that is then carried out against the heretic. Heresy is held to be 'a plague', a 'cancer', a 'poison' which must be 'excised' for the sake of the health of all (cf. Zagorin 2004: 44).

During the fourth century C.E., following the grant by the first Christian emperor Constantine and his colleague Licinus of legal toleration to Christianity and their imperial successors' decision to make it the sole legal religion of the Roman Empire, the Christian or Catholic Church, as we may now call it, approved both the Roman government's suppression of paganism as idolatry and its use of punitive laws and coercion against Christian heretics who denied Catholic teaching and formed schismatic churches. This initiated a development that led during the Middle Ages to the forcible conversion of pagan Germans and Slavs, Jews and Muslims at the hands of Christian rulers, and to the long Christian enmity toward the religion of Islam, which gave rise to the crusading movement of holy war in medieval Europe. It likewise led, because of the prevailing hatred of Jews as enemies of Christ, to frequent charges of ritual murder against Jews and to the instigation by

Catholic religious preachers of repeated massacres of Jews in
Europe. And it led also to the medieval church's legitimation of
religious persecution and its machinery of heresy hunting, the
creation of the papal Inquisition . . . and the killing of innumerable
fellow Christians whom the Church denounced as heretics.
(Zagorin 2004: 1–2)

Individualization One: The 'invention' of a God of one's own: Martin Luther

The 'heresy' of the Reformation – should we call it the revolution
of individualization? – for which Martin Luther 'stands' ('Here I
stand, I cannot do otherwise . . .') takes up this basic contradiction
in Christianity between individual faith and the religious church
tradition with its hostility to individual decision. Luther reconstructs it but fails to resolve it. On the contrary, he fills it with a
new tension. This 'Individualization One' takes place *within* religion. What this means for the politics of Protestantism is that
Luther 'only' redraws the boundary between believers and non-
believers, but does not do away with it altogether. This has the
consequence that the Reformation produces its own heretics,
while plunging Europe into endless wars of religion and ensuring
that even the 'heresy of the Reformation' is subject to conflicting
assessments by hostile value systems (a process that persists to this
day, as can be seen from Pope Benedict XVI's recent condemna-
tions of the Protestant churches in 2006).

The 'invention' of a God of one's own is perhaps the heart of
Luther's revolution. It was he who succeeded in the 'inconceivable', 'monstrous', 'heretical' task of providing a foundation for
the subjective freedom of conscience as opposed to church orthodoxy. What he did was to construct the individual's immediate
proximity to God by conflating the *'one'* true God with the
God *'of one's own'*. If the 'God of one's own' is taking His leave
from the churches at the beginning of the twenty-first century,
this second, global reformation on the part of the New Religious
Movements can be seen as a belated echo of Luther's self-
contradictory figure of the God who is both the one true God and
the God of one's own.

Taking Luther as his model, Hans-Georg Soeffner has traced
the pathway from collective worship to the Protestant variant of

individualization. His intention was not simply to follow a biographical pattern but to provide a sociological reconstruction
of a form of 'self-presentation'. Modelled on earlier forms of
collective worship, this involved mastering techniques of self-
examination or the emergence of a 'self' observing itself in a
manner that has since become second nature (Soeffner 1997: 20).
To phrase it in terms of my definition (see pp. 48–9), Luther sepa-
rates the adjective 'religious' from the noun 'religion'. To be religious has ceased to be simply the either/or of religion, in which
you are bound to the authority of the church. It defines instead
the individual's *attitude* to God. This allows subjective faith to be
decoupled from church authority and the sources of the certainty
of faith to be transferred to the personal encounter with a 'God
of one's own'. In consequence, the 'subjective meaning' of social
action (which Max Weber set out to explore) became a theme of
the theory and sociology of religion that was as important as it
was difficult to resolve (cf. Graf 2004: 100). On the one hand,
everything is based on the subjective sources of the certainty
implicit in the statement that 'I believe'. On the other hand, can
anyone understand a believer without a knowledge of that believer's 'own personal God'? Putting it in cosmopolitan terms, how
can we contrive to look into the heart of someone of a different
religious persuasion?

Whoever substitutes the self for the religious hierarchy as the
source of religious certainty achieves not only a change of perspective but a 'change of world'.[6] In Luther's case, the macrocosm of
the world is replaced by the microcosm of individual experience,
of conscience, the conflict between self-interest and necessity, and
so on.

> No longer is the *civitas* the battlefield upon which the armies of
> God and Satan meet. Accordingly, the war with 'Satan' is no
> longer to be waged by the polis or community. This war 'rages'
> within the individual. The war for the human being takes place
> *within* the human being. And at the same time he is (usually the
> sole) witness of this merciless struggle. (Soeffner 1997: 8–9)

---

[6] Similarly, in Fichte's philosophy of the self – as earlier on in Luther's religion
of the self – the external world is replaced by the 'non-self', which is represented
only by the consciousness of the self.

What is the special nature of a 'God of one's own'? In the first place, the individual is released from the bonds of traditional churchgoing and authority. With Luther, the individual is expected to abandon the protection of 'Mother' Church, and this spells the end of the protective representative who mediates between the individual and his God. 'Tradition is little or nothing, the immediacy of the "manifest word" as the immediacy of God Himself is everything' (ibid.: 13). One consequence is that 'the attention of the faithful is focused on faith, penitence, and mercy, on the individual's immediacy to God' (ibid.). This change leads to a revaluation of all values, both inner and outer, of both world and faith. The inner cosmos of a God of one's own gains priority as the source of salvation over the outer cosmos of the world.

> By concentrating on the immediate encounter with God, the cyclical and ritual order of time is dissolved into a chain of moments of decision and testing, while the cyclical succession of generations is dissolved into one person's individualization before God. The smallest unit of society – the individual – becomes, tendentially, the sole and thus the highest authority by way of the postulate of immediacy. (Ibid.)

Luther's stand at the Imperial Diet in Worms made this shift of priorities public. This stand is not the symbol of a new, collective, merely 'reformed' religious practice. Rather, he turns the inner religious transformation into something public and in this way he emphasizes the 'scandal', the 'heresy' of 'isolation' as the central quality of this type of religious subjectivity, which itself, in the shape of conscience – empowered by a 'God of one's own' – pits itself against the collective authorities. 'Thus I cannot and will not retract anything, because it is neither salutary nor safe to act against my *conscience*. So help me God' (ibid.: 14).

That is the one side of the question – the other side is that Luther sets *limits* to this freeing up of the subjectivization and individualization of faith authorities. In accordance with these limits, the immediate presence of God is tied to the immediate presence of God's *word*. Luther's own personal God is therefore not the do-it-yourself God of the twenty-first century, but the literal God of the Bible, the *personal* and *only* God who reveals Himself in the Scriptures. Paradoxical though it may seem,

Luther's 'own God' is identical with the one and only God of the Bible. Luther combines – not without contradiction – a subjectivized, individualized God with the monotheistic God-monopoly. The personal *and* only God remains committed to religious universalism. He, too, lays claim to absolute validity so as to be able to renew the elemental, basic experiences of individualized 'spirituality' in a controllable manner.

How does Luther manage to combine subjectivity and universalism in this personal God? By basing himself on an act of divine revelation in which the immediacy of the *text* coincides with the immediacy of *God*. Because their Protestantism is a monotheistic, world religion based on a book immediately accessible to individual believers, Luther and Calvin are compelled to draw a clear and, if need be, blood-stained line separating believers from unbelievers. The Protestants' 'unique', personal God revealed in the text fans their hatred of false believers, heathen, heretics and idolaters.

In this way, Luther 'transformed' the contradiction between individual and collective belief. The Bible (translated into German), the literal belief in the Scriptures, made possible the freedom of a Christian *from* the dogmas of the Catholic Church and simultaneously tied the believer into the either/or religion of the reformers. Both actions are grounded in the revealed word of God: liberation from the church *and* reintegration into the established reformed church – even though this self-contradictory halfway house between a 'good' and an 'evil', a 'true' and a 'Satanic' individualization of God was to prove neither convincing nor sustainable.

But even at the time, Luther's historical compromise solution to the contradiction between an individualized and a universal God required institutional props. Anyone who, like Luther, overthrows religious authority, undermines the (infallible) Pope and empowers the individual to take control of his or her own beliefs must clothe the isolated experience in a socially binding form. The symbolic activity in which isolated faith and religious community are brought together in an institution is the sacrament of *confession* (Foucault 1972; Hahn 1982). In the confession, where struggles between being and not-being, damnation and forgiveness are acted out, the narrative form of the reflexive self is born. This narrative form then goes on to acquire artistic authority in

Bildungsromane [novels of education], and secular authority in diaries and biographies.

The Catholic confessional is the meeting place of God, as represented by His church, the priest and the individual sinner. The act of confession presupposes that the penitent constitutes himself as a 'self' and thinks of himself as a 'person' who is able to exercise his 'liberty' and to distinguish between his own 'motives' and 'actions'. The turn towards the inner self is made even more radical if, as is the case with Luther, it is not just a person's acts and their consequences that are held to be 'sin' but also his motives and intentions, all of which have to be 'narrated' to his God if forgiveness is to be obtained. This is the starting point of that process of reflection with which the sinful believer torments himself and which is anticipated in the institutionalized confession as interiorized self-interrogation and self-censorship: Why do I want what I want? Why do I not want what I ought to want? Such reflections assume not just the form of silent monologue but also that of the verbalized 'confession' in the eyes of God, a social narrative of one's own wishes and actions. Is the individual an invention of the confession? Is the birth of the *legend* of the free, sinful individual a product of the reflection on oneself, the feeling of responsibility and the attempt to justify oneself in the eyes of one's own God which have been, as it were, 'conditioned' in the act of confession? Does the confession both presuppose and liberate the act of reflection on oneself? And does the socially authoritative narrative genre of 'self-reflexive biography' emerge – in secularized form – from this institutionally approved mode of self-reflection, self-observation and self-accusation?

Luther introduced a crucial change to the traditional Catholic model of the confession and endowed it with a structure appropriate to that change. This 'reformation of the confession' arises as a consequence of the individualization of God. In the classical confession, the Catholic Church, which thinks of itself as a 'sacred institution' and a 'sacrament', encounters the individual believer in the guise of the priest. It is just this that Luther rejects: praying and confessing are forms of God's immediacy and hence forms of dialogue with 'one's own personal God': 'He who to the end of his days retained and defended the confession at the same time radicalizes it and abolishes it in its ritualized, distanced, and protective form for the later realm of Protestant influence. Nor does the "Catholic" form of confession remain unaffected by these changes' (Soeffner 1997: 18).

> Thus the 'external Church' as a sacred institution is, in the Protestant view, relieved not only of legitimation and power, but also – far more significantly – of its influence on daily life, in which it formerly had been included in a pastoral, protective and advisory role. The Protestant parish, in which on the one hand each individual develops his unique relationship to God and in which, on the other hand, the community as a whole shows its tendency to control the individual members of the parish, is utterly different from the ritual and ritualized, institutionally organized, traditional community of the Catholic Church and its basically 'rational-systematic' form (Max Weber) of pastoral care. (Ibid.: 19)

This isolation *within* the religious community is evidently self-contradictory: does it not disguise the high degree of socialization whose product it is? The very 'reintegration' of the individual in the reformed church becomes the motor of isolation – and this perpetuates the contradiction. The consequence is that Protestants are exactly what the word says, namely chronic resisters, collectively socialized.

Above all, however, the individual preoccupied with himself and his own God is always at risk of losing sight of the social and political horizon. Social and political crises are transformed into internal crises and attributed to disturbances in the individual's relation to his own personal God. Disasters that engulf the world are explained by the fact that humankind 'has lost its peace in God' and its obedience 'to God' (ibid.: 28). From the vantage point of the observer, we are tempted to conclude that we are witnessing the birth of the autobiographical monologue, disguised as a dialogue with God. But it is difficult to halt the process of the individualization of God. In the final analysis, it is not any transcendental realm that is expected to provide answers to the agonizing problems of life, but the individual himself.

In his likeness to God and his nearness to Him, the individual discovers in himself the source of 'self-fulfilment', 'authenticity' and 'creativity'. All these qualities are easily identifiable as qualities that used to be reserved for a single being, namely God, in the Christian faith of the Middle Ages, including Luther's. The for the most part unconscious transfer of the attributes of the divine Creator to an immanent concept of the subject, together with the associated fantasies of omnipotence, self-justification, illusions – and disappointments – is characteristic of the God of one's own making in the context of the individual and his world. Thus we may speak of 'the self-reflexive, self-sufficient, autonomous, "emancipated" subject. And the Lutheran variant of this type, its emancipation or "liberation" according to the degree of "inner freedom", belongs to the new "Gods" and heroes who inhabit, in the mental configuration of the Enlightenment, the new inner Mount Olympus' (ibid.: 35–6).

The idea of the text as the site at which the *one and only* God of *one's own* is revealed contains the central contradiction of the Lutheran formula of individualization. This contradiction of what might be termed the monotheistic individualization of God is what breaks out fairly brutally in its treatment of 'heretics' guilty of the 'heresy' of publicly raising the question of the evident ambiguity of God's immediate presence in the text of the Bible.

The Christian critique of heresy: Sebastian Castellio

Martin Luther and John Calvin, the rebels who rose up against the 'institutionalized heresy' of the Catholic Church, were at least as Catholic as the Catholics when it came to fanatical intolerance. This provoked Voltaire to the assertion that of all religions the Christian religion was undoubtedly the one which should instil the greatest toleration, 'although so far the Christians have been the most intolerant of all men' (quoted according to Zagorin 2004: 3, 295).[7]

The English word 'tolerance' stems from the Latin verb '*tolerare*', which is defined as 'to bear or endure'. This means in the first place that the great word 'tolerance' points more immediately to a reluctant forbearance than to a wholehearted acknowledgement of the liberty and alterity of others. Furthermore, tolerance presupposes the possibility of withdrawing toleration – in short, of a ruler who concedes toleration but who may retract his magnanimity at any time. Tolerance, therefore, presupposes a minimal readiness to 'endure' a certain degree of religious coexistence and plurality. This minimal tolerance, which is not based on values,

[7] For the discussion that follows I am indebted above all to Zagorin as well as to Bainton 1964; Buisson 1892; Guggisberg 1997; and Pagels 1995.

recognition or Christian faith, is the product of insight into the principle of 'the lesser evil'. Bled dry by never-ending wars of religion, devastated and perverted externally and internally, the earthly regiment of kings and princes resolved on a lasting armistice and agreed for the most part on a pragmatic coexistence based on the principle of geographical separation.

By contrast, the church's laws of intolerance were based on the distinction between believers and unbelievers. Because in the Christian environment this distinction was drawn on the foundation of a shared experience of baptism and a community of believers, it easily became caught up in contradictions. Why should people who, like all Christians, know that God exists, that Christianity is the true religion and that the same moral ideas are present in all humankind because God has implanted them in each and everyone of us, why should such people be excommunicated or even brutally executed by the secular power at the behest of the church merely because they have cast doubt on an item of dogma or have merely given it a different interpretation?

Thomas Aquinas, a Dominican and one of the leading philosophers and theologians of the Middle Ages, justified this practice. Asked whether heretics should be tolerated, he answered with a determined No: for 'they deserve not only to be separated from the Church by excommunication, but also to be shut off from the world by death'. He explained with the aid of an analogy:

> For it is a much more serious matter to corrupt faith, through which comes the soul's life, than to forge money, through which temporal life is supported. Hence if forgers of money or other malefactors are straightway justly put to death by secular princes, with much more justice can heretics immediately upon conviction be not only excommunicated but also put to death. (Cited in Zagorin 2004: 43)

Deviations from the Christian faith, violations of church dogma, are far more than personal sin. They are a threat to society.

In his book *De haereticis* (1554), Sebastian Castellio became one of the first men to have the courage to criticize this fundamental institution of Christian intolerance, with its roots in the Catholic Inquisition and secular execution. With its appeal to Christian fraternity and the love of one's neighbour, this book was a beacon in the struggle for religious freedom and tolerance. He knew John Calvin and worked with him for a time, until the moment when he condemned Calvin's crucial involvement in the first execution of a Protestant heretic, Michael Servetus, in Lyons on 27 October 1553. The most scandalous aspect of this event in his eyes was the fact that Calvin, a Protestant in Protestant Geneva, should have had a Protestant publicly burned at the stake, evidently in collusion with the Papal Inquisition. In so doing, Calvin betrayed the Christian religion together with true piety and love of one's neighbour (Zagorin 2004: 93–5).

Castellio argued that the Bible was full of riddles which Christians have struggled to solve for centuries. It is a collection of words and sentences capable of a wide variety of interpretations. In this context, what is the meaning of the word 'heretic'? That was Castellio's question, and he replied: 'I can discover no more than this, that we regard those as heretics with whom we disagree and who dispute with us about the true interpretation of the Bible.' He goes on to refer to the plethora of sects and groups of sectarian believers who proliferated in his day and competed with one another, and who regularly looked down on those they disagreed with as 'heretics', with the consequence that a Christian who passed for orthodox in one town or region might be banished or burned at the stake as a heretic in another.

If we dig deep enough, so Castellio maintains, we can discern behind the lethal labelling of a 'heretic' the epistemological problem of religious truth (see pp. 41–2 above and pp. 190–1 below). If the church is tied to faith, Castellio contends, the Protestant Servetus was executed even though he spoke the truth, i.e. because what he said was the truth in his eyes, even if he was in error. All Christians believe in the truth of their religion. No one calls his own Christianity false. If different sects proclaim and practise different truths, what gives a Calvin the right to brand certain Christians as heretics and to condemn them to death? What justifies his claim that he alone is in possession of the truth? Is it perhaps because he utters the word 'God'? But others do likewise. If the matter is unambiguous, to whom is it unambiguous? In the end, only to Calvin. For others likewise believe their own beliefs to be unambiguous.

Must we not ask: Why are human beings ready to die for their Christian convictions? Are not Christian heretics the authentic Christians who bear witness to the truth even though – like Jesus of Nazareth – they are threatened with a martyr's death?

Finally, Castellio brings to a head the rebellion of Christian faith against intolerance, including the intolerance of the Protestant churches, by stating: 'If Christ himself came to Geneva, he would be crucified. For Geneva is not a place of Christian liberty. It is ruled by a new pope, but one who burns men alive, while the pope at Rome at least strangles them first' (quoted from Zagorin 2004: 116).

Calvin himself (writing in defence of the idea of the immediate accessibility of Holy Scripture) expressed anger at the claim that the Bible was obscure and enigmatic. However, he involuntarily conceded the point by producing so many commentaries on it. He daily took issue with other writers, writing and disputing with the aim of clarifying the scriptures, while simultaneously assuring us that everything is perfectly clear. This did not mean, according to Castellio, that there were no certainties, no core truths in Christianity. Thus it is certain that Jesus Christ is the Son of God and that he did everything written about him in the New Testament. In *The Art of Doubting* (1563), Castellio places great emphasis on the word 'art' in the title. How are we to distinguish, he asks, between belief and doubt, truth and error? Why is it essential to have an *art* of doubting? People often sin because they believe where they should doubt and doubt where they should believe. They are ignorant of what they should know, and think they know what is unknown and perhaps even unknowable. Moreover, they persist in the belief that they can act in this way without affecting their salvation. The evils come not from doubting. The justification of doubt lies in the fact that it is highly dangerous to accept as certain things that are uncertain because it is precisely this that costs heretics their lives.[8] The evils, however, that flow from not doubting what should be doubted are as great as those that come from not believing what should be believed. If the Christian churches had doubted, they would not have brutally slaughtered so many holy Christians for accepting false beliefs in good faith.

In 1558, in one of his replies to his adversaries, Calvin denounced Castellio in the following words: 'You wish to subject the mysteries of God to a judgement according to human perception, and you make reason, which by blindness extinguishes all of God's

---

[8] On the relation between knowing and not knowing in the world risk society, see Beck 1999: Chapter 7.

glory, not only the leader and teacher, but dare to prefer it to Scripture' (quoted from Zagorin 2004: 141). This controversy likewise shows how the dialectic between the fundamental Christian principle (the free choice of faith) and the historically dominant and no less fundamental church institutions (the Inquisition, the burning of heretics) leads to violent bloodshed: on the one hand, on behalf of the individual's freedom of religious belief; on the other hand, to restrict that freedom and turn it into its opposite. The Inquisition has been overcome. But the role of the churches in a world of religious plurality still awaits clarification. The American Jesuit philosopher John Courtney Murray characterized the attitude of the Catholic Church to religious freedom as 'intolerance wherever possible, tolerance wherever necessary' (quoted from Zagorin 2004: 309). Notwithstanding this, Christian morality has elevated individualist morality into a fundamental principle, and this principle cannot be abandoned except at the price of forcing Christianity to abandon itself. This makes it impossible to denounce individualism as the enemy of Christianity. To combat individualism is simply to reinforce it. What needs to be discovered is how to resolve the paradox of an individualization process that combines Christian features with church institutions and to ensure that the resulting collectivity has the right balance and the right mode of being.

A God of one's own is a religion in which man is both God and a believer.

> But this religion is individualistic, since it has man as its object, and since man is, by definition, an individual. Indeed there is no system whose individualism is more uncompromising. Nowhere are the rights of man affirmed more energetically, since the individual is here placed on the level of sacrosanct objects; nowhere is he more jealously protected from external encroachments, whatever their source. . . . There is no reason of State which can excuse an outrage against the person when the rights of the person are placed above the State. If, therefore, individualism by itself is a ferment of moral dissolution, one can expect to see its anti-social essence as lying here. One can now see how grave this question is. For the liberalism of the eighteenth century, which is, after all, what is basically at issue, is not simply an armchair theory, a philosophical construction. It has entered into the facts, it has penetrated our institutions and our customs, it has become part of our whole life, and, if we really must rid ourselves of it, it is

our entire moral organization that must be rebuilt at the same time. (Durkheim 1969: 22)

John Locke's model of tolerance

Is one's own personal God a *public* God? What attitude does the religious individual adopt towards the commandments of the church, the laws of the state or the norms of society? The answer given by John Locke in his *Letter Concerning Toleration* (1689) is based on the Protestant conviction that true religion is *inward*, it consists in faith, in conviction; for the foundation of religion and of church identity lies in the sovereignty of subjective belief – and not outward forms of behaviour and their consequences. To put it somewhat colloquially, Locke's principle of tolerance is: 'Believe what you will, but do not impose your beliefs on others!'

In other words, the space in which the individual's religious freedom can unfold is one where the private realm is marked off from the public one. And this is achieved by mutual agreement between the state and its citizens, whatever their religious, secular or even anti-religious convictions happen to be. In Locke's view the state that is neutral on religious matters may not impose restrictions on its citizens' beliefs. The corollary of this, however, is that rules that have not been promulgated with a particular religious community in mind and that represent universal social norms must be binding on everyone. What is vital to a religion and what is superficial emerges from the separation of 'inner' and 'outer'. Matters that are irrelevant to individual belief include, for example, road-building or the food supply, and so on. The fact that the state organizes such externals involves no 'genuine' restriction on religious liberty because that liberty lies in subjective belief not in outer circumstances. Nothing that concerns the supra-individual public can impugn the authentic, true, private, inward individual religion of a God of one's own. Thus a compromise is struck between the freedom of all citizens as far as public activity is concerned and their religious freedom. This compromise does not mean that the plurality of religions can run riot in the private sphere, but that it can run riot *only* in the private sphere.

Admittedly, in the context of the headlong onrush of industrial capitalism, this acts as a 'functional' brake on the de-restriction of religiosity. What it means is that by effecting the definitive separation of private and public and by resolutely keeping his or her distance from science and the economy, from public affairs and politics, the Christian surrenders the world to the modernization process. This spells the end of any resistance on the part of the religions to advances in science and research or in general to the global expansion of capitalism and the risks and costs associated with that expansion. Religion is confined to the religious sphere, and that sphere is to be found in the private realm. In short, systems are differentiated functionally and the entire process has a green light!

Locke's hedging round of religion aspires to a neutral definition of religious tolerance and liberty. In actual fact, however, as the child of his age, what Locke sees is the variety of *Protestant sects* in England. To that extent, it is unsurprising that the abstract term 'tolerance' contains, often without making it explicit, the particular background consensus of Protestantism. The society of the personal God who has been banished to the private sphere is not society as such, but *Protestant* society. It is this God that underlies the idea of a secularized and individualized religion whose claim to public attention is reduced, not to say, 'castrated'.

Activities such as road-building that are 'neutral' and 'external' in the Protestant world-view may easily ignite almost intractable communal conflicts. That is the situation in Israel, for example, where a planned North–South bypass running through an Orthodox suburb in Jerusalem encountered the implacable opposition of the local population. Dominated by the liberal Meretz Party, the city council attempted to blunt the protests of orthodox Jews by putting forward a compromise proposal (in line with Locke's ideas of tolerance). Specifically, they offered to vote for the closure of the section of the bypass passing through that suburb on the Sabbath, if in exchange the Orthodox Party agreed to public transport operating in secular parts of the city on the Sabbath. Such a proposal presupposed the Protestant dilution of religion and had forgotten the intransigent attitude with which many orthodox believers seek to maintain their religious claims even in the seemingly 'insignificant externals' of religious faith.

Looked at in this way, it becomes obvious that, far from being neutral and tolerant, the public space created by the Lockean model can be seen to be partisan and intolerant since it was defined in Protestant terms. Locke's tolerance model assumes that religion is individual, private and divided into the various confessions in a way that is not shared – or not yet shared – by Orthodox Judaism, Orthodox Islam or Orthodox Catholicism.

There is a further objection to Locke's understanding of the constitution of the public and private spheres. There is no universal agreement about what is 'external' – in other words, religiously irrelevant; it varies according to the contexts of the different religions. Bodily matters such as circumcision or kosher food are not external, but internal to religion; they form the ferment that brings the religious community into being, that helps to make sacred the social ties that render a religion 'mobile', 'transportable' and 'fit for a diaspora'.

Much of what passes for externals in the minds of Protestant reformers appears to others as an essential constituent of faith. From a sociological standpoint, kosher food means that Jews will not eat with non-Jews (in the absence of further arrangements). In this sense, we must accuse Locke's idea of universal tolerance of being 'blind to the needs of particular religious groups'.

> Locke's religiously neutral state, which has been the basis of the liberal interpretation of the relations between religion and the state, is not religiously neutral at all, since it works with a Christian, specifically Protestant conception of religion. The Western world is blind to this fact since it thinks it inconceivable that one might speak of religion in any other way than as an inner faith. (Dellwing 2007)

And yet, with the emergence of nationalism in the nineteenth and twentieth centuries, the political abstinence characteristic of the Protestant narrative of religion was decisively abandoned: 'In Germany, Protestant theologians frequently thought of the hoped-for unity of the nation as the completion of the Reformation' (Graf 2004: 130; see also pp. 184–6 below).

Individualization Two: The welfare state

Institutionalized individualization refers to two contexts which historically come to the fore in successive periods but which may also overlap and reinforce one another. We are speaking here of Christian individualization and the institutionalized individualization of the *welfare state*. There are thus two historically distinct but comparable forms of interiorized institutional individualization: namely the *Christian confession* and the acquisition of *social rights* (which, like fundamental civil and political rights, are addressed to the individual). Both forms compel us to reflect on ourselves and to assume responsibility for social crises. This shows clearly how powerfully religion has helped to mould institutions and mentalities in Europe without this being reflected explicitly in the underlying religious traditions at work. Christianity may be said to have evaporated into the basic social rights of the welfare state, and this very disappearance can be regarded as a mark of its success.

Welfare-state individualization is an empirically testable, core element of my theory of individualization (Beck 1992, 1999). The authority that decides whether individualization hypotheses can be falsified or not is not to be found in the contingent mindsets and behaviour patterns of individuals (and in the corresponding qualitative and quantitative studies, see, e.g., Beer 2007), but in the *connection between individualization and the state*. Fundamental civil rights, fundamental political rights, fundamental social rights, family law, divorce law, but also the neo-liberal reforms of the labour market (Brodie 2007) – in all these fields we can see the historical trend to institutionalized individualization in ways that can be proved or disproved empirically. For the addressee of these (fundamental) rights and reforms is the individual and not the group, the collective. Thus from this perspective what we see is the historical and empirical basis from which to test individualization theory. This basis was established, first, by the introduction of fundamental civil and political rights in the nineteenth century, their restriction (to men) followed by their de-restriction (the inclusion of women) in the twentieth century, and, second, by the growth, expansion and dismantling of the welfare state in Western Europe after the Second World War, in particular since the 1960s and 1970s, not just within a single nation-state but across all frontiers.

What we see here (analogously to the paradox of Christian orthodoxy, see p. 100 above) is the *irony of the welfare state*. This irony is that the class struggles of a class society result in the acceptance of the welfare state and with it the principle of individual claims and contributions – with the consequence that individualization is made permanent and class, the internal structuring principle of modern societies, declines in significance. By analogy we can say that in the Christian churches the principle of individualized faith is made permanent – with the paradoxical consequence that the churches' monopoly of truth and faith is eroded and the frontier between the new religiosity and the new irreligiosity becomes blurred. Shakespeare's statement in *Hamlet* that 'There are more things in heaven and earth . . . Than are dreamt of in your philosophy' can be applied with equal validity to the new hybrids formed by religious sects, forms of atheism, esoteric beliefs and self-help therapies. Half a millennium or so after Shakespeare we might reply with G. K. Chesterton: 'When people stop believing in God, they don't believe in nothing – they believe in anything.'

In order to discover the strides made by this institutional individualization since the second half of the twentieth century we need to conduct various historical analyses. In particular, we need to consider which aspects of individualization are to be found expressed in the social semantics of the law and the actual practices of the judiciary (against the backdrop of public discourse and political debate), as well as in the current or future reforms of the welfare state and the labour market. In so doing, it would make sense to draw a distinction between the *opportunities* and *constraints* on decision-making arising from institutionalized individualization. At the beginning of the twenty-first century the welfare state is characterized by a general outsourcing of key institutions which had brought relief to the individual in the first modernity and given him or her a sense of security and orientation (Lash 2002). This can be observed in the family, in particular in changes in the workplace (Sennett 1998). At the same time, a sort of insourcing has been taking place. Many characteristics, functions and activities that were previously the prerogative of the nation-state, the welfare state, the hierarchical organization, the nuclear family, class or the centralized trade union have now been displaced either outwards or inwards: outwards to global or international institutions; inwards to the individual.

What emerges from this is that institutionally individualized decision-making opportunities and constraints can be distinguished only analytically since they are not self-evident in actual reality. If we make use of welfare-state legislation to provide a test case to falsify individualization theory, we must focus our attention not just on the liberation from constraints, but must include also the new constraints on that liberation (and then also the liberation from those new constraints, etc.). This means that we need to inquire into *de*-individualizing tendencies in the changing legal environment. All three questions – those of institutionally individualized decision-making *opportunities*, institutionally individualized decision-making *constraints* and *de*-individualizing tendencies – mark out the *ambivalent space* characteristic of the different waves of institutionalized individualism.

Beyond the normal family

Under what conditions and in what sense can we speak of a metatransformation brought about by institutionalized individualism, and what consequences does it have for religion? Since we find ourselves in virgin territory here, it may be advisable to clarify the question by inspecting the more thoroughly researched metatransformation of the *family* (Beck and Beck-Gernsheim 1995, 2002; Beck-Gernsheim 2002). Until the 1960s, Western societies possessed a universally recognized 'natural' model of the family, one corresponding (more or less and allowing for differences of living conditions, class and religion, etc.) to reality. This *model of the normal family* consisted of an adult couple with their own children; the adults were of different sexes, i.e. man and woman; they were married and remained married until death did them part; a division of labour existed between them: the man was gainfully employed, the 'breadwinner', the wife was responsible for the family and the home. It goes without saying that there were exceptions to this pattern – a few brave souls consciously chose other ways of life, others put up with them as best they might. These other ways of life were regarded as *deviant* and were comparatively rare; they were the product of unfortunate circumstances and external constraints, such as the turmoil of war and the resulting dislocations.

The situation of the family has undergone a radical change in the conditions created by, and as a consequence of, institutionalized individualization. The normal family as we have described it has by no means disappeared, but its role and its forms of authority have been 'de-naturalized' – there now exist numerous other forms alongside it. What we now find is 'a juxtaposition of different forms which, it is claimed, are or ought to be equally valid' (Lüscher 1994: 19). Above all, however, the normal family has lost its status as the norm. As a result, deviant forms have become more prevalent. Furthermore, once-deviant forms of cohabitation have come to be regarded increasingly as normal and acceptable – both socially and in law. What now prevails is not just diversity but the *normalization* of diversity, and this is reflected both in family law and in the view of family members and (finally) even in the sociology of the family. We are witnessing a meta-transformation of the cultural conditions of life. More and more regulations have been introduced that transform collective guidelines into individual choices. This applies particularly to the reordering of relations between the sexes in marriage. In many countries there has been a fundamental reform of the relevant legal provisions. We can take the changes in German law as an example (see table).

Original version of the Civil Code, in force since 1.1.1900	Marriage Law Reform Act, in force since 1.7.1977
§1354 The husband has the right to decide in all matters concerning the joint lives of the married couple; in particular, he determines their dwelling and place of residence.	Abrogated
§1355 The wife assumes the husband's surname.	The marriage partners can decide to take either the husband's or the wife's surname to use as their joint surname.
§1356 The wife has ... the right and the duty to oversee the care of the joint household.	The marriage partners shall conduct the affairs of the household by mutual agreement.

Moreover, in Germany, as in other Western countries, many other legal provisions have been added, all of which tend in the same direction (e.g. Mason et al. 2001; Röthel 1999). Further instances of amendments to the marriage laws include the easing of the divorce laws, the improved legal status of children born out of wedlock, the improved legal status of long-term relationships outside marriage, the increasing recognition of homosexual relationships. What all these changes have in common is the growing reluctance on the part of the legislature to prescribe any particular way of life. Paradoxically, this development sets a spiralling number of constraints in motion which might easily have been foreseen. If gay or lesbian couples marry or enter into a civil partnership, does this imply that they have a right to parenthood, adoption or to avail themselves of the latest developments in reproductive medicine? If a woman is not compelled to take her husband's name on marriage, what names shall their children be given? If more and more people embark on second and even third marriages, how can an equitable distribution of assets be achieved between partners, ex-partners and ex-ex-partners and their various children?

This *institution* of marriage provides *empirical* evidence of decisive importance for assessing the validity of the individualization thesis, and, as has been shown by a number of contemporary studies by Ulrich Herbert and others (2002, 2007), there have been dramatic changes: within around fifteen years the paradigm change we have described has taken place in almost every European society at roughly the same time. Moreover, these changes have taken place not just among a few scattered groups but throughout society in the space of a single generation. Such a comprehensive shift in the opportunities and risks of personal choice from institutions to individuals over such a brief time-span is historically without precedent. This process has been continued in the concept (whether social-democrat or conservative) of the '*active welfare state*' which has come to prevail in all Western nations and which combines three principles: the development of human capital (education), the ascription of individual responsibility, and integration into the labour market. We glimpse here the deepening of the institutional production and reproduction of the individualized individual – and at the same time, an example of the way in which individuals are saddled with the impossibility of finding biographical solutions for systemic contradictions.

'Reflexive individualization' or 'manipulated individualism' and 'anomic privatization'

What is the relationship between the theory of institutionalized individualization and other theories of rampant individualism? Anthony Giddens (1990) emphasizes that the individual can benefit from the increasingly abstract and globalized structures of an advanced modernity. Alain Touraine (1995), in contrast, fears that these structures have been reinforced by scientific advances so that the individual ends up as the appendage of a more powerfully rationalized production system, leading an alienated existence as a 'consumer unit'. In my view, the structures of the (first) modernity of the nation-state are far from being as stable as Giddens promises or Touraine fears. Precisely the opposite is the case: they become eroded, they disintegrate and, in the vacuum that arises, the different players find themselves in an unfamiliar context of increasingly radical, cosmopolitan inequalities and the impossibility of excluding cultural and religious others. This situation forces them back into the horizons of their own experience and reflections from where, beset by insecurities and ignorance, they have to learn to explore their new scope for action without coming to a sticky end in the process.

Comparable differences in perspective can be discerned in other theories (cf. Elliot and Lemert 2006), such as those of a 'manipulated individualism' (variants of which can be found in Max Horkheimer and Theodor W. Adorno, and later, in Michel Foucault), or in the theories of 'anomic privatization' (as can be seen variously in Daniel Bell, Richard Sennett, Christopher Lasch, Robert Bellah, Robert D. Putnam and Arlie Hochschild). In the first variant, heteronomy and heteronomous control are replaced by a conditioned autonomy and self-control. In the second, it is assumed that globalization and individualization subvert the moral integrity of private life, while individualism degenerates into self-obsession and gives rise to an unfettered narcissism. My argument cuts the ground from beneath this criticism since the distinctions and assumptions on which it is based are negated by the way in which individualization and cosmopolitanism intermesh.

Institutionalized individualization is reflexive in the sense that individuals engaged in constructing their own lives and their social and biographical identities cannot appeal to pre-existing models. They are forced to learn how to create a biographical narrative of their own and continuously to revise their definition of themselves. In the process they have to create abstract principles with which to justify their decisions. The notion that the 'personal lives' of isolated individuals are controlled utterly by social mega-institutions – the state, science, capitalism, the culture industry – is dubious, if only because these institutions are fluid. On the other hand, individuals – or 'dividuals' – are by no means completely identical with or fully integrated into the networks of society. Caught up in the elimination of tradition brought about by the individualization and globalization process, individuals are condemned to transform themselves into ingenious tinkerers and do-it-yourself creators of their own increasingly unviable identities. Their lives become a 'world of worlds' from which nothing is excluded and where decisions constantly have to be taken in haste. In the world risk society, individuals have lost the necessary distance from themselves to make reflection possible. They are simply no longer in a position to construct linear, narrative biographies. They spend their lives balancing on a circus high wire between divorce, losing their jobs, permanent self-praise and flexible entrepreneurship. They are not artists creating themselves, but bunglers cobbling an identity together. They improvise, amalgamate and construct *ad hoc* alliances in order to cope with inexorable demands, such as ferrying a child to the nursery or substituting a menu of one's own for the 'weekly poison'. Everything is always on the point of breakdown. Whether it is a question of the ingredients for the evening meal, flight safety, care for the sick, old-age insurance, the EU, the university, peace, the climate or the Middle East, we find ourselves forced to live in a world full of risk in which both knowledge and life opportunities have become uncertain in principle. This is the New Immediacy – 'the culture of immediacy' (Anthony Elliott and Charles Lemert; John Tomlinson) – which imposes automatic responses where in earlier times reflection may well have been possible. Everything comes too close for comfort; stimuli have to be promptly, immediately resisted, ruled out and held in check. A state of emergency has become commonplace and normal. We are looking at a completely normal state of chaos, the normal fragmentation of an individualized existence.

These constraints and opportunities of individualization are ultimately linked to the rapid expansion of media cultures, the expansion of the virtual world and the revolutions in information technology which, by blurring and mixing boundaries, ensure that even the most blinkered worlds acquire a shimmer of alternative horizons and symbolic possibilities – and they do so to a degree that until recently was unknown and even unimaginable.

The consequences of individualization and cosmopolitization cannot be confined to the private sphere. They become pervasive in the world of work (where the principle of flexibility triggers constant changes in the organization of the workplace), the world of party politics (voter fickleness, voter abstention), trade unions, and not least the churches. In the case of the latter this is seen, for example, in the exclusive diversification and individualization of groups of believers and globalized religious movements (such as the evangelicals) which dissolve the boundaries between church, sect and individual mysticism and spirituality, and lead to new kinds of combinations and demarcations.

Beyond normal religion: The motley assortment of New Religious Movements

The upshot of these processes is that at the birth of the twenty-first century, we are experiencing the paradox that religion is both declining and on the rise. Europe's cathedrals are in fact inspiring, magnificent and empty. It is a mistake to attribute this to the waning influence of religion. The opposite is also true. Religious themes and conflicts have risen to the top of the agenda both in politics and everyday life and in the personal, existential experience of ordinary people. This does not find expression in the mass spread of patience and humility. In the eyes of many people the idea of God is linked to terrorism, hatred and discrimination against homosexuals. Clergymen, nuns and priests who have established a *modus vivendi* as mediators between the sacred and the secular and who function in a religious routine with its Sunday sermon, baptism and funeral service find that their world has lost all its meaning – much like the trade unions, who have seen their power melting away.

Admittedly, all that lasts only as long as they fail to take to heart the paradox of secularization (see pp. 22–6 above), according to which the terrestrial disempowering of religion has become the basis for the vitality of religiosity. 'Robbed' of the onerous duty of producing certainty (thanks to the separation of science and religion) and of legitimating rule (thanks to the separation of religion and the state), religions have succeeded, above all in secular society, in gaining a new function and authority as 'a school of morality'. This can be seen in the case of parents who do not themselves go to church and who regard themselves as sceptics (e.g. in the Prenzlauer Berg district of Berlin) but who nevertheless choose to send their children to nurseries run by the churches so that they will be inducted into the *social morality* of individualization. Not just the morality of 'Develop your own personality', but also that of 'Have respect for the dignity of others'. In this way, children are taught to distinguish between individualization and egoism; they acquire the model of a 'responsible self', which includes a sense of responsibility towards others. Interestingly, even the Chinese regime of authoritarian state capitalism has discovered the meaning of religion and religious education as an antidote to the moral anarchy that is breaking out with 'predatory capitalism' and 'predatory communism'.

More specifically, the question of how the world religions and the various New Religious Movements react towards one another in the environment of individualization and cosmopolitization calls for what Peter Clarke refers to as a 'cosmopolitan gaze' (Clarke 2006). Ernst Troeltsch, Max Weber's friend and rival, expanded the latter's distinction between church and sect by adding an ideal type of religiosity or individual spirituality which he called 'mysticism'. A century ago, Troeltsch was exercised by the question of whether the already perceptible decline of the churches would lead to a future without religion or whether signs were emerging of new religious forms of life beyond the churches and sects. He considered this question from a specifically European point of view. His fear was that Europe 'would not succeed in calling into being a new religious form of life but that it would also prove unable to live without one'.

Here at the latest it becomes clear that individualization and cosmopolitization pose the question that has haunted the entire history of religion, namely the question 'Who are we?' And in the age of self-chosen Gods with its unshackling of religiosity and spirituality, the question acquires an unprecedented urgency. The hope is that by drawing a distinction between the 'good' church and the 'evil' sects, it will be possible once again to ring-fence the divisive pronoun 'we' that in the past has triggered so many wars of religion. For many years, the churches and the great religious communities in other countries have regarded 'sects' as potentially immoral, asocial and irrational, and treated them accordingly. By giving this act of exclusion a scientific veneer, theology and sociology side with religious monopolies and not simply on the question of obedience to a particular faith. On the contrary, they also absolve the churches and indeed themselves of the need to take these New Religious Movements seriously and to analyse them in the context of the shifts in the power and significance of the cosmopolitan religious field.[9] The third – supplementary – concept introduced by Troeltsch, that of a free-floating mysticism, anticipated the individualization of religion. It opened people's eyes to the fluid nature of a liberated religiosity and spirituality, to the simultaneous process of merging and delimiting, of explicit and implicit religiosity, of traditional religious communities and New Religious Movements.

In determining the limits of religion, Troeltsch's distinction between churches and sects, on the one hand, and religiosity and spirituality or mysticism, on the other, can be taken further. If in the first case we have an either/or regime, in the second we have a motley assortment of 'both this and that'.

Churches and sects may well overcome such distinctions as class and nation; they divide the world into believers and unbelievers. The latter are ultimately denied the dignity of human beings since they reject the 'true God'. The self-chosen God of individualized religiosity, in contrast, does not recognize unbelievers since He does not recognize the existence of any absolute truths, hierarchies, heretics, heathen or atheists. In the subjective polytheism of a 'God of one's own choosing' there is space for many Gods. What religions and churches, imprisoned in their claims to religious truth, regard as not simply morally reprehensible but also logically impossible is put into practice here. In their nomadic

---

[9] Max Weber had of course realized that the concept of the sect had to be kept separate from the denominational prejudices of the church; but that scarcely affected its polemical character, which arose from the need to forestall schismatic developments.

search for religious transcendence, individuals are both believers
and unbelievers at the same time. Indeed, the meaning of a God
of one's own lies precisely in this 'love of one's enemy', which may
be thought of as an expansion of one's religious horizon. This
subverts the division into believers and unbelievers, with its vast
potential for violence; the 'unbelievers' become an integral part
of one's own experience of faith. The vertical axis consisting of
the refusal to recognize the religion of others is transformed into
a horizontal axis of recognition. That is the kernel of the religious
practice implied in the statement that 'I am in search . . .'.

Only in this way is it possible to recognize what is involved in
the interaction between the old religions and religious movements
and the new ones. It is nothing less than *'a religious reformation
on a world scale'*. (What would Luther think of it? Does it represent the fulfilment of his hopes or of his worst fears? Or of both
at once?) As a global reformation, it can only be understood 'in
the context of the emerging global society' (Clarke 2006: xiii).
And even if there are no clear figures – not least because the basic
concepts of church 'membership' and 'belonging to a church' are
somewhat vague – we may take it as read that the New Religious
Movements are 'global religions in their own right' (ibid.). They
represent the diversity characteristic of the modern world.

This motley assortment of religious movements opens the door
to new contradictions. Is the search for spirituality no more than
a paradoxical attempt to set limits to the never-ending process of
individualization? Luther had sought to restrict the liberated individualization of God from a universalist standpoint by equating
'textual immediacy' with 'God's immediacy'. That synthesis is
now disintegrating. The question arises whether the individual
made in the image of God has become God the father of his own
personal God, finally pushing the coordinates of spiritual illumi-
nation into the realms of the esoteric and the absurd.

But this is not the only possible interpretation of these New
Religious Movements. Insofar as we can sum up these highly
diverse movements under one heading, they represent in many
respects a radicalization of the narrative of a God of one's own,
which can now continue to be written in the spirit of an existential
experiment as a novel of education of private religiosity and spirituality *outside the confines of any church*. This can be seen in the
epistemological rewriting of key religious concepts. The place of

faith, redemption by the grace of God, is now taken by subjective *knowledge* arising from experience and experiment. The concept of *sin* is secularized and its function is taken over by the concept of *ignorance*, while the idea of *paradise* as the future home of the Blessed is replaced by the concept of *self-fulfilment* in the here and now.

Communication with one's chosen God who has escaped from the controlling hand of church authority thus radicalizes the subjective basis of experience, activity and sense of responsibility. Whoever thinks about religion from within this conceptual horizon reflects about him- or herself. And, in what is no more than a slight exaggeration of the situation, either this may lead to the therapeutic culture of peace-loving wellness spirituality, or else it can motivate people to become suicide bombers for revolutionary purposes.

A God of one's own transforms religion into a 'religion of self', into competing 'religions of the true self'. This leads ultimately to the elimination of the distinction between heaven and hell. Life on earth no longer has boundaries; the heaven the believer aspires to discover and conquer lies within the grasp of the unfettered self. Many seekers believe that exploring their own consciousness in line with the demands of subjective spirituality can lead to a direct, unmediatized contact with the sacred in all its forms. It is from such contact that we might see the emergence of the power to transform not just the inner self, but also the world. The New Religious Movements bring with them a *subjectivization of utopia and revolution*. It is increasingly unusual to find the ideal equated with the future kingdom of God and even more unusual to identify it with the gradual or radical reform of society. All the more frequently, however, do we find that the ideal is something the individual imposes on him- or herself. One is supposed to discover in the kingdom of one's own life the very thing that in earlier times was deemed to dwell in paradise: what is sought today is *paradise now*, in the here and now of one's own life.

The task today is not so much to win God's attention and help, as was preached by the religions of old; people's efforts nowadays are directed at sharing in the creative powers of their inner God.

Only the cosmopolitan gaze is able to appreciate the novel hybrid and (latently) *polygamous forms of religion* that have come into existence despite the insistence on monogamous religious membership and that were often smiled at tolerantly or dismissed as blasphemous by the traditional churches (Graf 2004). We now find Swiss Catholics who have no difficulties believing in both Christ's resurrection and Buddhist reincarnation, a Catholic shamanism that allows the living to conduct a remarkably friendly relationship with the dead. And likewise there are Arab mullahs, Chinese scholars, Japanese bonzes, Tibetan lamas, Hindu pandits, who preach fatalism and predestination, ancestor worship and worship of the venerated ruler, the gaiety of pessimism or redemption through self-realization. This makes it very clear that the New Religious Movements do not replace the old; they merely reshape them in their understanding of such concepts as transcendence and faith, good and evil, and so on.

What this leads to – with the believers initially – is a 'subjective cosmopolitization' of the religions. Grace Davie has coined incisive phrases to describe the zombie-like, 'both/and' forms of hollowed-out church façades behind which secularization steadily advances in Europe. She speaks of 'believing without belonging' (Davie 1994). This can be contrasted with 'belonging without believing', but also with an all-inclusive third hybrid form of 'multiple believing with belonging', i.e. hybrid beliefs combined with the purely conventional membership of a church.

Statistics show that in the present, as in the past, people are *born* into a religious community in Germany and other European countries and are socialized in those communities by their parents. They then remain in those communities unless they leave them or change their faith. What that means, however, is an open question. Many take advantage of the profusion of creeds on offer as need arises, without formally leaving their original church and indeed without formally joining a new one. The either/or decision to convert is subverted and people simply live the *inclusive life of a plural monotheism* or an improvised mishmash of old religion and new religiosity, esotericism and New Age practices.

It is a return in altered subjective form of the founding age of the great world religions in which the 'grand narratives of the human race' became intertwined and were spelled out in a missionary spirit – in the Middle East, in India, China and in Europe. The religious, cosmopolitan spirit of the world society has from its very inception been part and parcel of religion – unlike the spirit of capitalism. The 'globalization' of the religions is nothing new historically. On the contrary, it is a defining feature of religion (see pp. 50–1 above).

One example of the new forms taken by religion is to be found in the pages of the internet. What we find there is a simply overwhelming bazaar of meanings where individuals can stroll around and pick and choose from what is on offer. Alongside this explosion of virtual religion, a swelling flood of publications on religious topics, together with the offerings of cinema and television, all contribute to a fundamental reconfiguring of institutionalized religious landscapes – although some may find this superficial and arbitrary.

> Two out of three French teenagers born into Catholic families have never been to mass or Sunday school. But they will without a doubt have seen movies such as *Little Buddha*, *Seven Years in Tibet*, or *Witness*. They will have made contact, through the intermediary of films, with the world of Jewish festivals or Ramadan, or with the themes of New Age trends and spiritual ecology. And their first exposure to the Gospels might well have been a successful popular musical. They will thus have discovered, albeit in the most anecdotal and unreliable fashion, the existence of diverse cultural, religious, and spiritual worlds that would of course have been unknown to their grandparents. (Hervieu-Léger 2006: 63)

This obviously raises the question of how traditional churches and individualized new religiosity relate to each other quantitatively and what social structures influence this. As Pollack and Pickel (2008) show in their empirical study of the structural changes in the religious sphere in Germany, religiosity outside the churches is clearly more popular among the younger generation than the older generation, in both eastern and western Germany. Women, too, are more likely than men to engage in the search for post-church religiosity. The greater the degree of education, the greater the distance from commitments to a traditional church, and the greater, therefore, the eagerness to discover new religious movements and the readiness to involve oneself in them. The same may be said of an urban lifestyle: it encourages people to distance themselves from the churches and adopt syncretist religious beliefs (ibid.: 621–2).

In parallel to religious individualization – especially in the European centres of institutionalized individualization – a worldwide process of de-localization and de-traditionalization may be said to be taking place in the great religions. This forces them to respond to the global expansion of modernity as well as to the resulting intellectual challenges provided by mutually inter-penetrating and hybrid religious organizations – right down to deformed or synthetic cults of an esoteric or terrorist kind. These may be decoded as an entrepreneurial search for politico-religious meaning and condemned as contributing to the mass production and consumption of religious symbols. At the same time, whereas historically the world religions have operated in isolation from one another, they are now forced to compete and communicate with one another in the boundless space of the mass media. These conditions of religious globalization break through the hermeneu-tic circle of diversified but inward-looking world religions and force them to develop a new *'cosmopolitan hermeneutics'*. In consequence, they will have to make their symbols accessible in a process of mutual exchange for the benefit of all concerned.

In times of reflexive modernization, the world religions can no longer rely exclusively on their own traditions. They must reflect the myriad strands of the past, present and future that are inter-woven with the thick texture of the world. From now on, what matters is to make the 'impure', that is to say, hybrid origins of religious cultures visible – in contrast to the fantasies of purity characteristic of both occidental and oriental ideologues. This holds good for the origins of the world religions but equally for the cosmopolitan 'spirit' of the world society that will decide the fate of religion in the modern world (see Chapter 6).

The relationship of religion to anti-modernity, post-modernity and the second modernity

We can distinguish between three great modes characterizing the acquisition of religion in the modern age: (a) the *anti*-modern, (b) the *post*-modern and (c) the *second*-modern mode. And indeed, at the heart of the unease and insecurity that is gripping the world of the religions is the fact that they must all confront these alter-natives. They are forced to decide between anti-modern, post-modern and second-modern trends, lines of tradition and visions of the future. Alternatively, in this debate about modernity they have to rule out the extremes, or combine them or else bring them into a state of peaceful coexistence by constructing an inner plurality. This makes it possible for the great religions to split up – indeed, some of them even empty themselves of content, wither away, or are taken over by others; new permutations emerge and struggle to achieve institutional form in transnational space. For unlike nations and states, religions are 'global players' – not unlike mobile capital and the campaigning movements of civil societies.

Anti-modern fundamentalism

Anti-modern fundamentalism is of modern origin. It springs from the *intersection of postmodernism and post-colonialism* as well as their reciprocal confirmation of each other. The era of post-colonialism begins when the colonized cultures, societies and religions seek to liberate themselves from the influence of Western imperialism. This liberation succeeds when the former colonies appropriate for themselves the postmodern repudiation (of the grand narratives) of Western modernity. As the critique of Western modernity, postmodernism empowers post-colonialism, intellectually at least. The door that opens here swings in two opposing directions: a fundamentalist anti-modernity on the one hand, postmodern religious diversity on the other.

On the one hand, *modern* arguments in favour of a religious anti-modernity can be distilled from the combination of post-colonialism and postmodernism. Such arguments advocate a return to a pre-colonial, pre-modern fundamentalist basis of religious truths and practices. This reaction will be both modern and anti-modern, insofar as it uses the postmodern to reject modernity and asserts for that reason that there is only *one true* religious narrative, only one true religious path to the true conduct of one's life and the formation of society and politics (whoever defines and sanctions this for the benefit of whomsoever). But since there is no escaping the universal presence of plural religious truth claims, these claims cannot be done away with by turning a blind eye. On the contrary, such rejection simply overwhelms them, and this in turn provokes a militant, anti-modern reaction in pure self-defence. Religious conversion makes it possible to take up arms against the colonial, imperial, relativist, nihilistic 'barbarism of modernity'. Taken to its logical extremes, this leads to the terrorism of Al-Qaeda. There is also a hybrid form of anti-modern, post-colonial and *individualized* religiosity, namely religiously motivated terrorism. This terrorism presupposes individualization, as well as transnationalism, and arises therefore from a modern blending of extremes (pre-modernism and anti-modernism), but does not arise in any sense from a renewal of tradition.

Moving in the opposite direction, the connection between post-colonialism and postmodernism opens the door to the ubiquitous dissemination of a global religious pluralism and to various other forms of reaction.

Postmodern religiosity

Postmodern religiosity puts a question mark over modernity *without* wishing to revert to the origins of fundamentalist religiosity. Religious postmodernism breaks with at least one basic principle of the secular, first modernity, namely with the hierarchical order of scientific knowledge and religious belief – in other words, with the doctrine that modern science is the only form of objective knowledge of the world. The postmodern world begins where both religious and scientific knowledge have lost their innocence and where the resulting relativism produces a new equality between religious and scientific knowledge (or faith). Thanks to its progressive self-demystification, even scientific knowledge stands unmasked as a speculative interpretation of the world, one based on faith (faith in its ability to decipher the world), and unable to deliver the final truth about reality. There are innumerable disputes about this in the various branches of science and their respective philosophies. But the controversies themselves point to the postmodern coexistence of a (scientific) knowledge and (religious) belief, each of which is relativized by the other.

Putting belief and knowledge on the same plane in this way seems at first sight to lead inexorably to a radical cultural and ethical relativism. Postmodernists celebrate this absolute relativism because they regard it as the end of the totalitarianisms, which seemed to lead more or less inevitably to justifying the use of force against people with different beliefs. Even if no violence is threatened, the claim to absolute truth kills the dialogue with others.

A truth that is valid once and for all – whether it be scientific or religious in origin – favours inhumanity in all dealings between human beings.

On the other hand, this same 'dictatorship of relativism' seems to point the way to the ultimate catastrophe of humankind. For it compels us to abandon the clear distinction between good and evil, between us and other people, and to leave human beings to face the dangers created by civilization on their own and without guidance.

Religious postmodernism is based on the assumption that it is intellectually impossible to choose between 'truths'. To that extent we can and must make our choices pragmatically – and we do so from the standpoint of 'what does me good'. Truth, beauty, goodness and love – are all 'in the eye of the beholder'. The paradox of religious postmodernism can be summed up as follows: the cultural, subjective fluidity of religious convictions undermines the minimum of certainty that individuals require in order to form a personal identity as believers who have to assume responsibility in all aspects of society.

Individuals demand the right to choose their own spiritual path. In other words, the authenticity of their personal search is more important to them than their assent to 'truths' of which the world religions claim to be the guardians. There is an obvious objection to this. Is it possible to conceive of individualized religious narratives that guarantee the necessity of 'divided certainties'? Is it in fact the case that an 'eclectic' involvement with religious plurality can provide support and a foundation *in itself*? Does not the construction of 'one's own' God lack a connection with something 'outside itself', without which the demand for 'redemption' has no legitimacy? How far is the personal aspect of a God of one's own choosing capable of establishing the binding force of the religious that would negate that element of the personal in the God one has chosen? What keeps the conscious mind alert to the fact that the foundations of a personal religiosity can *only* be won and defended through public, political intercourse with others? How may the pitfalls of the privatization of religion be avoided and *public* forms of religious practice be enabled and developed to take on an active social role and to be in a position to take up the struggle socially and politically against an unjust and self-destructive civilization?

Does the fashionable closeness of individualization to the esoteric perhaps express the constant sum of religious energies, the
indispensable necessity of a transcendental framework for one's
personal life? And is it conceivable that postmodern religiosity is
concerned neither with being religious as such nor with membership of a religious community, but merely with a need to discover
the combination of religious practices and symbols conducive to
one's own wellbeing, one's happiness and one's life?

Religiosity in the second modernity

Between the two poles of a postmodern, anti-modern religiosity,
on the one hand, and the promises and threats of a postmodern
religiosity, on the other, we glimpse the vision of a *cosmopolitan
religiosity of the second modernity*. This religiosity negates the
other two, i.e. both postmodern absolutist relativism and the
privatization of religion. This vision is based on the actually existing *historical impurity of the world religions*: the recognition that
they are intertwined, that they are both other *and* the same.
Learning to see and understand themselves through other people's
eyes does not mean that the religions must sacrifice their own
special nature, nor that they must all merge in a decadent, value-
neutral, secular relativism. On the contrary, they enrich their own
religiosity, mutually reinforce one another, and in this way they
can practise and develop anew the public role of religion in the
post-secular modern era – without falling prey to the snares of a
fundamentalist, religious anti-modernism.

'Cosmopolitan' means changing the religious viewpoint, the
internalized 'as-if conversion', the practice of 'both/and', the ability
to see one's own religion and culture through the eyes of another
religion and the culture of other people. How and to what extent
can this 'cosmopolitan spirit' of the world society be said to have
a *realistic* chance of becoming a reality?

5

The Irony of
Unintended Consequences
How to Civilize Global Religious
Conflicts: Five Models

Religion has attracted worldwide public attention in the light of the conflicts of the twenty-first century, which some have militantly dramatized as the global 'clash of civilizations' (Huntington). Noteworthy among these conflicts are the fundamentalist religious revolutions in a number of Islamic societies, the powerful mobilization of the dominant Protestant right wing in the USA, and the aggressively triumphant progress of the evangelical Pentecostal movements and Protestant sects in many countries of the Third and Fourth Worlds. I shall here – without any claim to be systematic or comprehensive – propose five models for civilizing global religious conflicts: (1) the *model of unintended consequences*: civilizing the religions by individualization; (2) the *market model*: God's commodity form; (3) the model of the *religiously neutral constitutional state* (Jürgen Habermas); (4) the model of the *'world ethos'* of religion (Hans Küng); and, lastly, (5) *methodological conversion* (Mahatma Gandhi).

The individualization of religion and the 'spirit' of the world society

We can condense our previous observations into a contradiction. On the one hand, the civilizing of the potential for world religious conflict calls for the world religions to civilize themselves. On the other hand, the universal closeness of different faiths to one another forces believers to sharpen their own profile, to define the limits and make more dogmatic the core beliefs of their religions by means of which they proclaim the recognition of religious others as equal but different. It is difficult to see how such a contradiction can be overcome through conscious action, and it may even be insuperable. If so, it may be worth our while to inquire whether the concept of unintended consequences may help us to civilize the world religions.

The unintended-consequences model can be explained by analogy with Max Weber's thesis of the spirit of capitalism. As is well known, Weber identified religiously motivated 'worldly asceticism' as the driving force which produced – as its unforeseen and unintended consequence – the tyranny of the 'spirit' of capitalism with its rational insistence on the continual maximization of profit. This spirit produces an unending process of 'creative destruction' (Schumpeter). How was it possible – that is Max Weber's question – for the 'Protestant ethic', i.e. 'the most absolutely unbearable form of ecclesiastical control of the individual which could possibly exist' (1974: 37), to put individuals in the position in which their economic activity would enable them legitimately to break 'rationally' with the restrictions of traditional societies? His answer (not really grasped by commentators on Weber) is based on the distinction between two polar forms of religiosity, namely the striving for the holy (utopia) and for the sacred (taboo).

Weber shows in detail that the utopian force of the radically individualized search for the holy compels individuals to change the world by following the maxims of worldly asceticism and profit maximization. If the Calvinist individual is to acquire God's grace (which cannot be 'earned'), he or she must break with the traditional social order based on sacred taboos.

This contradiction between *holy* and *sacred* – the subjectivity of the *holy* casts doubt on the taboos of the *sacred* order – is worked through in the *framework* and *on the ground* of institutionalized religion (Calvinism). Today, in the course of our transition to the second modernity, the unintended consequences of the individualization of faith turn against the dogmas of the institutionalized religions. Individualization arises from the collapse of religious truth systems – or at least from their decay – and liberates individuals from the pre-existing 'religious federations' (or religious civilizations) to which they had been assigned. It is this liberation that compels (or enables) them to discover or invent a 'God of their own'.

The talk of a 'God of one's own' presupposes – as I have shown – a radicalized religious freedom. What a 'God of one's own' means here is a God who has not been assigned to us at birth. Nor is He the collective God whom all members of a major religion are forced to venerate. He is a God one can choose, a personal God who has a firm place and a clear voice in the intimate heart of one's own life. *This* individualization of God breaks with the basic assumption that human beings can be categorized uniformly in accordance with a once and for all inclusive system of an either/or religious choice. This religious division of the world population into what is mainly a territorial, geographic pattern of distribution satisfies the monocultural ideal of purity according to which people belong to one and only one of a number of clearly demarcated groups that are defined for preference by religion or civilization. This stress on purity fosters two grave dangers. It blinds people to reality, in particular to the subjective reality of people's faith. Over and above that, it fails to realize that this very eradication of diversity – in other words, the imposition of a homogeneous identity – is itself an essential component of that 'martial art' in which sectarian conflicts inevitably culminate.

The doctrine of the impurity of cultures

We arrive inexorably at a misunderstanding, indeed utter incomprehension, of the world we live in if we adopt the standpoint of a yearning for purity. We need each only question ourselves in order to discover that we all regard ourselves as the members of different groups which we belong to all at once and without contradiction. The same person can have a German passport, come from the Caribbean, have an African pedigree, be a Christian, an archliberal, a woman, a vegetarian who goes jogging in the morning, a superb cook, a feminist, a heterosexual but one who is an advocate of homosexual rights, a cinema-lover, an environmental campaigner and, not least, someone who is convinced of the significance of astrological signs and who misses no opportunity to drive everyone round the bend talking about them. Every man and woman is a crazy patchwork of identities. The individual decides about their relative weighting, depending on the situation at a particular time and in a particular context. None of these identities needs determine the others.

If this is true of our social relations in general, it applies with particular force to the individualization of the religions. As empirical studies show, practising Catholics in France, Belgium or Italy who play an active part in the community have a firm belief in reincarnation (in contrast to official Catholicism). Norwegian or Danish Lutherans who feel great loyalty to their national church are at the same time fervent champions of nature myths derived from the teachings of spiritual ecology and cultivate a life in harmony with nature in which humans do not enjoy privileges vis-à-vis other creatures. And there are Jews who claim that the authentic meaning of their relation to the Torah is to be found in Buddhist meditation. In this way, believers of every conceivable background open up new religious freedoms for themselves. They re-cast pre-existing religious world-views and develop composite religious identities in the various stages of their personal spiritual journey.

These subjective searchings and the composing of individual religious narratives represent conscious breaks with the ideal of purity to be found among the clerical guardians of the truths of institutionalized national churches. What is astounding is that people who feel free to take these liberties continue to call themselves 'Christians'.

What are the unintended consequences of this deregulation of organized systems of religious belief? Does the individualization of God serve as an antidote to the much trumpeted clash of civilizations and cultures – if only because religions cease to exist in their familiar form?

In the past the ideal of pure religious identities was fraught with potent and indeed dangerous consequences for the world community. As the individualization of belief gains ground in religious life and the experience of the world, purity will increasingly be sidelined and even replaced by the ideal of impurity. The self-conscious anarchy of the religious allegiances that are being formed in part behind the façades of the main religious labels (Christians, Muslims, Hindus, Buddhists, etc.) serves to defuse *structurally* (that is to say, not intentionally, but as an unintended consequence) the potential for violent clashes between rival religious truths. It thus represents an important step in the direction of the cosmopolitan coexistence of ancient and modern global religions. For the 'impurity' of faith includes other people's religiosity and becomes the source of an individualized experience of God.

'Most people are other people. Their thoughts are someone else's opinions, their lives a mimicry, their passions a quotation' (Oscar Wilde [1973: 169]). Let us imagine the scenario in which religious freedom might in fact be radicalized and practised so that individuals could communicate with one another without coercion. In such a scenario, personal 'solutions to the problem of faith' and hence (to take the thought to its logical conclusion) an *inner* world-religious multi-religiosity might well arise in one's own life and beliefs. In that event, the intransigence of global religious conflicts would be moderated, as individualized faith became disseminated beyond all frontiers and grew in influence. Paradoxically, the 'heresy' of a religious 'mishmash' is best able to guarantee the principle of freedom from violence in the dealings of religious communities with one another. It does so as an unintended consequence. The individualized plurality of religious and other identities and ties provides a foundation for the utopian ideal of the renunciation of violence in global international relations. People's thoughts and experience have led to the cross-fertilization of the world religions and that is now woven into their narratives about and belief in a 'God of their own'. In consequence, the religion of others is not merely 'tolerated' (i.e. it is not merely regarded with indifference or as an unwanted but inevitable reality); it is held rather to be an *enrichment* of one's own religious experience. This could conceivably lead to a paradoxical 'duty', based on self-interest, to appropriate the rights of other religions – in tune with the maxim that *'freedom of religion is the freedom of other people's religion'*. The institutionalized religions' passive reliance on their monopoly of truth, the exclusion of believers in other faiths, would in that case be anathema on moral grounds.

As a rule, the reductionist insistence on purity is accompanied by obscurantist views of world history. What is generally overlooked is the importance of cross-fertilization in the history of religion. Such interpretations of history are devoid of the conception of harmonizing dialogues. Instead we see the paradox of a shared history that contains cross-fertilization and differentiation at the same time. Thus Europe's appropriation of the legacy of antiquity was mediated in part by Islamic Arab culture. Perhaps we should refer to the Islamic influence on Europe following the conquest of Spain as the 'first Enlightenment', as Johann Gottfried Herder proposed in the nineteenth century. There can be absolutely no question of an 'original purity' of the world religions, if only because in many places Islam was closely bound up with 'the' Christian West and 'the' Jewish world. An appropriate world-historical overview would have to distinguish between different *kinds* of impurity. The plurality of religions has always existed: slavery, crusaders, empires, colonialism.

What is historically new, and what finds expression in the increasingly subjective nature and increasing individualism of faith in our time, assumes one face in the post-colonial world and another in Europe. In such post-colonial cultures as South America or Africa, and partly also Asia, the New Religious Movements express the confidence of religions liberated from colonial ties. The 'both/and' elements of a religion, derived from one's own faith and the faith of others, are nothing new here. They have their origins in the enforced diversity that the open violence of slavery and colonialism has raised to the level of a norm. What is new is the *post-colonial self-confidence* with which these age-old amalgams of 'superstition' and licensed religiosity make their voices heard. In European modernity, by contrast, a key distinction introduced in the first age of modernity collapses as a consequence of these movements, namely the distinction between secularism and religiosity. This leads to the hybrid forms of 'secular religion' and 'religious secularity' (see pp. 19–21).

What is 'new' about the 'religious spirit' of the world society at the start of the twenty-first century can be described by reference to the distinction between cosmopolitanism and multiculturalism. *Cosmopolitanism* conceptualizes the experience of 'both/and'. *Multiculturalism*, or, more precisely 'plural monoculturalism' (Sen 2006), conceives of, and practises, identities in accordance with the pure logic of 'either/or'. The existence of distinct religions and cultures is conceived in accordance with the insular monocultural model – chiefly in the framework and space of nation-states.

An additional factor is the assumption that the corresponding collective identities (Germans, say, or Turks), as traditionally established, form part of the dowry of their origin – in other words, choice is precluded! If a young couple decide to establish a family going beyond the boundaries of their religion and country, that is a 'cosmopolitan' initiative. If these young people come from conservative families, whether native or immigrant, and their parents do everything in their power to prevent their marriage, we might interpret their actions as a 'multicultural' chess move whose intention is to keep their particular cultures 'pure'. In such cases, the much-vaunted 'tradition' often plays a role. There is the implied suggestion that this 'tradition' is more valuable than the freedom of the younger generation to marry and choose their own religion. Even the so-called 'communitarian' philosophies rely on this argument. The preservation of a clearly distinct, 'pure' identity has priority over an insight into the realities of multiple, interwoven identities.

What distinguishes cosmopolitanism as the doctrine of the impurity of all cultures, religions and identities is its *realism*. This emerges clearly when we realize that the world today oscillates between *interaction* and *isolation*. The realism of the cosmopolitan gaze exposes the capacity for violence inherent in the illusions of isolationism.

The use of the relevant 'experts on religion' to get a grip on religiously motivated terrorism results in an increase in power for Islamic clericals and other members of the religious establishment – precisely at the point in time in which the political and social role of Muslims (democratic rights, for example) should be strengthened in civil society.

> What religious extremism has done to demote and downgrade the responsible political action of citizens (irrespective of religious ethnicity) has been, to some extent, reinforced, rather than eradicated, by the attempt to fight terrorism by trying to recruit the religious establishment on 'the right side'. In the downplaying of political and social identities as opposed to religious identity, it is civil society that has been the loser, precisely at a time when there is a great need to strengthen it. (Sen 2006: 83)

Religion and morality

The individualization of faith ultimately ends up denying the rarely questioned *equivalence of religion and morality*. Almost all political positions proceed from the assumption that with their resources of motivation and legitimation, the institutionalized religions are the starting point of moral behaviour. In recent times, we often encounter the idea, even in secularized Europe, that without the institutionalized belief in God no one can guarantee that people will behave morally. Political rhetoric goes even further. It proclaims that it is the 'Judaeo-Christian values' that are to be understood here, even though the term 'moral' seems to possess varying and even contrary meanings. These values are said to characterize 'Europe' or the 'West', and it is commonly suggested that without them there would be no reason to pass laws that would establish a human and just order of things.

Of course, criticizing the tenets of a religion is generally taboo. Only from within the force field of *religion* and *faith*, that is to say, in the age of individualized faith, is it possible to identify a vantage point from which to judge what a religion requires of its followers. It then turns out that these requirements are often profoundly irrational and often incompatible with the elementary expectations of a human morality. The proponents of religious definitions incline towards subordinating morality to the dogmas of the religion, thus detaching it from the realities of the lives of suffering humanity.

Such a *conflict between religion and morality* can be seen in abundance, and indeed to excess, in Africa. In the sub-Saharan countries alone, the AIDS epidemic wipes out millions of people every year. Nevertheless, church officials active there keep on doing their 'duty' and preaching that condoms are a grave sin even in communities where the AIDS tide is still on the rise. And this is done from motives of 'Christian charity', even though the preachers concerned know all about the horrific sufferings to which this policy leads. And moreover, they are the only people who are in a position to explain to people what effect condoms might have.

Like the activists of non-religious organizations, people whose commitment to others is rooted in individual faith do not call on the religious authorities to help spread ignorance and death. They distribute condoms. It would surely be more to the point to condemn the idea that a person's actions are 'reprehensible' if he preaches against the use of condoms in a culture plagued by AIDS. Whoever does that equates faith and religion, and, as a religious conformist, he implements the dogmas of the church without taking individual responsibility. Such acts carried out without an individual God can, in extreme cases, deaden a person's sensibility and judgement. Conversely, a good man may perform *fewer* good deeds than he might have done if he had obeyed the dictates of his conscience rather than the internalized commandments of the God of the *church*.

In moral terms, the individualization of faith should be more highly valued than mere obedience to church doctrines because, in the final analysis, the believer him- or herself is the only person who can decide what is morally right and good – and even what is morally right and good about the dogmas of religious morality. Frequently, the moral precepts and teachings of religion correspond to our own individual impulses and experience. But then again in texts codified in the religious tradition, we come across demands by God that make us shudder: if a man discovers that 'the tokens of virginity be not found for the damsel [his bride] . . . the men of her city shall stone her with stones that she die' (Deuteronomy 22: 20–1). People whose religious experience and faculty of moral judgement are rooted in the subjective narrative of a self-chosen God can feel nothing but horror on reading this in the Holy Scriptures. On the other hand, it may be pointed out that Islamic terrorism ignores all the prohibitions on violence in the Qur'an. In short, separation from clerical authority and the individualization of faith may well have devastating consequences in that religion.

Religiously motivated civil resistance: Henry D. Thoreau

Individualization must not be confused with moral relativism. But here we find the crux. The separation of state and religion has long been an established fact; in France it is over one hundred years old. The question of how an individualized religiosity can acquire a rebellious, public voice in the post-secular world refers us back to the radical ambivalence of religious moral absolutism. This can be seen, on the one hand, in the worldwide political impact of *Civil Disobedience* – that is the title of the world-famous essay by Henry D. Thoreau[1] – while, on the other hand, we can find it articulated in the terrorist threats of an Islamism aspiring to world power.

---

[1] See Klumpjan and Klumpjan 1986 for the following account.

Thoreau belongs to the narrow circle of early critics of America. It is a remarkable fact that in its most radical forms the rampant anti-Americanism current today is part of the 'American dream'. Thoreau was a follower of the American Socrates, Ralph Waldo Emerson, and his New England Transcendentalism (which is broadly related to the German philosophical idealism of Kant and Fichte). Since in Thoreau's eyes politics and society had manifestly failed, a search for self and self-reform offered the only way out. The world of politics had almost ceased to exist for him. It appeared to be unreal, unbelievable and meaningless.

But the retreat to 'self-reform' had been cut off because moral criteria are sharpened in the course of the search for self and even the citizen who withdrew into the fortress of his own self was made into an accomplice of the 'monstrous injustice of slavery' (Lincoln) by the state. Thoreau wished to convince Americans that in this situation a citizen had not only the right but the moral duty to refuse obedience to the state. 'How does it become a man to behave toward this American government today? I answer that he cannot without disgrace be associated with it. I cannot for an instant recognize that political organization as *my* government which is the *slave's* government also' (Thoreau 2001: 206). (The discourse of Islamists is likewise socially revolutionary, aimed at 'justice'.)

Slavery was legal at the time and had the approval of a majority of Americans. Thoreau's *Resistance to Civil Government* (this was the original title of his revolutionary essay) had to try to cast doubt on its *legitimacy*. Thoreau could expect sympathy neither from his fellow citizens nor from any influential political party nor from church authorities – since all of these had either approved of slavery or silently acquiesced in it.

The legitimacy which his public indictment set out to undermine derived from religion: the justification of the American government before God. Because slavery could not be called unconstitutional, Thoreau was compelled to appeal to a law that stood above 'the highest law in the land', namely God's commandment. Whoever followed the inner voice of this absolute 'higher law' might claim that 'He who lives according to the highest law is in one sense lawless' (Thoreau 1993: 25, 27 February 1851). (The Islamists preach the same message.)

For Thoreau the matter was as clear as day. Anyone who did not wish to become the moral accomplice of a slave state had to act publicly without slipping into the vicious circle of violence and (public) counter-violence. He would have to choose the path of peaceful revolt that would strike at the heart of the state's claim to power. He would have to practise civil disobedience, and that meant refusing to pay his taxes.

Thoreau saw himself subjected to all the abuse that even today would be heaped on the 'highhandedness' of anyone who ventured to carry out an act of civil resistance. In a democracy such resistance is said to be superfluous; indeed, it is thought to imply *contempt* for the will of the democratic majority and to amount to an attempt to impose its own deviant opinion in a dictatorial manner. Thoreau replies to this criticism by arguing that if he has justice, i.e. the voice of the one and only God, on his side, he has no need to wait for majorities: 'I think that it is enough if they have God on their side, without waiting for that other . . . [majority]. Moreover, any man more right than his neighbors, constitutes a majority of one already' (Thoreau 2001: 212). (Cf. Islamism.) On the other issue he retorts: 'If I have unjustly wrested a plank from a drowning man, I must restore it to him though I drown myself.' Ethical and democratic relativists find this 'inconvenient. But he that would save his life, in such a case, shall lose it. This people must cease to hold slaves . . . though it cost them their existence as a people' (ibid.: 207). In the contradiction between law and the state, on the one hand, and morality, in other words, absolute ethical principles, on the other, there is no middle way. We must decide for one thing or the other.

According to Thoreau, the crucial issue here is how to introduce the power of a religiously based absolute morality into the public arena. The strength of the state rests ultimately not on its monopoly of violence but on the 'voluntary servitude' of the citizenry. What empowers the state is the self-imposed incarceration of citizens who are over-eager to comply with state power. That power can be withdrawn from the state by those whose action has been legitimated by their experience of 'their own God'. Needless to say, whoever rises up against the laws and thus excludes himself from their scope should not be surprised if the laws are used against him: 'The proper place today, the only place which Massachusetts has provided for her freer and less desponding spirits, is in her prisons, to be put out and locked out of the State by her

own act, as they have already put themselves out by their principles' (ibid.: 213).

Civil disobedience became the model for the return to the
public arena of religious voices and actions morally fortified by
the individualization of belief. The history of its impact is overwhelming. It includes the resistance Mahatma Gandhi organized
against the British Empire; the Civil Rights Movement in the USA
in which Martin Luther King denounced and fought against the
racism of the southern states; and the resistance to the Vietnam
War which based itself on Thoreau's beliefs. Many of the Americans conscripted for war service sent the call-up papers back
without any explanation except for a copy of *Civil Disobedience*,
which they enclosed and in which the words 'Vietnam War' were
substituted for 'Mexican War'. Demonstrators who had been
arrested read out in court and to the police the sentence quoted
above that prison was the only proper place for a morally upright
American.

Like the religions themselves, individualization itself has two
faces: it can be used to justify both freedom from violence
and the right to use violence. If we exclude the middle way
– in other words, the decision in favour of passive resistance
– the structural similarities of Thoreau's position with that of
Bin Laden are blindingly obvious. The distinction between laws
that have 'only' a democratic legitimation and a hypermorality
based on the immediate access to God that empowers the
individual to carry out acts of resistance may have effects in
two directions. It may in some cases strengthen the will to
engage in civil resistance, while in others it may lead people
to sacrifice their own lives and to drag other randomly chosen
fellow human beings to their deaths in obedience to 'God's
command'.

To sum up: even the individualizing of belief cannot rely on the
power of unforeseen and unintended consequences to initiate, let
alone guarantee, the civilizing of the conflicts involving the world
religions.

If a growing number of actors pursue strategies of rhetorical esca-
lation in many areas of religious conflict, the radicalization
of symbolic conflicts is unavoidable. In the pantheon of the early
twenty-first century, the liberal deities of consensus have fallen

into the minority. Many ecstatically savage, power-mad gods will stage new dramatic struggles among the pluralistic religious territories of the future, and in particular, many of the devout will regard the readiness to resort to violent measures as the mark of true service to God. (Graf 2004: 66)

Who are cosmopolitanism's cultural others?

If the relation to one's religious others is the fulcrum around which the changing circumstances of the religions revolve, we have to ask the question: Who are cosmopolitanism's cultural others? An initial answer is implicit in the observation that cosmopolitanism has room to tolerate traditionally antithetical positions with all their contradictions. Cosmopolitanism presupposes the dualisms and antitheses which go to make up the world of religious and ethnic antagonisms. But it effects a 'perceptual switch', what Nietzsche would have called a transvaluation of values, in three respects:

- It does not do away with disagreements but gives them a positive evaluation. Genuine diversity and unity, integration and homogeneity form the cosmopolitan horizon of expectation.
- The goal is not the elimination of differences and disagreements, but rather their denaturalization, denationalization and depersonalization. In other words, the seeming realism of these disagreements is replaced by the realism of the way they are blended together.
- This diagnosis of a religious amalgam and the individualization that results from it robs antithetical positions of their function of bringing politics into being. Cosmopolitanism as the antithesis of antitheses uncovers the hidden essentialist background of the friend-or-foe attitude towards religious or national others. Its significance lies precisely in liberating differences of opinion from the insanity of the binary friend-or-foe pattern of thinking.

But this does not yet provide an answer to the question of the cultural others of cosmopolitanism: Is the enemy of cosmopolitanism included in the cosmopolitan recognition of others? And won't the hostility that others show cosmopolitans force the latter to deny *this* otherness of the others, and to answer hostility with hostility? Does it mean, therefore, that cosmopolitanism will be refuted by the *dilemma of tribalism*? All attempts to open up the ethnic ghetto, to deprive ethnicity of its power of definition, appear to produce ethnicity and reinforce it. The crucial point here, therefore, is that there can be a radical divide between one's own estimate of the otherness of others and that of outsiders. Those who declare their support for (religious) cosmopolitanism can be turned into Christian, Jewish, Hindu, etc., others by other people's violent actions. To undermine this argument we shall have to test the extent to which the commodity form of God aids and abets religion's potential for violence involuntarily and as the unintended consequence of an attempt to civilize.

The market model: God's commodity form

The invisible hand of the market can be a powerful ally in the pacification of global religious conflicts.[2] The two processes – the individualization and cosmopolitization of religion – are not merely given an impetus by the market model; they are as good as brought to fulfilment by it. This development has costs, of course, not least the fact that the coupling of God and the commodity form is considered to be blasphemous. 'Thy money perish with thee, because thou hast thought that the gift of God may be purchased with money.' With these words Peter doomed all attempts at commercialization to perdition from early on (Acts 8: 20; see also Zinser 2006). Furthermore, all religious exchange contradicts the Christian doctrine of God's absolute nature, the absolute claims of ethical norms and the tenet that divine grace is not for sale. Sale means (or presupposes) availability, and is incompatible with the doctrine of predestination. Looked at in this way, the commodity form of God is the most radical of all forms of a God of one's own choosing because He can claim to be neither absolute nor unique (in that form). For as a customer, the believer can evidently choose between various God-offers (or non-God-offers) in turn, just as he or she might choose between

[2] In what follows I summarize the extensive literature and the debate on the economics of religion: Berger 1963; Bruce 1999; Graf 2004; Iannaccone 1997; Moore 1994; Zinser 2006 – to name but a selection.

different massages, refrigerators, TV films, shampoos, restaurants or porn films.

There is, however, an inner connection between the market-ability of religious belief and its individualization. Religious economics are based on the assumption that the individual's freedom of choice in religious matters has become a reality. This means that in the United States the churches had to come to terms with something that was not at all to their taste. The Catholic Church in particular found it very difficult to transform itself into a voluntary organization, and this meant a drastic change in its dealings with its 'customer base', as well as its relation to the great religious communities. In this respect, American society is a model in which the fundamental right to the free choice of religion became a founding myth of the state.

In Europe, on the other hand, the market principle of individual choice was only partly implemented. In the first place, the Christian churches and the European states still constitute a union based on cooperation. In the second place, the choice of religious creed was restricted initially to the Christian churches. Only much later did it become possible for people to opt for non-Christian religions. And not until recent decades have people started to think of religious freedom of choice as the right to *provide* a religion. Alongside the free choice of religion we now find the free offering of religions not tied to one of the established churches. Together the free provision and the free choice among these offerings constitute the developed religious market.

In Europe a profound change is underway at present from a culture in which people acquire their religious belief simply by 'inheriting' it to one in which a religious creed is freely chosen and consumed. For instance, the ceremony of 'confirmation' has changed from a more or less prescribed rite of passage for young people in Christian families into a matter of personal choice for groups of all ages. In this way, the Christian churches are adapting themselves to their non-established counterparts. The voluntary principle (the market) is starting to assert itself independently of the constitutional norms and organizational forms of the churches.

The second aspect of religious freedom – the freedom to put a religion on offer – is (as we can also see from the American case) the gateway to *religious cosmopolitization* within the framework of the nation.

By 'pluralization' I understand the coexistence of different, frequently contradictory world perspectives and value systems in a space where they directly interact. 'Cosmopolitization' is a special case of pluralization; it may be said to exist when old and new global religions and religious movements start to overlap in utterly different contexts, manifest themselves in novel or traditional ways, compete or interact with one another, contest each other's privileges or mutually dispute each other's legitimacy or legality. In other words, cosmopolitization refers to the way in which the macrocosm of the world religions is refracted or mirrored in the microcosm of the nation and the community. In this sense, modernization does not drive secularization, but is the motor propelling a conflict-ridden process of religious diversification in a variety of national contexts. There is nothing inevitable about this process, of course, but, confronted by the new, global media of communication, it is hard to put definite religious and governmental strategies in place to stop its advance, at least in the de-territorialized space of the internet. The religious other is currently very much present in the minds of almost everyone, not necessarily as an enemy – and that is an important point – but rather as an *alternative* not just to the religious way of thinking but also to the way in which believers understand life and the world, and seek to give them shape.

The logic of the market does not only make national frontiers fluid and thus – as in Germany, for example – represent a threat to the monopolies of the Protestant and Catholic churches. The expansion of the number of religious creeds on offer, beyond the boundaries of churches and nation-states, has sent shock waves through society (and unleashed defensive reactions). This is because even atheists who have left the Christian churches still remain Christian atheists.

At the same time, the logic of the market breaks with the logic of conversion (see Bruce, Moore, Zinser). It is not necessary to leave your own church or religious community to consume religious services to mark particular circumstances, life crises, etc. The market model means that the either/or associated with the pre-existing church monopoly is replaced by both/and. Religions on offer are selected much like other offerings in the marketplace; they are tried out, changed and combined. What is trying the patience of Europe at the moment is, in the language of the market, Islam's right to make a public offering – what consequences this right will have is hard to predict at the present time. There is some evidence that European societies will have to rethink their view of the relations between church and state in a quite fundamental way: for example, by a 'de-nationalizing' of religious freedom. Not all Muslims are radical Muslims, but Muslims who think of themselves as European Muslims in the various countries of Europe and who wish to organize themselves as such cannot be forced to 'assimilate' on the pattern of the European national churches. In this sense, the struggle for the soul of European Islam is a struggle to ensure the victory of the free-market principle in religious matters in Europe.

Over and above that, the model of the free market has two major consequences for the pacification of global religious conflicts (consequences that are interconnected, as Zinser [2006] points out). If it is correct that the universal history of religion is the history of lunatics who are always at each other's throats, in actual fact or potentially, then the logic of the market is in *essence peaceful*. While the market may make possible, and may even renew, the tendency towards missionary imperialism, it does not do so by military conquest, but through the strategies of the marketplace. In this sense, Immanuel Kant grasped the situation two centuries ago when he wrote:

> For the *spirit of commerce* sooner or later takes hold of every people, and it cannot exist side by side with war. And of all the powers (or means) at the disposal of the power of the state, *financial power* can probably be relied on most. Thus states [and religions – Ulrich Beck] find themselves compelled to promote the noble cause of peace. . . . And wherever in the world there is a threat of war breaking out, they will try to prevent it through mediation. (Kant 1970: 114)

We thus witness the emergence of a kind of *'religious imperialism of the spirit of commerce'*, which those who wish to acquire the services of the religions and esoteric or New-Age offerings endorse by their acts of purchase and consumption. What this points to not least is a readiness to succumb to the temptations of religion: in other words, to practise a kind of masochistic self-interest that satisfies its religious needs in the wellness offerings of the religious-esoteric world-consumer society in a manner that at once condemns and confirms that society.

What follows from this? The fire of religion could well be extinguished by the commodity form of God. Admittedly, there is an evident risk that religion might be extinguished along with the fire. It is possible, of course, that those who have intoned the Song of Songs of market forces in the domain of religion are right to prescribe this drastic remedy as a way of curing the fanaticism of religious violence, whether potential or actual. It would be a mistake to banish this antidote from the great pharmacopoeia of humankind. But between the extreme alternatives – religion kills or the market kills religion – it must surely be possible to discover (or rediscover) a third way, and that third way is one we should now go in search of.

The model of the religiously neutral constitutional state: Jürgen Habermas

In addition to an examination of the religious denominations in their dealings with their co-religionists and followers of other creeds, it is important to scrutinize the ways in which religion interacts with the neutral constitutional state and secular citizens respond to the religious revival in society, politics and the public sphere.

> As the example of the United States shows, the modern constitutional state was also invented with the aim of promoting religious pluralism. Only the ideologically neutral exercise of secular governmental authority within the framework of the constitutional state can ensure that different communities of belief can coexist on a basis of equal rights and mutual tolerance, while nevertheless remaining unreconciled at the level of their substantive worldviews or doctrines. The secularization of the political power of the state and the positive and negative freedom to exercise one's religion are two sides of the same coin. They protected religious communities not only from the destructive effects of violent interconfessional conflicts but also from the hostility towards religion of a secularized society. The constitutional state can defend its religious and nonreligious citizens from each other, however, only when their civic interactions are not based on a mere *modus vivendi*: their coexistence within a democratic system must also be founded on conviction. The democratic state is sustained by a legally unen-

forceable form of solidarity among citizens who respect each other as free and equal members of their political community. (Habermas 2008: 2–3)

What Habermas calls for as a way of regulating conflicts arising from the absolute, mutually exclusive claims of religious truths is nothing less than a civility that transcends entrenched religious differences. All creeds must accept and indeed positively affirm a religious and intellectual pluralism, and not just as the lesser evil. It follows that it is wrong to deny 'rationality' to religious voices in the public sphere from the outset. Habermas defends Hegel's thesis 'that the major world religions belong to the history of reason itself' (ibid.: 6).

Behind this we can glimpse the concept (at least within the horizon of European secularism) of the *'post-secular society'*. As long as secular citizens continue to regard religions as archaic remnants, freedom of religion means no more than a kind of natural preservation order for endangered species. In such circumstances the separation of church and state ceases to make any sense. In the shadowy space formed by forbearing indifference and in the light of scientific criticism, the contents of religious creeds melt like glaciers under the influence of climate warming. Secularism, however, is based on a belief in its monopoly of truth, namely that of scientific truth, which admittedly has become reflexive in the course of scientific observations of itself in the world risk society. In other words, it is shot through and undermined with self-doubt. When it is made into an absolute, secularism finds itself caught up in a universalist circularity which is blind and, in particular, blind to the cosmopolitan recognition of the otherness of other traditions of belief, their history, their humanity, their oppression, their dominance, their dignity and the burden of their suffering. In contrast to secular modernity, the post-secular variety is already en route to the cosmopolitan society. In it the norms governing a tolerant and hence necessarily indifferent society guaranteed by universal laws must cease to be accepted only with reluctance; instead they must be internalized and defended as guarantors of one's own religious traditions and communities (Habermas, ibid.; see also pp. 190–1 below). For all the interlocutors who are party to religious disagreements that means undergoing a profound historical learning process and change in mentality. The secular society must become post-secular, i.e. sceptical and open-minded towards the voices of religion. Permitting religious language to enter the public sphere should be regarded as enrichment, not as an intrusion. Such a change is no less ambitious than the general toleration of secular nihilism by the religions.

This is evidently a model not of pre-established religious harmony, but rather of constitutionally regulated religious *conflict*. This was illustrated in exemplary fashion in 2007 by a sudden upsurge of passions in a Germany which is still predominantly Christian. Muslim religious communities decided to take the right to religious freedom inscribed in the constitution at its word. They demanded that the Protestants and Catholics who share Christian Germany in a somewhat unfraternal spirit should agree to grant equal rights to Islam, evidently looking to the 'religiously neutral' state and its democratic organs for support. This created a dilemma for the system of the semi-nationalized, bipartisan religious organization of Christianity in Germany. Either an incomplete secularization will be retained or else secularization will be further developed. In the latter case, the far from modest privileges of the Christian churches will have to be abolished – from religious instruction in the schools, on through the church tax and right down to the seats reserved in the Broadcasting Council for church representatives. A consistent separation of state and religion of the kind that is customary in France and for which Habermas has provided a blueprint would undoubtedly be the best solution, for in the final analysis non-Christians are also citizens with a right to freedom from religion. Such a demand is probably not capable of fulfilment in Germany in the foreseeable future, however, but to state that fact shows just how thoroughly institutionalized Christianity has become as well as revealing the uncomfortable truth that the apparent neutrality of the state is really an illusion. Yet because the Basic Law guarantees the equality of religious denominations it is unavoidable that Muslims too should be given equal rights. Remarkably enough, even unchristian or anti-Christian secular citizens in Germany find it hard to envisage the possibility that the state might levy a Muslim tax or that Muslims should be entitled by law to a seat in the Broadcasting Council. And incidentally, that would involve a process of 'organizational assimilation', since other world religions and the New Religious Movements would also find themselves having to put up with the same sort of bureaucratized corset as the semi-nationalized religious organizations.

But, we might ask, would we not be right to say that Habermas's blueprint for the constitutional regulation of religious conflict in post-secular society is still imprisoned in the micro-optics of the constitutional *nation-state*? Does it therefore not lack a dimension that embraces world society as a whole? No, Habermas takes one further, decisive step. In his search for a globalized constitutional patriotism he decouples the universalist idea of a constitution from its concrete version in the nation-state. Having done so, he is able to discover empirically many examples of constitutions detached from the state in a variety of forms. Examples are provided by economic constitutions, the constitution of the EU, of the UN, the WTO and the WHO, etc. This leaves the door open for the idea of a *political constitution for the multi-religious world society*: that is to say, for the extension of the

> '*bürgerliche Verfassung*' (i.e. the type of constitution which had recently emerged in Kant's day from the American and French revolutions) from the national onto the global level. This marks the birth of the idea of a constitutionalization of international law. The extraordinary thing about this farsighted conceptual innovation was the implication that international law as a law of states would be transformed into cosmopolitan law as a law of individuals. For individuals would no longer enjoy the status of legal subjects merely as citizens of a nation-state, but also as members of a politically constituted world society. (Habermas 2008: 314)

This programmatic decoupling of state and constitution does have one consequence, however. According to Habermas, we are speaking here of a constitution of the world society without a world republic, without a world government, and therefore without a world state capable of enforcing its will. This is the vital new historical element for a religiously mobilized global society: since the civilizing of global religious conflicts can no longer be delegated to nation-states to impose their will (as in the first modernity), the civilizing process must be entrusted to the *self-civilizing* capacities of world religions (as in the second modernity). This means, on the one hand, that in the cosmopolitan constellation the reciprocal demonization of those who have other beliefs or none at all is immediate and without restraint. On the other hand, the state mechanisms that enforced tolerance and that made the Peace of Westphalia possible in the first place have now failed. For the Peace of Westphalia did not come into being because the religious denominations were inspired by their inner irenic disposition to agree mutually to recognize one another. Rather, the political powers concerned had tired of identifying themselves with one or other denomination and of resolving their disputes by force of arms. It was they who introduced the separation of church and state and thus brought about an armistice between religious denominations that were incapable of achieving peace on their own. It is this factor that is lacking in a global society without a world government. In consequence, the pressure grows on *all* large religious communities to improve their mutual understanding of the normative and legal conditions underpinning their coexistence with, alongside or in opposition to one another on the basis of equal respect for all. Admittedly, Habermas does not ask the crucial question of how – in the absence of an impartial regulator – an exclusive and zealous form of monotheism *might be able* to transform itself in the course of its conflict with an alien religion into an inner, stable form of religious tolerance that would encourage the development of a forbearing and peaceable nature. In other words, the problem is to discover how we might preserve a sense of the historical openness of conflict and hence too of the productive nature of friction and confrontation, which bring forth their own forms of regulation. For only in that way can we manage not to offend against the oldest of all rules for conflict regulation, which states that we must adopt the standpoint of our interlocutor, instead of persisting unthinkingly in the pseudo-certainties of a universal European particularism.

The blueprint for a universal world ethos: Hans Küng

Many people (religious organizations as well as religious believers) attempt to draw the teeth of religious conflicts throughout the world by claiming that they all speak of the common belief of all monotheistic religions in the same God and by emphasizing the shared Abrahamic roots of the three great world religions.

Does this mean that there is what Hans Küng (1990) calls a universal 'world ethos' that underlies both the world religions and more individualistic spiritual searchings? Yes, there is, is his answer.

> Japan is ethnically homogeneous and it demonstrates how three different religions – Shintoism, Confucianism and Buddhism – can live together in peace and in many instances can even merge. Even Islam, which expanded chiefly in the wake of military conquest in the Middle East, India and North Africa, reached South-East Asia by peaceful means, following in the footsteps of traders, scholars and mystics. Moreover, as early as the fifth century BC, China had produced a historically important, ethically inspired humanism. The expression '*ren*', which corresponds to our '*humanum*' (human), is a central concept in this Chinese tradition. Similarly, Confucius was the first person to formulate the golden rule of reciprocity: 'Never impose on others what you would not choose for yourself.'[3] This golden rule also appears in the Indian tradition. In Jainism it takes the following form: 'A man should treat all creatures as he would like to be treated.' In Buddhism we find: 'A condition that is not pleasant or beautiful for me must be the same for another, and how could I burden another with a condition that is not pleasant or beautiful for me?' In Hinduism it is asserted: 'One should never do that to another which one regards as injurious to one's own self.'[4]

That is the core of morality.

> This golden rule is also to be found of course in the Abrahamic religions. Rabbi Hillel (60 BC) said: 'That which is hateful to you, do not do to your fellow.' Jesus expresses this in a positive form: 'And as ye would that men should do to you, do ye also to them likewise.'[5] Islam too has the same idea: 'None of you [truly] believes until he wishes for his brother what he wishes for himself.' These trans-cultural ethical rules are a structural component of a common humane ethic, regardless of what we call it and make the idea of a profound gulf between 'Asiatic' and 'Western' values more or less irrelevant. (Küng 2007: 8)

---

[3] *Analects* XXV.24 (trans. David Hinton).
[4] Brihaspati, Mahabharata (Anusasana Parva, Section CXIII, Verse 8).
[5] Luke 6: 31.

How are we to distinguish between what is in fact pretty obviously a religious *universalism* from a religious *cosmopolitanism*?

Universalism means: religious differences are smoothed out so that what they have in common is actually a lowest common denominator. Cosmopolitanism, in contrast, emphasizes the dignity and the burden of difference, the indissoluble alternation of interweaving and opposition of universalism and particularism (Sznaider 2008). From the standpoint of (European) universalism, one's own God is the *universal* God. The universal God, however, is the *Esperanto* God who scorns the particular features of the religious languages and traditions and discards them in favour of an Esperanto religiosity. That is a wrong track, since a lowest-common-denominator universalism disregards the unique nature of the world religions and offends against their dignity.

The universal God is, moreover, the *conquering* God, the God of the Crusaders. The others – the 'heathen' – must be 'saved' and converted in what is understood to be their own best interests. The universalist God – this is the bitter lesson of history – is the God of colonization, the 'white man's burden'.[6]

Methodological conversion: Mahatma Gandhi

According to John Dunne in his book *The Way of All the Earth* (quoted by Esposito, Fasching and Lewis 2006), the age in which it would be possible to found a new religion is now past. The conquest of the world by some religion or culture or other is no longer necessary. What is needed rather, is, an answer to the question: How can competing religious certitudes and the stereotypes of others embedded in them coexist in a confined space or in the closeness created by the media without losing their identity, their dignity and their memory? An experimental cosmopolitanism is needed, a spiritual adventure in which people practise what Dunne refers to as a 'passing over' into the religion and culture of others that makes it possible to see the world of one's own religion through the eyes of others. When we then return to our own

---

[6] See pp. 54–7 above and pp. 167–8 below; for a critique, see Spaemann 1996.

religion and culture, enriched with insights into not just the other religion and culture but also our own, we might succeed in experiencing the new closeness not simply as a threat but also as enrichment.

Mahatma Gandhi's religious biography and worldwide influence provide a good illustration of the way in which this adventure can take the form of a *'methodological conversion'*. As a young man, Gandhi went to England to study law. This 'detour' to a country at the heart of the Christian West did not estrange him from Hinduism. On the contrary, it deepened his understanding of it and his commitment to it. For it was in England that, at the suggestion of a friend, Gandhi began to read the Bhagavad-Gita in the English translation by Edwin Arnold under the title of *The Song Celestial*. This reading proved to be an eye-opener and he followed it up with an intensive study of the Hindu text in Sanskrit. He was also deeply impressed by Arnold's book *The Light of Asia*, a retelling of the life of Buddha. Reading this through the eyes of his Western friends, he was moved to discover the spiritual wealth of his own tradition.

The seeds of Gandhi's worldwide influence in the liberation of India from the colonial yoke of the British were sown in England, but blossomed during his years of study in South Africa, and finally bore fruit after his return to India in 1915. This kind of 'passing over' and 'return' illustrates how the individualization of faith can create, enrich and empower *both* the individual and the institutional, public authority of the religious voice.

The question of the conditions governing the possibility of a religious cosmopolitanism must not be confused with the wishful thinking that projects the researcher's cosmopolitan intentions onto reality. The conversion model is no one-way street. Anyone who has learned to conduct his or her life in a number of religious cultures simultaneously – in other words, anyone who has been 'converted' to the values and contradictions of freedom and consumerism in the West – can take advantage of this talent for 'passing over' to practise religiously motivated violence with expert cruelty. The terrorists of September 11, 2001 are an apt illustration of this.

Revolution?

In the light of the 'withering away of the premises' underpinning the first modernity of the nation-state and industrial capitalism, many observers look to the emergence of an alternative proletariat. This is to be found in the 'rainbow coalition' or, as Hardt and Negri call it, the *'multitude'*. It is the 'average migrant' and 'political Islamism' who function here as the 'gofers of the world revolution', to use Bertolt Brecht's term. If it is right to say that in the second modernity boundaries merge and become blurred, it is the 'average migrants' who embody the blurred frontiers between religions, states and nations. If they are to survive, the average migrants must become frontier artists (evading the frontier, exploiting the frontier, establishing the frontier, crossing the frontier, and so forth) and they can easily come crashing down from the high wire of the frontier they are balancing on. From a nationalist standpoint it is not possible to regard potentially criminal immigrants as the avant-garde of a mobile transnational population. Nor is it likely that these mobile populations will be seen as actors rehearsing a cosmopolitan form of existence. They appear instead as wilfully unruly because they resist assimilation.

This is not to suggest that they should be regarded as the desirable subjects of a cosmopolitan revolution. It is not just their numbers and the consequent difficulty of integrating them organizationally that militate against such a conclusion. The chief point is that it is a fallacy about cosmopolitanism to believe that the contradictions arising from the transnational situation imply that 'average migrants' have a cosmopolitan outlook and mode of action. The opposite is no less plausible and may in fact be more likely, namely re-ethnicization and religious fundamentalism. And yet the 'average migrant' embodies the very model of an experimental cosmopolitanism *from below*, of a cosmopolitanism of the *powerless* who must combine a minimal change of perspective, dialogical imagination and ingenuity in their dealings with the contradictions which are part and parcel of the border regime if they are to survive at all.

> The new type of an everyday migrant cosmopolitan hones his skills in coping with an alien environment through the frontier experiences of acculturation and ethnicization. In immigrant societies,

migrants inevitably become experts in the system of cultural distinctions that turns them into ethnic outsiders, above all in its
commonplace aspects in daily life. At the foundation of these
experiences we find the reservoir of 'labels' for one's own use: for
example, for a temporary strategic self-ethnicization or for the
many forms of ethno-mimicry that enable the migrant to adapt to
multiculturalism in order to outwit it. . . . Cosmopolitanism of this
kind neither enjoys the pleasures of difference nor suffers from its
drawbacks. Culture and identity here are not autonomous horizons
that call for widening in the spirit of a training in world citizenship. On the contrary, they are inseparably bound up with a long
history of hegemonial cultural and identity politics that inevitably
form part of one's own subjective history. Thus cosmopolitanism
of this kind does not envisage utopian conditions of a paradisal,
post-national kind, but, at best, a variety of precarious hetero-
topias that construct a practical and political dream of a better
life across the frontier, in the realm of what is possible. (Römhild
2007: 620–1)

No doubt, the worldwide resonance of the terrorist outrages of
political Islam and the subsequent insecurity and anxiety of the
West signal the potential global threat represented by this politico-
religious movement of modernized anti-modernity. But that very
fact also points to its limits. It does indeed promise to restore the
dignity of everything that has been steamrollered by the Western
modernization process. But it has no answer to problems of the
world risk society that are themselves the product of the civilizing
process – except to advocate the abandonment of modernity.

We can of course retreat into a counter-modernity in the spirit
of Catholicism and strive to continue refurbishing the principles
of dogmatism with a never-flagging Counter-Reformation zeal
('Purgatory', etc.). But in that event, we would fail to answer the
key question about where a revived Christianity would find the
intellectual strength to imagine a *better modernity* that might
arise from the heart of a reflexive modernization.

6

Peace Instead of Truth?
The Futures of the Religions in the World Risk Society

Introduction: 'Clash of universalisms'

Up to now, the answers we have considered to the question of how to civilize global religious conflicts have been far from convincing. If the constitutional state proves unable to control the mutually exclusive truth claims of the monotheistic religions in the framework of the nation-state, and the unforeseen consequences of individualization and the market remain ambivalent, there will be nothing for it but to explore the possibility of religion becoming a cosmopolitan actor. What must the world religions do to help civilize the religious potential for violence that has been rampant in Europe for at least the last three hundred years?

Religious history has been the history of its globalization since its inception (Chapter 3). As far as Christianity is concerned, it was Paul, a Hellenistic Jew, who did more than anyone to convert the Jesus movement from a Jewish sect into a global religious movement with a universalist claim: 'Go ye into all the world' (Mark 16: 15).

Conceptualized, globalization of religion means 'crusades', 'overcoming blood bonds', 'colonialism', 'universalism' and 'denigration of the religious other', etc. This globalization has not been imposed, it is *missionary work*. '[T]he Church is missionary by her very nature' was Pope John Paul II's summing up in a missionary encyclical of 1990. Globalization is globalizing *labour*, religious *labour*; it means labouring away at religious others and against them; it is worldwide labour at the borders with others, or, more accurately, a highly contradictory form of frontier labour. For centuries, religions have been vast, transnational wall-building and wall-demolishing projects – operating against one another, with one another, and across ethnic, national frontiers and even continents. And they have been deeply intertwined with the ruling powers in the periods of their dominance. To be sure, we may with equal justification put the heretical question whether or not the clocks of religious history have stood still because, like infinite loops, these 'faith industries' carry on their conflicts timelessly.

All the components of the labour of religious globalizing – the elimination of social and political frontiers, as well as the construction of the boundary dividing right belief and wrong – relate to the horizon of the world society. Neither the destruction of national frontiers nor the construction of religious frontiers can be implemented or even conceived of merely in the framework of the nation-state. The religious decoupling of society and nation bursts asunder the territorial and ethnic dimensions of the concept of society and acts out its own drama within the framework of 'humanity'.

What is the meaning of 'inter-religiosity', the contiguity and interpenetration of the world religions, in the twenty-first century? It flows into a – by no means temporary – clash of universalisms. Its obverse is seen in the tendency to denigrate the followers of other faiths as unbelievers or heretics and to question their human dignity. In the course of the thick communicative discourse of the world, all believers or unbelievers, whatever the nature of their belief or unbelief, find themselves transposed both into the home-land of believers (or atheists) and equally into the potentially outlawed condition of the unbeliever (in the eyes of religious others). This pigeon-holing arouses and nurtures diffuse anxieties that can become religiously charged and may culminate in an explosion of violence.

The linkage of nation, religion and violence characterized the nineteenth century and culminated in the experiences of the world wars of the twentieth century. These dangers, which have not been eliminated, have been overlaid and reinforced by the terrors of a possible nuclear war and the world risk society in general. *The extent to which truth can be replaced by peace is a question that will decide the continued existence of the human race.*

In this final chapter this thesis will be explored in three stages:

1. If we acknowledge the irrevocable reality and significance of religion in the modern world, a change of perspective will become essential. We shall have to move from the statement that 'religion has ceased to play any role in world politics' to the assertion that 'religion plays a key role in world politics'. Does that imply a victory for the fundamentalists or does it mean the start of a shift towards a cosmopolitan way of seeing?
2. Whereas this section explores the hypothesis that religion is not just part of the problem but also part of the solution, the second part inquires whether, in the age of the nation-state with its world wars and the Holocaust, the churches – especially in Germany – betrayed the claims of Christian universalism.
3. In conclusion, the third section discusses how far truth can be replaced by peace: Can religion be legitimated as an agent of mobilization and modernization in the world risk society?

Victory of the fundamentalisms or cosmopolitan turn?

The clash of religious universalisms – the cosmopolitan constellation – takes place not in the abstract, in global realms or in the external macrocosm, but in the innermost heart of one's own life. The 'soul' has become the stage in the battle for the human dignity with which fellow believers of different countries, nations, classes and castes are credited, while that dignity is denied to believers in other religions. The consciousness of this change lags behind reality because people still think in national terms which insinuate that the only important 'containers' in which affairs are conducted are those of the respective nation-states.

In 2007, the Spanish undersecretary of state for foreign affairs, Bernardino León, had an unexpected encounter with reality that brought home to him that the world was very far from conforming to his ideas of how it was supposed to be. He became entangled in a diplomatic nightmare that ought not to exist but which corresponds with increasing frequency to the reality of the cosmopolitan constellation. The problem centred on an Italian ship off the coast of Senegal that was carrying out a check on a North Korean boat under Spanish command on which a Russian crew was attempting to smuggle 300 Indians and Pakistanis illegally into Spain from Guinea. The boat was seized in the course of an EU operation coordinated from the Canaries.

Globalization is more than an economic process. It produces new kinds of de-nationalized subjects and life-situations, new categories of rich and poor, at the top and the bottom of society, all of which undermine the premises of those of our attitudes that are rooted in the nation-state. On the one hand, there are international finance elites sitting in global cities such as Hong Kong, São Paulo or Frankfurt who spend their days in hot pursuit of streams of money with the click of a mouse, as if the globe were their personal plaything. On the other hand, there are illegal Mexicans who slave away in meat factories in the American state of Iowa in order to save up enough money to send home to enable their families to pay for the basic necessities of life.

And then there is also the entirely normal, but unfamiliar city of Stuttgart. How many people know that in Stuttgart around 200,000 people, roughly one-third of the population, were born abroad? Or that around 40 per cent of the children of pre-school age come from immigrant families? Or that in every second marriage at least one partner is a foreigner? Or that the city contains people from roughly 170 countries, speaking over 120 languages? And that this profoundly cosmopolitan Stuttgart promotes a whole range of transnational ways of life from within Europe and beyond its frontiers under the leadership of a Christian Democrat mayor who is immensely proud of the city's achievements?

We all live in Stuttgart now. But we do not wish to acknowledge the fact. Why not? Our view of the world is *essentialist*. We think and act according to clearly defined categories of frontiers and nationalities: one country, one passport, one national identity – that is the secular version of the Trinity. And this is what has been falsified by the cosmopolitan constellation.

To gain an adequate understanding of the reality in which we live, we need a cosmopolitan gaze, one that can focus on the way in which borders have been abolished or become porous, become blurred and *at the same time* have been re-established or newly erected. We need a *cosmopolitan realism* – the national gaze is a backwards-looking idealism; the cosmopolitan gaze is realistic because it places the dialectics of borders, the fears and opportunities this creates, at the centre of our attention.

Avishai Margalit (2007: 9) tells the story of how years ago he had been given a book of photographs with the title *The Family of Man*. In it you could see human faces of every skin colour, with unusual physiognomies and exotic clothes, doing all the things that people always do throughout their lives: being born, working, dancing, quarrelling, making love and even laughing. An older woman of his acquaintance whose judgement he respected looked through the volume and said: 'It's kitsch!' Margalit took some time before finally coming round to her view.

For this volume of photographs was based, as is often the case, on the assumption that in the final analysis human beings are all the same beneath the surface of their cultural diversity – everyone descends from Adam and Eve – we might call this belief Adamism or Eveism. This universalist belief that we are all the same under the skin is not just sentimental, it is something even worse, namely utterly false, if only because it misunderstands the particular source of its notion of sameness, something that painfully emerges from the clash of universalisms. It is our white, European or German sameness that we have at the back of our minds and that leads us to judge 'others', changing them into 'strangers' even though they may be fellow nationals (who hold the same passport as us).

A clear distinction should be made between the sceptical realism of the 'cosmopolitan gaze' and a *normative* version of cosmopolitanism. It would be important to establish that (and why) the cosmopolitan constellation does not automatically produce cosmopolitans but instead (1) anti-cosmopolitan fundamentalists and also why, even if only through a crack in the door, so to speak, (2) it creates the opportunity for a cosmopolitan turn. Against this background, it might become possible to bring about a revised view of the history of religion. Instead of thinking of it as a history of the victims who have succumbed to the imposition of modernization, we could inquire (3) whether we might go beyond disenchantment and a linear history of secularization to construct a history of religion as the history of the active reformation of a modernity that is always placing itself at risk.

Reflexive fundamentalism

The cosmopolitization of the religions is the source of resistance to them. This constellation apparently transforms nationally defined spaces into cross-border battlefields with a worldwide reach and communicative echo effects (see the 'Danish' controversy about the caricatures of Muhammad). Under the impact of this process, the universalist claims of Western modernity, like those of Christian revelation, find themselves exposed to fundamental criticism. This is achieved, on the one hand, by decoupling modernity from Westernization, since this denies the West its monopoly of modernity. On the other hand, the certitudes of Christian revelation are forced to confront the certitudes of the revelations of Islam and other faiths. The result is that the contact between the different religious faiths and their mutual interpenetration end up undermining the foundations of their faith.

> Of course, by definition Islam is universal, but after the time of the Prophet and his companions (the Salaf) it has always been embedded in given cultures. These cultures seem now a mere product of history and the results of many influences and idiosyncracies. For fundamentalists (and also for some liberals) there is nothing in these cultures to be proud of, because they have altered the pristine message of Islam. Globalisation is a good opportunity to dissociate Islam from any given culture and to provide a model that could work beyond any culture. (Roy 2004: 25)

The worldwide expansion of divergent religious fundamentalisms unleashes confrontations and politicizations, and leads in part to bitter conflicts that deploy the discriminatory language and stock of symbols characteristic of the duel between scepticism and faith. What is at stake here is a 'transfer of ideas and conflict of meanings, osmosis and resistance, paradoxically all happening at the same time. . . . We would need a history of interactions to give us an inkling of the ferocity of interfaith conflicts and the aggressive nature of cultural disagreements within particular creeds' (Graf 2004: 43).

The cosmopolitan constellation – in other words, the availability of a diversity of cultural, political and religious symbolic worlds – is seized on gratefully by monotheistic religions struggling to establish their collective identities. This is because it gives them access to totalitarian ideological attitudes. If the clash of civilizations coincides with political or economic crises and conflicts, it may well culminate in explosions of violence (Eisenstadt 2006a: 59).

This shock discovery that the universal religions are *far from universal* has been driven by the cosmopolitan process worldwide. The ensuing series of enduring earth tremors this has caused has triggered fears (of foreigners) and thus encourages fundamental religious movements to extend their political activities. They acquire their power from the creeping and in fact irreversible growth of cosmopolitanism, which – measured against the normal rules of the national and international order – is played out in the half-light of society as a breach of the peace and perhaps even as a violation of the law. If the worlds of religious or secular faith are transformed into battlefields of conflicting certainties, this may well lead us to the conclusion that – not to put too fine a point on it – the rules governing order in nation-states are surreptitiously being bludgeoned and destroyed.

The cosmopolitan gaze teaches us that the growth of cosmopolitanism is irreversible but that anti-cosmopolitanism wins out. The fundamentalist religions of the present are *not* original fundamental religions but modern, partly reflexive modern movements that have learned how to swim in the tide of cosmopolitanism (the mass media, the internet and the weak points of Western civil society) like fish in water.

Such 'fundamentalist movements' have four main distinguishing features: (1) the rediscovery of unquestioning acceptance; (2) the unwavering belief in the totalitarian immediacy of God; (3) the demonization of believers in other faiths and none; and (4) transnational networks and operations.

The rediscovery of unquestioning acceptance. It is evident that the clash of religious universals must trigger reciprocal attacks on the respective canons of revealed certainties. Comparisons, responses and justifications are demanded and become indispensable, where hitherto a circular self-certainty had prevailed. In other words, the cosmopolitan constellation creates pressures to provide justifications and rationales that fundamentalist religions typically react to by resolving to defend their beliefs even more militantly. In other words, in an age when the certainties of belief have increasingly come under fire, fundamentalist religions do everything in their power to reinstate an unquestioning acceptance.

As Mark C. Taylor (2006: 6) reports, new forms of 'religious correctness' have developed (the latest version of 'political correctness') even in the liberal strongholds of religious studies.[1] The more religious students become, the less they are prepared to submit to critical reflection about their faith and the more determined they are to dismiss doubts and questions about their beliefs arising from a diversity of historical, sociological and psychological perspectives.

This means that in the cosmopolitan constellation a new sociological distinction is emerging – in all religious traditions. A distinction is being drawn between a category of believers who seek to restore the unquestioning acceptance of their faith tradition by refusing more or less militantly to entertain doubts of any sort and a group of believers who accept the need imposed by interdenominational constraints to reflect upon and justify their faith. The distinction between believers and unbelievers, which can act as a threat to the human dignity of the members of the various religious communities, is overlaid by internal and interdenominational disagreements between religious currents and groups who find space for doubt and even welcome it as a way of revitalizing religious life, as opposed to those who do not share this view and who barricade themselves behind the constructed 'purity' of their faith.

> In pluralist religious markets the winners are the providers with strong brands. Aggressive God-selling and the provision of a rigorous, hard-line religion generally enjoy greater success than the conventional marketing of products with a high degree of ambiguity and latitude of interpretation. If we take an example from the highly developed religious markets of the two Americas, it can be shown that a growing number of consumers show a preference for hard-line religious products. In the United States, the old mainline Protestant churches are among the losers. The winners are the

---

[1] 'Distinguished scholars at several major universities in the United States have been condemned, even subjected to death threats, for proposing psychological, sociological or anthropological interpretations of religious texts in their classes and published writings. In the most egregious cases defenders of the faith insist that only true believers are qualified to teach their religious tradition.'

unswerving conservative providers of the 'religious right'. An analogous situation is to be found in several societies of Latin America where conversion to charismatic groups and sects is depriving the Roman-Catholic Church of many members. The great success of such sects and, more generally, of the many charismatic Christian movements is probably best explained by the fact that hard-line religions have a lot to offer consumers. By demanding a high degree of religious commitment, thick-textured community spirit, the strict observance of moral norms and considerable financial support, they provide the people who congregate in them and who feel insecure in a pluralist, uncertain world with a strong, stable identity, a crisis-resistant interpretation of the world and the age we live in, well-ordered family structures and thick networks of solidarity. The heaven of their authoritarian God the Father is a haven of irrefutable, self-evident truths where everything is clear and straightforward, a situation already anticipated in this world. (Graf 2004: 28–9)

The totalitarian immediacy of God. What is the source of the militancy of the new unwavering certainty seen everywhere in the return of the Gods? From Islamic fundamentalism and American evangelism to Hindu nationalism, the call for total conformity and absolute submission to whatever particular variant of divine revelation one chooses has suddenly become 'popular' (not to say 'modern'). Against the backdrop of the God who has now become 'one's own', all doubts are suddenly quelled and suppressed by the claim of the totalitarian immediacy of God – a 'direct line to God'.

Religious fundamentalists follow the path mapped out by the secularization process radically to its very end. They do so by displacing the supreme authority of the 'objective world' into the realm of the 'subjective world'. This means the expulsion of God from nature and raising humanity to the status of the measure of all things. From the standpoint of scientific rationality there can be no 'natural knowledge' of God, and, as the authority providing the basis for the scientific rationale of faith, theology must be banished from the sphere of science. In the course of a transvaluation of all values, religion is reduced in the final analysis to a blind subjective faith that can now be transformed by a (more or less reflexive) fundamentalism into a totalitarian certainty in the immediacy of God.

Demonization of believers in other faiths and none. The message of salvation that emanates from the world religions has brought humankind the greatest hopes and the bitterest disappointments – the promise of salvation to those in the community, threats of perdition to those on the outside. The religions preach peace (to those within) and sow dissension (among those without). On one point they are agreed: the demonization of religious others or of secular, atheistic modernity. Faced with the choice between truth and peace, the fundamentalist opts for truth – at whatever the cost.

That is the contradictory twofold promise of the religions in the globalized world: they hold out the promise of an ethics that builds bridges for a world of strangers but also opens up new chasms and abysses. It is the felt connection between the new religiosity and barbaric violence engendered by the mass media that has contributed to the return of the Gods to the public arenas. The ubiquitous presence of religiously motivated terrorism staged by the mass media reminds us of the way the Cross was used for centuries to stir up and legitimate anti-Semitism and the persecution of heretics. Nowadays, too, the resurrection of faith goes hand in hand with a public health warning: Religion can kill you!

The Catholic Church has been engaged in a never-ending process of counter-reformation down to this day – embodied at present in the figure of Pope Benedict XVI. Currently, when dealing with fellow Christians of other denominations, it has been more deeply preoccupied with upholding its own absolutist truth claims than with the Christian obligation to be mindful of the teaching 'Blessed are the peacemakers'. The Pope calls for a Christian Europe and is keen to promote its cause. He therefore excludes 'Islamic brothers'. Battling against the 'dictatorship of relativism', he defends the Catholic hierarchy of truth with a kind of card-game logic in which faith trumps reason. Christian faith trumps all other types of faith (especially Islam). Roman-Catholic faith is the ace that trumps the faith of all fellow Christians. And the Pope is the supreme trump in the truth gazette of right-thinking Catholics. He of course has no wish to give offence with this hierarchy of truth. But he either cannot see, or prefers not to see, that with this strategy *peace is replaced by truth* in this highly sensitive, indeed vulnerable relation between religions, *and is damaged in consequence.*

Little wonder is it therefore that in the West the spirit of the age leans towards a sort of ever-shifting pantheism. The place of belief in the One God has been taken by esoteric mini-cults, Romantic paganism. As Heribert Prantl puts it in his lapidary judgement, 'At any rate, it cannot be said that in the West people have no faith. On the contrary, they will believe almost anything' (Prantl 2006: 4).

And yet, the opposite is partly true too. The Catholic Church is neither a state nor an NGO; it is a mixture of the two – a quasi state-like, non-governmental organization with global reach and a global voice that, in accordance with its understanding of its own peace mission, it raises for the good or ill of all humankind and in defence of humanity. In fact, like a latter-day Marx, Pope John Paul II spoke out on behalf of the poor of this world and against exploitation by capitalism following the collapse of communism. He criticized the war in Iraq in the presence of its commander-in-chief, President George W. Bush. And amid the general confusion of the clash of universalisms, it is of all people Pope Benedict XVI who speaks out publicly in support of the maxim: 'In addition to faith, the highest value of all believers should be reason instead of violence.'

Transnational networks and operations. Those who proclaim an *anti-cosmopolitan* fundamentalism are compelled to act from within the terrain of cosmopolitanism. This is what makes them dangerous, and it means that they involuntarily further the advance of the very thing they combat: cosmopolitization.

There would be little surprising about the term 'anti-cosmopolitanism' were the negation to be understood as the return of the old, the pre-modern, instead of as the product and *integral* part of the second modernity, its *bastard offspring*. The adjective 'cosmopolitan' has to be attached to the concept 'anti-cosmopolitanism' – so that we must speak of cosmopolitan anti-cosmopolitanism. This means that in the case of the Islamic terrorism of Al-Qaeda we are talking about something that became possible only in societies where an inner cosmopolitization had already occurred and could ingeniously be turned against itself – organizationally, militarily and ideologically (Beck 1993: Chapter 4; Beck 2004: 171ff.).

What is meant by the normative cosmopolitanism of the religions?

Cosmopolitanism must be stripped of its kitschy overtones. That can be achieved with the aid of a sober, sceptical, realistic scrutiny of the contradictions and paradoxes of anti-cosmopolitan religious fundamentalists. Such realism has to prove its worth on the question of the normative value of religious cosmopolitanism.

It is often said that a Christianity that becomes tolerant may as well give up the struggle. 'What is true of nations applies also to religions and religious denominations. There can be no strong identity without the clear concept of an enemy' (Graf 2004: 35). This may well have been the situation at the time of the merging of nation and religion in the nineteenth century and during the world wars of the twentieth century, but it has ceased to be true at the start of the twenty-first. The opposite applies now: *there is no strong identity without a willingness to recognize the religious otherness of others.*

For, given the irreversible process of religious cross-fertilization and faced with civilization's potential for self-destruction, the cosmopolitan alternative is steadily acquiring contours, and a growing number of public voices are prepared to speak out in support and approval. At the macro-level the problem is how to strike a balance between two opposing trends that paradoxically are present simultaneously: the exchange of ideas between different religious denominations and the need to establish boundaries between them. And further, it is an open question whether religious intolerance at the top can learn from syncretist tolerance at the bottom. The historical record of interaction thus acquires its biographical pendant, which surfaces once more beyond the bounds of churches and religion in the '*bricolage* of a self-chosen God'. Two principles of tolerance define the normative framework of religious cosmopolitanism: (1) the principle of ethnic and national religious tolerance and (2) the principle of interdenominational religious tolerance.

The principle of ethnic, national religious tolerance. 'Love the sinner, not because he is a sinner, but because he is a man.' This was St Augustine's stated view. It means that the recognition of a human being must be uncoupled from what he or she does, believes and what place he or she occupies in society.

> Thomas Aquinas echoed this sentiment: 'We must hate in sinners what makes them sinners, and love what makes them men.' This represents the formula of an enduring right to exist that is valid for every human being and is based on a respect established by God: everyone is to be loved in the final analysis, independently of status, education, race, nationality and even of sinfulness. All human beings retain their enduring dignity even if they are dragged before the courts to answer for their misdeeds: love your enemies, but detest whatever evil is in them. The justification of this view lies in the parable of the wheat and the tares,[2] which the sociologist Rainer Forst regards as a central pillar of Christian ideas of tolerance: 'No man shall venture a judgement on earth that God alone can judge.'

This means that executing someone for blasphemy is not acceptable – a highly controversial issue at the present time.

> What is permitted is a 'mixed' society; everyone must live together in a state of mutual recognition. . . . From a Christian standpoint, the only circumstances in which it is permissible to speak of a church – in the sense current in the early church – are those in which members of different nations come together, people from the entire inhabited world. According to the Frankfurt sociologist Karl O. Hondrich, Christianity is the home of an ethic of brotherhood that embraces the whole of humankind, and this signifies 'a tremendous achievement on the part of a prophetic religion of redemption and a major affront to all known morality', which always 'gave priority to one's own clan'. (Angenendt 2007: 583–4)

The principle of a transethnic, transnational tolerance breaks with the primary power of blood ties, and this may be thought of as offering an almost revolutionary resistance to the worldwide trend towards re-ethnicization and re-nationalization. This transcendence of frontiers and hierarchies characteristic of Christian tolerance liberates emancipatory impulses that can be traced back to the anti-slavery movement.

[2] Matthew 13: 24–30.

But here too we perceive a dual aspect: only in a universalism that obliterates all frontiers – as do Christianity and the Enlightenment – can the blackness of Blacks, the Jewishness of Jews or the femininity of women become a 'particular' feature that is felt to be morally inferior. Whoever proclaims Christian equality limits or expunges the otherness of others. All those who refuse to endorse universalism condemn themselves to exclusion. In contrast, those who proclaim a universal morality and truth always detect chaos and disorder when universalism is rejected and fear the subversive power of ethnic particularisms. Anyone who criticizes universalism, so they imagine, fails to acknowledge the higher morality that distinguishes it and thus finds him- or herself condemned as a particular being hostile to morality.

The principle of interdenominational religious tolerance The cosmopolitan tolerance of religion can be seen not just in its dealings with ethnic others but even more strongly in its treatment of the dualism of faith or lack of faith. The clash of universalisms is paralleled by the clash of religious missionaries who regard the adherents of other faiths and none as the legitimate targets of their efforts at conversion and who believe that 'saving' their souls is in their own best interests. Even the assurances that such conversions must – of course! – be entirely 'voluntary' and be brought about without 'the use of force' give expression to the breach of the peace that they are committing worldwide. Hence what is decisive for this principle of interdenominational tolerance is not just the guarantee that only peaceful means may be employed, but, far more importantly, the offence caused by the attempt to proselytize as such has to be retracted, while the beliefs of those who belong to other faiths or none must be respected. The law of this version of religious tolerance could be summarized in the formula: conversion is good, missionary work is bad (however difficult it may be to draw a clear distinction here).[3]

Alongside the conflict between believers who denounce one another as unbelievers and cast doubt on their human dignity, there is a further, equally bitter conflict between believers and secularizers, who mutually demonize one another. The believers

---

[3] On this point, see 'methodological conversion', p. 160 above, as well as 'peace not truth', pp. 190–1 below.

attack 'secularists' belief' as a misconception, while the secularizers treat their religious fellow-citizens as mythical beasts who have escaped from the museum and who exclude themselves from active participation in the process of modernization. In both cases, equality and human dignity are questioned. We might perhaps say that the real conflict can be located in the polarity of secularism versus religiosity. The secularists insist that religious citizens must decide whether in cases of doubt they will accept the neutral state together with its secular rationality as legitimate or whether they will persist in their loyalty to their faith. In this sense, the question of cosmopolitan tolerance implies the further question about whether the secularizers will tolerate religion and the religious believers will tolerate secularism.

The recognition of the otherness of others is itself an alterity that must fight for recognition by others – as against the ties of blood and nationality, and against a universalism that rejects tolerance. How can religious cosmopolitanism ensure the acceptance of its own otherness – its image of multiethnicity and multinationality? Certainly not by means of 'postmodernist tolerance'. It should be noted that we are talking here about a strategy of tolerating otherness simply by virtue of making otherness an absolute and without any uniting, binding network of norms. This stance combines the principle of likeness with the relativist principle that different points of view are incommensurable, and, if we take this line of thought to its logical conclusion, it makes it impossible to construct any criteria of classification. It is very clear that without a 'universalism of tolerance', religious cosmopolitanism threatens to degenerate into an indiscriminate religion for all, for those who believe in other faiths and those who believe in no faith at all.

Human rights are intolerant of the infringement of human rights. In this sense, a cosmopolitan religious tolerance stands in need of *in*tolerance. The recognition of the otherness of others presupposes an intolerant attitude towards those who refuse to recognize others' otherness. The abolition of slavery calls for intolerance towards slave owners and slave traders as well as towards those who tolerate them. The recognition that migrants are made in God's likeness presupposes an intolerant attitude towards those who refuse migrants human rights and dignity. Indiscriminate tolerance – even towards fundamentalist intolerance – is a retrograde step.

The symbolic systems of the religions are profoundly Janus-faced – they may serve to legitimate both cosmopolitanism and anti-cosmopolitanism. But there is an age-old tradition of experience with a global, multiethnic world society and a related cross-border, state-transcending organization that has grown up over centuries and that dismisses as meaningless the very things that the nation-state has regarded as its *ne plus ultra*, namely frontiers, nationality, the exclusion of foreigners with different coloured skin or different political convictions. Religious communities have long memories of the fact that their humanity is defined not by these antagonisms but by the overcoming of them. The world religions have succeeded – paradoxically by calling upon their own tradition – in producing answers to the cosmopolitan constellation of the second modernity. They have understood how to develop a version of *cosmopolitan theology* that was comparable to the earlier wave of feminist theology or liberation theology. This theology drew upon cosmopolitan visions of medieval Catholicism (which had been forced to retreat or had simply been disposed of step by step from the sixteenth century to the nineteenth), and cultivated at the heart of its faith and its organization a way of treating unbelievers in a purified spirit of internationalism. Religion – or, more accurately, specific religious (in this case, cosmopolitan) traditions – is not merely part of the problem but perhaps also part of the solution.

We see here with exemplary clarity that the religious theory of the second modernity breaks with the tradition of hostility towards tradition characteristic of the first modernity and its theoreticians. One possibility is the reflexive acquisition of a *religious critique of modernity as judged against the yardstick of tradition*. Such a critique would remind us of the individual's likeness to God, and thus help to overcome the essentialism of a modernity based on national identity (i.e. a critique of a national vision). At the same time, it would help to consolidate the recognition of religious (or non-religious) others in the spirit of furthering the cause of peace (i.e. a critique of the humiliating treatment of those of different faiths or no faith at all). Not every tradition provides us with a yardstick for the critique of modernity, but only those that (like cosmopolitanism) have proved their worth in the foundation of modernity. Thus what we understand by the religious critique of modernity is playing off the modernity of the cosmopolitan tradition against the obsolescence of a modernity based on the nation-state with its false universalisms.

Sociological change of perspective: Religion as co-builder of modernity

The theoretical approach to the sociology of religion developed in this book argues that religion is globalization, religion is ambivalence, and religion can or might develop from the object or victim of demystification into an agent of reflexive modernization in the world risk society. This approach contradicts all existing theories and research methods in the subject. Of these, some follow in the footsteps of the classics and endorse the idea of the relegation of the Gods to fusty museum-status as predicted by classical secularization theory. In so doing, they persist in ignoring the crisis of modernity that has been provoked and rendered visible by the return of the Gods. Others busy themselves with sweeping up the broken shards of the hopes for secularization and sorting them, interpreting them and trying to glue them together again. But this surely prompts further questions: What is left of modernity if religion does not disappear but instead assumes a key role in world politics? If religion had a globalizing effect in its origins, what role will it have in the emerging world society? How can the dialectic of simultaneously overcoming and erecting boundaries be deployed for the cosmopolitan renewal of modernity?

Religion is obviously a swindle! That is the judgement to be found in more or less moderated form at the heart of the shabby treatment meted out to religion by sociology and political science. Max Weber recognized the plurality of the religions more clearly than anyone, but with his formula of disenchantment – more modernity means less religion – he banished religion in the modern age to a backwater of increasing irrelevance. Marx's celebrated dictum that 'religion is the opium of the people' was Marxist modernity's declaration of war on a superstition that legitimated existing forms of domination. Even Émile Durkheim, who devoted so much attention to religion, does not investigate its role as an agent and architect of modernity but only its secondary effect: religion constitutes the 'cement' that holds members of society or the group together.

This consistent process of abstraction which treats religion as the agent and architect of the modern world can be found as far back as the philosophers of the Enlightenment; from Immanuel Kant to Jean-Jacques Rousseau as well as political theorists from John Stuart Mill down to Ernst Gellner – they all agree that alliances forged by the world religions can lead only to absolutism and intolerance. And in fact, for a long time the Catholic Church was closely linked with anti-democratic elites in almost every country of the world. It fought capitalism, liberalism, the modern secular state, democratic revolutions, socialism, human rights, the women's revolution and the sexual revolution – and was never on the winning side. It is hardly to be wondered at, therefore, if over the centuries the Catholic Church has developed a philosophy of defeat.

And yet, historical research on the religions of various European societies in the long nineteenth century has shown that

many churches reacted with remarkable astuteness to the traumas of a modernization they experienced as a succession of crises. They revitalized long-forgotten cultural practices and rituals and so helped the many losers in the modernization process, baffled by obscure and threatening developments, to acquire a new, stronger identity. They took dramatic social crisis-phenomena seriously, turning to welfare and social work agencies and well-organized charitable organizations to establish networks of communitarian solidarity and create new life-enhancing opportunities for people who found themselves on the margins of society. In other churches, relevant sections of the clergy, the most important part of the functioning elite in all denominations, were prepared to undertake deep reforms of the traditional stock of symbols and theological doctrines so as to improve communication with new segments of civil society and adapt old religious signs and images so that citizens might construct their new value heaven. Classical examples of this are German cultural Protestantism and Reform Judaism, which originated chiefly in Germany but were subsequently exported to other countries in Europe and above all to the United States. Some churches reacted uncertainly and defensively to these highly contradictory historical developments, while others went on the offensive. Comparative studies by Hugh McLeod, the British social historian of religion, have revealed the huge diversity in attitudes towards different aspects of the crisis and responses to it among the functional elites of the churches in different European countries. (Graf 2004: 27–8)

The change in perspective involved in thinking of religion as one of the contributory factors in the construction of modernity shall now be explored in two stages. On the one hand, in the central European context in the nineteenth century, the modernization of religion meant the 'nationalization' of religion in open opposition to Christian universalism (nationalizing of religion). On the other hand, to what extent can we replace truth by peace? (Peace instead of truth? Religion as an agent of modernization in the world risk society.)

The 'nationalizing' of religion and the methodological nationalism of the historical sciences

What is the relationship between transnational and interreligious tolerance? We can give something of an answer by combining religious individualization and cosmopolitanism: individuals are detached from secular and clerical hierarchies and placed before the God of their own choosing (Chapter 4). Because people's likeness unto God establishes their human worth and their rights, once they are forced to face up to the voice of conscience as embodied in a God of their own, neither status nor nation nor race nor age has any significance. Compared with liberated individuals' need to prove themselves in God's eyes, all else pales into insignificance.

This kind of individual freedom of faith is possible only in the encounter with cultural and religious others. Only when we all grant to others the very same freedom we demand for ourselves – the complete freedom to decide in favour of a particular faith or indeed against all faiths! – will the freedom to believe have substance. It is based on the mutual tolerance of the different religions.

The principles of tolerance should be thought of as 'potential' (see pp. 100–2) that other currents of faith with different historical regimes may oppose, welcome or combine with historically potent leading ideas. From the end of the eighteenth century on, it was essentially the idea of the nation that was always linked to religion. The clergy, academic theologians and representatives of cultural studies acted as a chorus for this idea, so that all resistance to the project of the 'national identity of religion' was eliminated as 'traditional', 'unmodern' religious interpretations of Christian traditions.

This turn towards the national negates both principles of tolerance. It is open to criticism using the yardstick of early and medieval Christianity since it leads to (1) the naturalizing of intolerance and violence. Admittedly, this criticism has hitherto been half-hearted since methodologically it has been unable to break out of (2) the nationalism of the historical sciences.

The 'nationalizing' of God leads to the naturalizing of intolerance and violence

Talk about nationalism as a 'substitute religion' trivializes the transformations of the nineteenth and twentieth centuries. It conceals not only the 'Germanicization of Christianity' (Bonus 1911) and the role of Protestant elites in the nationalizing of theology and the theologization of the nation. What have been overlooked above all are the consequences of this project for religious tolerance, for the internal and interdenominational association with others, consequences that endure to this day. For the fusing of religion and nation does away with *both* principles of tolerance – the principle of ethnic and national tolerance *and* the principle of interreligious tolerance.

Whoever imports a national either/or into Christianity abandons the Christian universalism that recognizes no distinction between nations and races, and at whose heart lies the individual's sovereign faith that exempts him or her from all other ties. The antidote to the demonization of national others and nationalist intolerance is the idea of Jesus Christ, which is synonymous with tearing down all ethnic and national walls.

The 'nationalizing' of God is no superficial process. It encompasses, but also poisons the fundamental concepts and fundamental symbols of the Christian religion that are calibrated to transnational tolerance.

'In National Socialism', according to the Protestant theologian Richard Karwehl, writing in 1931, ' . . . we are confronted with a secularized eschatology.' In this eschatology 'Jewish messianism' is replaced and surpassed by 'Germanic messianism'.

The National Socialist movement is said to have

> borrowed its key concepts from the Church and transformed them by sleight of hand. Original sin has become a sin against blood. The likeness to God has become the primordial image of the Aryan. The expulsion from Paradise is the debasing of the race by 'crimes against blood'. The Party programme is immutable and infallible, like the dogmas of the Church. The Kingdom of God is to be replaced by the Third Reich. (Schreiner 2003: 32–3)

To the outside world the 'nationalizing' of religion replaces the friendly image of Christian fellowship with the hostile image of the national other whose own Christianity becomes meaningless. Within Germany the national conscription of God was undertaken in order to exclude and even do away with religious others. In this way nationalist Protestant pastors gained their supporters from the illusion that the National Socialists were essentially an anti-Catholic, anti-ultramontane party which would help them to attain a religious monopoly. The point of this Protestant sanctification of the nation is that the nation can transfer the 'naturalness' of national conflicts to the naturalness of 'intolerance' towards national and religious others. Thus an appeal to God comes to underpin an essentialism in which *in*tolerance and the violence it produces are deemed 'necessary' or tolerable, since religions, like nations, can realistically be expected to generate stereotypes of the enemy.

The first victim of nation-based religious intolerance was interdenominational tolerance. In 1933, the Erlangen theologians Paul Althaus and Werner Elert produced an expert opinion on 'The admission of Christians of Jewish origin to offices of the German Evangelical Church'. In it they stated that

> According to the teachings of the Reformation, the external order of the Christian Church ... had to comply not only with the universality of the Christian Gospel but also with the historical and national (*völkisch*) organization of Christian human beings. Christians had to recognize that fate had decreed 'biological ties to a particular nation ... in people's minds and actions'. (Quoted according to Töllner 2007: 57)

Moreover, Elert thought it self-evident that 'a Christian had actively and resolutely to help maintain the *biological purity of German blood* that is both demanded and encouraged by our laws' (ibid.: 58). In this way, even in the eyes of the Confessional Church (*Bekennende Kirche*), persecution of the Jews right up to and including deportation became a

> new confirmation of a Jewish destiny that had been fixed as early as the Bible. The aggressive anti-Semitism of Protestant congregations hastened to comply with the anti-Semitism promulgated by the state. Matters went so far as to lead to the prohibition of Christians wearing a Jewish Star at divine services in a number of parishes. The small number of 'non-Aryan' parsons found themselves especially stigmatized inside the Church, and even the Confessional Church did not always come to their aid. There was no public outcry following the so-called *Kristallnacht* in November 1938, nor were there any official statements on behalf of the Church as a whole, although there were a number of individual protests. . . .
>   Catholics tended to take a back seat because of the international character of the Roman Church, but became no less nationalist in their outlook after 1900. (Angenendt 2007: 557, 478)

In 1939

> a number of Protestant state churches established the 'Institute for Research into and Elimination of the Influence of Jews on German Life' in Eisenach – an institution whose true history did not emerge clearly until after the fall of the Berlin Wall in 1989. Over forty professors of theology, in addition to a number of provincial bishops and church presidents, were among the most active in this enterprise. At the opening ceremony it was stated: Just as Luther overcame Catholicism, so now Protestantism must overcome Judaism. They propagated a Christianity that would be defined by Teutonic culture and which accordingly proclaimed that Jesus was an Aryan. One of the spokesmen, the exegete Walter Grundmann, declared that Judaism was a violent and immoral religion, a religion that knew only of submission and servitude; judged Christ to be a Galilean and hence a non-Jew; and regarded the New Testament as alien and false, a book that needed now to be purified. The Eisenach Institute, lavishly equipped with both financial and

human resources, published a de-Judaized New Testament, as well as liturgical texts, developed a broad range of activities, acquired seven Swedish (!) doctoral students as late as 1943, and organized lecture series until February 1945. Catholic scholars joined in with expressions of interest. One such was Karl Adam, who became famous in later years for helping to pave the way for the Second Vatican Council. After the war, almost all those involved were allowed to retain their academic or clerical posts or else embark on new ones. (ibid.: 558)

The methodological nationalism of the historical sciences

Religious studies and theology. 'Methodological nationalism' refers to the unthinking adoption of principles of political nationalism and their insertion into the language and point of view of the scientific observer (Beck 2004, 2005). In this context, it means that now, as previously, the logic of dividing people into friend or enemy still holds good for nations as for religions, a logic that shows its 'realism' in excluding the alternatives of transnational and interdenominational tolerance from the realms of the possible. This explains why Protestant theological nationalism has persistently impregnated its understanding of religion with nationalist ideas and given a nationalist twist to its politics down to the present day. This can be seen in the adoption of the distinction between 'us' and 'others' in the religious context itself.

> Distinctions between 'us' and 'others' are of fundamental importance for every construction of religious identity. They assume their shape not just in carefully dramatized theological precepts, but also in symbolic codes designed to establish distinguishing features. Stereotypes of the alien other have been inscribed in every religious group identity – prejudices about 'the Jews', 'the Catholics', 'the Freethinkers', or 'the Muslims'. Stereotypes of others are supposed to stabilize the mechanisms of inclusion and exclusion in the course of daily communication and cooperation. Amid the diffuse diversity of religions, prejudices generate a new transparency and a general clarity. Even if at times this process reaches the point where taboos are broken and the limits of political correctness are breached, it should be emphasized that no stable collective religious identity can be produced without a vigorous rejection of other creeds. (Graf 2004: 37; see also 35)

In the present case, the diversity of 'us' and 'others' that is so essential to the understanding of the religious denominations is reduced to a *single* variant and a *single* logic: the either/or of nationalism. In fact, it is important to make systematic distinctions here. We must distinguish between differences (a) from others in one's *own religion* (heretics, schismatics); (b) from members of *other religions* (Jews, Muslims, Hindus, etc.); (c) from members of *other nations* (ethnicity, nationality); as well as (d) from *secular others* (those indifferent to religion, anti-religious parties or movements, secular fundamentalists). The point of distinguishing between these modes of distinguishing is that each obeys a different *logic* of exclusion and inclusion. In consequence, religiously based inclusions and exclusions can be decoded only in the way they overlap, in their mutual delimitation of one another, their internal contradictions and dependence on historical context.

This leads to a key thesis. The 'Carl-Schmitt temptation of religious studies' is false. According to Schmitt, the nationalist either/or predominates in religious dualisms: in other words, the problems involved in differentiating between religions can be understood on the analogy of the either/or logic of whether nations are friendly or hostile. This model enables us to speak of a methodological nationalism in parts of religious studies and theology.

It would be desirable to analyse this systematically and in detail, but here we can only make a few points about it. The duality of orthodoxy versus heresy to be found in particular religions is not primarily designed to exclude religious or national others, but is a prophylactic to preserve religious identity. It may be said to involve *the threat of exclusion in order to achieve inclusiveness*. I have no wish to deny that this threat is more susceptible to violence than a mere process of delimitation of one faith vis-à-vis another. But even if

> members of another religion were unwilling to convert, they were granted a special status, namely that of a tolerated religion. One's own religion was, and remained, the primary and self-evident religion; but other religions were tolerated because coercion against them had been renounced. They were granted the right to exist, admittedly with restrictions on their appearance in public and

frequently on their general legal status, in addition to increased liability to taxation. (Angenendt 2007: 99)

All world religions have to come to terms with ethnic and national others, and their treatment varies according to historical conditions and the nature of the religious links. Thus the Jews actually invented the sacred bonding of country, town, people, temple and faith, and then encountered outside the ghettoes a Christendom that for its own part had ceased to think of itself as free of ethnic and territorial ties. This historical dialectic teaches us that the exclusion of the national and the ethnic cannot be treated as a model that can be transferred to all religions, let alone regarded as their 'essence'. That would be equivalent to the category error of *confusing religion with the nation*. A given religion can define the boundaries of nations and nation-states inclusively or exclusively. Indeed, it may even make a virtue of including national others as a way of distinguishing itself from other religions. Over and above that, as we can see from the history of Christianity, marginal regimes may well change their position over time.

The fusing of religion and nation at the threshold of the cosmopolitan second modernity constitutes a barrier to perception and an obstacle the 'national churches' have to overcome in their efforts to assert themselves in the worldwide competition between religions. Similarly, the resistance and fear that Islam generates in Europe doubtless owe their origin to the fact that it has become one of the present-day global migrant religions.

A tendency for different denominations to *overcome* both internal and external religious differences can be observed as a result of the opposition to *secular others*. Thus in (European) societies where secularism predominates there is pressure for Christian and non-Christian religions to work more closely together (cf. Joas 2007a: 983).

The social sciences. In national thought-paradigms it is often asserted that cosmopolitanism is in favour of solidarity between all human beings. But we only feel committed to people – so the argument continues – with whom we share a common identity. However, since identity presupposes a clear opposition to something (friendship is the daughter of conflict), a cosmopolitan identity is nothing but a square circle, a self-contradiction.

Such arguments ignore the source of transnational attachments. We do not have to embrace everyone and everything (as Beethoven so movingly encourages us to do in his setting of the Ode to Joy). Many people who identify with foreigners are attracted by particular aspects of their lives. Thus German Christians collect money for suffering Christians in Africa; writers defend persecuted writers in other countries; scholars communicate with 'foreigners' more than with their colleagues at home, etc.

Religion is a particular mode of experience with which to establish social ties, networks and biographies that transcend national and ethnic boundaries. This compels social scientists to confront the question of which *research rubric* to choose: *nation* or *religion*? In effect this predetermines what will have priority and why – ethnic identity and ties to their country of origin or religious bridges and pathways that lead across frontiers. In the latter case, the religious slot, an Islam in the process of globalization has attracted massive attention. The same may be said of the triumphal progress of the Pentecostal movements and Protestant sects in South America and Latin America more generally, as well as in Africa, etc. But much of this research fuses religion and ethnicity – as Nina Glick Schiller and her associates have shown (2006: 614f.). Even if Protestant movements and networks think of themselves as part of a transnational, transethnic religious landscape, without laying much stress on ethnic and national boundaries, social scientists persist in classifying believers according to their membership of ethnic and national groups. The result is an incoherent narrative in which the subjects and objects of the sociology of religion who think of themselves as belonging to a Christian parish and community and who define themselves essentially as Christians find themselves defined by sociologists as religious Americans, Mexicans, Brazilians, Africans, Nigerians, etc. The situation is similar in Europe, where sociologists speak of an 'African Christianity' or 'South American Christianity', which are largely determined by the development of African or South American ethnic and national communities.

It becomes clear here that methodological nationalism starts out from a highly dubious premise. Either the sociologist selects a national (or ethnic) research rubric and thus implicitly and without any authority ascribes a greater determining force to territory, ethnicity, nation and state than to the religious self-situating and self-description of believers in a transnational society of religions; or else he or she opts for religion as the research category of choice. The first case excludes the very factors that occupy the centre of attention in the second case and whose importance is confirmed in exemplary fashion by the successes of the Pentecostal movements (they include something of the order of a quarter of a billion human beings – in other words, one Christian in five). Their emergence cannot be explained in terms of their territorial, national or ethnic origins and contexts, but only by recognizing their religious practices, which treat these other ties as adventitious and surmountable. Their success is that of a *cross-border* religious community *whose identity lies in the human imagination.*

Like Muslims, Pentecostalists are part of a network emerging in mega-cities and tending recently to congregate in mega-churches.

> They differ from Jews and Muslims in one important respect. This is that they are based on voluntary association rather than ethnic identity. . . . This chimes with the origins of Christianity and their more recent origins as volunteer groups separate from the state. Today, they contribute to a global trend towards religious communities that are lay-centred, conscience-orientated, participatory, pluralist, decentralized and voluntary. (Martin 2007: 444–5)

Replacing truth with peace: Religion as an agent of modernization in the world risk society

Peace instead of truth

In a civilization that is putting itself at risk, the key theme of violence and tolerance comes to a head in the question: How can we establish tolerance *between religions*? How can we bring ourselves to recognize religious others as others (and not as like us) and stop belittling them as fighters for the 'true faith', robbing them of their human and religious dignity? This question combines the historical vindication of religion with fears for the future existence of humanity.

It might be supposed that believers and the elites of the different religions were looking for answers, were it not for the fact that intolerance towards the historical dignity – and suffering – of other religions is the obverse of one's own absolutist revealed truths and that doubting those truths, not to mention abandoning them, might end up bringing the entire edifice crashing down. The effect of this is that the intolerance with which the monotheistic religions treat one another, despite their verbal assurances to the contrary, mainly appears as an acceptable 'lesser evil' and is justified as such.

The revealed religious truths that constantly contradict one another and cast doubt on the other's credentials exist only in the plural not the singular. In the light of the clash of universalisms this fact can no longer be concealed. On the contrary, it has become part of everyday experience and an existential theme of humankind everywhere.

In addition, peace acquires a new priority vis-à-vis truth because the *one* truth jeopardizes not just truth but the continued existence of humankind. Thus, giving priority to peace is a matter not of an unreal utopia of 'peace everlasting' but a question of how to civilize modernity, given the vast growth in its potential for self-destruction as a consequence of its past victories. Truth takes aim at harmony; peace at conflict. There are two priorities: truth on the one side; peace on the other.

Thus the question is not how to replace truth by peace (or vice versa). The problem is how are we to set both truth and peace as priorities? At the same time, we must resist the temptation to restrict the scope of the question. This dilemma cannot be 'resolved' or 'sublated', to use Hegel's term. Nor can it be fully stabilized – perhaps just made more stable than before. Are there precedents in the history of religion that could usefully be appealed to? There are indeed. On the one hand, the history of religion is familiar with the model of a 'tolerated religion'. This arose from the situation in which Judaism, Christianity and Islam all claimed to possess the absolute truth and also thought of themselves as universal religions, while at the same time proclaiming freedom of worship. On the other hand, there is the model of a 'double religion' which emerged from the European reception of Egyptian religion in the eighteenth century.

Tolerated religion. As far as the category of 'unbelievers' is concerned, the monotheistic faiths drew what they thought of as the crucial distinction between those who 'only' held other beliefs and the *apostates*, those who betrayed God, a group they regarded as enemies and treated accordingly. This distinction coincided with the difference between 'tolerable' and 'intolerable'. The model of a 'tolerated religion' presupposes both coexistence and differentiation, and applies both to adherents of the monotheistic faiths and to apostates.

> Given what is held to be the structural violence of monotheism, we might well have expected a permanent state of war. By way of a solution, the three monotheistic faiths cultivated a judicial practice that had originally been developed for the Jews in antiquity, namely that of a tolerated religion (*religio licita*). Where different religious communities live together the predominant faith allows other religions to exist and permits their adherents to practise their own faith among themselves, as well as conferring civil rights on them. At the same time, it imposes certain restrictions, increased taxes being the chief among them. The aim was to curb the instinct of both individuals and masses to indulge in violent acts of 'religious cleansing'. (Angenendt 2007: 102)

It must be admitted that this compromise notion of a 'tolerated religion' was, as church history shows, unstable in the extreme and susceptible to pogroms, as well as to the persecution and expulsion of the believers of other faiths. It not only presupposed a minimum of denominational peaceableness, but also required an executive authority – a state – which would intervene to protect religious minorities from violent attacks by the majority religion.

Double religion. Jan Assmann (2007) provides an account of the emergence of the tolerance model of a 'double religion' in the course of the discussions about Egyptian religion in the eighteenth century.

> The information about the Egyptian written culture that was coming to light led the eighteenth century to develop the idea of a 'double religion'. This consisted of the generally accessible outside of the polytheistic popular religion and the inside of a philosophical monotheism accessible only to initiates. Ordinary people worshipped the many gods in the belief that they presided over the laws, handing down rewards and punishments and defending the state against enemies internal and external. By contrast, the initi-

ates devoted their worship to the hidden, one-and-only deity on whose enthroned image in the temple of Sais was inscribed, according to Plutarch: 'I am everything that was, that is and that will be; no mortal man has ever lifted my veil.' This sense of a dual allegiance as citizen of the state and citizen of the world, Catholic and philosopher, corresponded to the intellectual situation of an age which, having experienced the first breakthrough of globalization, was learning to think in cosmopolitan terms and to experience the nations of this world as a community. At the same time, this was something of a re-enactment of the life feeling of late antiquity when a similar experience of a globalizing coming together of the nations in the Roman Empire had resulted in similar ideas. In *Isis and Osiris*, a treatise much read in the eighteenth century, Plutarch had written at the beginning of the first millennium that 'just as the sun and the moon and the heavens and the earth and the sea are common to all, but are called by different names by different peoples, so too that one rationality (*logos*) which brings order into all things and the one Providence which watches over them, are revered among different peoples, in accordance with their different honours, forms of address and sacred symbols'. Like the author of the text of Mozart's *The Magic Flute*, Celsus could argue in his tract against the Christians that 'it makes no difference whether we call God "the Highest" or Zeus or Adonai or Sabaoth or Amun, like the Egyptians, or Palos, like the Scythians'. The birth of the first 'world religions', Judaism and Christianity, with their commitment to the One God, whose Name was unique and not interchangeable with any other, coincided with its opposite, the emergence of a world religion in the true sense, which admittedly could never come into being as a religion but only as the cosmopolitan wisdom arising from the hidden convergence of all religions. (Assmann 2007: 350–1)

The idea of a 'double' religion, according to Assmann, was taken up later on by Mahatma Gandhi (see pp. 160–1 above). But how are we supposed to think about two different aspects, two different concepts of religion in this model of religion (in the singular)?

The recognition of the religious truth of others burdens cosmopolitanism with a contradiction. It must, on the one hand, acknowledge the assertion of absolute truth because this is the core of other people's truth. On the other hand, however – and likewise by way of recognizing the religious truths of others – it must perforce deny the absolute validity of both one's own truth and that of others.

This ensures that the model of a double truth diminishes the worth of the truth of the individual religions, as opposed to the one truth common to all religions which cannot possibly be identical with the many truths of those religions. We must now consider two possibilities. Either the one truth that is common to all religions, a universal truth, does in fact exist. Admittedly, such a truth is open to the suspicion that it is no more than the 'universalized' version of the (more or less overt) particular truth of a given religion. Alternatively, there can be no such thing as a *purely* religiously based cosmopolitanism in which the absolute claim to truth of a religion (namely *my* religion) can provide the framework in which the religious truths of others are 'tolerated'. But if there can be no such thing as a *purely* religiously based cosmopolitanism, then the one truth that is common to all religions must be the *cosmopolitan* truth based on the recognition of the otherness of other religions, inclusive of their truths.

To formulate this slightly differently: The relations of cosmopolitan truths to one another call for a cosmopolitanism of the religions that is based not on immutable truths, handed down to humankind, but ultimately on rules, treaties, procedures (human rights, the rule of law, etc.) that have been agreed by people among themselves. This once again poses the question: Why should the 'Holy Fathers' who base the legitimacy of their 'sovereignty' on (partly contradictory) divine certitudes regulate their relations to one another on the basis of self-demystification? And above all, *how* should they go about it?

The parable of the ring. In his play *Nathan the Wise* (1779), Gotthold Ephraim Lessing mapped out the problem of tolerance between the world religions in exemplary fashion. The heart of the play, the famous *parable of the ring*, contains a plea for the equally deserving priorities of peace and truth that fits well with the model of the double religion. Lessing is not guided by the philosophy of truth; indeed, he had a profound distrust of the dream of one truth that philosophers had pursued throughout history. What discredited the idea of truth in his eyes was his insight, as surprising as it was logical, into the law that always converts the one truth into *my* truth. For, in the case of truth, it is never just a matter of the truth, but, according to Lessing, of *humanity* or, as we would have to say today: *peace.*[4]

Lessing's play focuses our attention on the conflict, we might even call it the contradiction, between truth and peace. He knew that the humanity of peace, which was in his eyes the greatest possible good, presupposes the truth, even the absolute truth. But truth is a risky business. One has, as it were, to put up with absolute truth – for the sake of peace.

But God forbid that the *one and only* ring should ever fall into the hands of one person![5] That would be the Hell of a single universalism that had buried all the other universalisms beneath it. Hence both must exist simultaneously: the one-and-only ring *and* the many rings that every son who has inherited a ring from his father believes to be the one-and-only ring. Every ring is the 'one-and-only' ring – which in fact does not exist. This explains why no one can know which ring is the true one-and-only ring. Everyone knows, however, that there are many one-and-only rings and that they own one of them.

If Lessing had had to choose between the one-and-only ring and none, he would have chosen the latter. In his ring parable it turns out that even if a one-and-only ring had ever existed in the past, it has now been lost for ever. In fact it has disappeared in the welter of one-and-only rings that the religions of humankind

---

[4] This is my own interpretation, which I go on to explain *as if* Lessing had elaborated it in this way in his ring parable. Remarkably enough, Sloterdijk (2009) makes use of a similar method, a fact I discovered only after the completion of this book.

[5] [In Lessing's play the hero Nathan is asked by the Sultan to tell him which of the three major religions, Judaism, Christianity or Islam, is the true one. Since expressing a preference for Judaism might put his life in danger and since fudging the issue is out of the question, Nathan answers with the parable of the three rings: A king in a foreign land owned a ring that made its owner pleasing in the sight of God and man. Having been passed down through many generations, it came into the possession of a king who had three sons whom he loved equally. Not wishing to show a preference, he had two further identical rings made and gave one to each son. After his death the sons could not agree which of them possessed the true ring and was therefore the rightful heir. Since the true ring had the power to make its owner beloved by all, the judge they consult ruled that the identity of the true ring could be established only by practical action: each son should strive to liberate the 'power of his ring' and act so as to make himself loved. (Trans.)]

require and that are indistinguishable from one another. If the one-and-only ring really existed, the outlook for world peace would be bleak. To put it another way: Lessing perceives the contradiction between the one truth and the cosmopolitan recognition of the many truths of religion. But Nathan's 'wisdom' consists in defending and facilitating both priorities, that of an absolutist religious truth *and* that of peace.

God as mediator. The model of the double religion formulated in the parable of the ring can appeal to God as mediator, as peacemaker. Religion here becomes a kind of proof of identity and membership. Its purpose is, on the one hand, to join together a number of nations under one canopy and, on the other, to tolerate and respect the coexistence of different religious communities. The religions capable of peace and their theological interpreters exploit the multidimensionality of truth, the art of ambiguity, the deployment of ambivalence and the interplay of levels of meaning in the contextualizing of what is said and what is left unsaid. In sociological terms, they exploit the distinction between the formal and the informal and the conflicting opportunities this distinction offers to enable them to develop a *pragmatics and a practice across boundaries so that opposing sides may both profit.*

This brings irony into play since irony gives people a breathing space, whereas the clash of absolutes is stifling. On his visit to Turkey in November 2006, Pope Benedict XVI seemed to have been inspired by Lessing's 'heretical irony'. The television pictures prove it. He entered the mosque and, with his gaze turned inwards, he moved his lips. Was he actually praying in the mosque? Was he meditating? What was he murmuring?

This was the parable of the ring in action. The different, highly subtle and in religious terms highly explosive interpretations of this event all stand in for the versions of the one-and-only ring which everyone claims to possess. The Muslim world was convinced that the Pope had been praying. This shatters the truth of Catholicism with its claims to be grounded in exclusivity and purity, and this means that relations between Catholics and Muslims have to be built on new foundations. Perhaps so. For Catholics too wear their own ring with pride. They are convinced that the Pope did *not* pray, that he may have been meditating, but that he was merely moving his lips wordlessly, thus preserving the integrity of Catholic teaching. In German kindergartens it is once again possible to forbid Catholics to utter a prayer together with Muslim children and to do so with a clear conscience.

The most striking feature of this event was the active silence of Pope Benedict alias Nathan the Wise. In this instance, it was the action of words not spoken that was the element of interdenominational cosmopolitanism. This is based on *both*: the coexistence of the one-and-only truth with that of the many truths that makes possible the priority of peace.

The voices of religion in the global arena or: How are we to civilize civilization?

The clash of universalisms is evaded by distinguishing between different levels in practice. We must distinguish between the level on which the dogmas and absolute claims of the world religions encounter one another and the levels of successful, pragmatic cooperation that have long since developed in the actually experienced thick texture of the world religions on the spot. Beyond all demarcation battles and wars, the *surplus value resulting from the practice of cooperation* has prevailed. This means that groups intolerant of other faiths' theology can nevertheless work together with them creatively to bring their own separate projects to fruition. Theological experts and their endless quarrels could well be advised to learn from this empirical experience.

Everywhere we see agitated debates about the 'problem' of Islam in a 'secularized' Europe. These debates give expression to the fear of foreigners and the impossibility in principle of a 'multicultural life together'. At the same time, people ignore the reality of cooperation in which orthodoxy plays no part. This can be seen best of all in the United States, above all in the big cities. Although talk of the way in which religious fundamentalists mutually blockade one another is ubiquitous, and although such views are constantly underpinned by the sensationalizing accounts of outrageous incidents in the mass media, it is obvious that an everyday pragmatism of a religious commonsense has long since provided the foundations for cooperation between religious denominations and secular institutions, not least because the benefits for all participants are plainly visible. This applies to educational projects as well as to charitable support for the poor, the protection of minorities or work on behalf of (legal and illegal) migrants.

Whoever believes that the thesis of the surplus value resulting from interdenominational cooperation is false in principle can learn a thing or two by noticing in how many places interdenominational pragmatism is taken for granted and how successfully it has been institutionalized. Forums and active programmes have come into being with which to bridge the gulf separating religions from one another and from the secular realm. This process tends to take place on an informal level. Religious communities create the grass-roots of a 'religious secularism' that strives to erode the rigidities and the barriers erected by the established 'public' (state-organized) churches. Although the differences and frictions between the world religions are not annulled at the level of either communal or global civil society, they are transformed so that they become capable of cooperation and attuned to success through the recognition of their specificity.

Can we also separate dogma and practice on the world stage in the search for pragmatic solutions to the challenge of the 'world risk society' (Beck 1999)? There is some evidence that we can. There is no doubt that it is hardly possible to overestimate the potential of the religions as cosmopolitan actors – not just because of their ability to mobilize billions of human beings across barriers of nation and class, but because they exercise a powerful influence on the way people see themselves and their relationship to the world. Above all, they represent a resource of legitimation in the battle for the dignity of human beings in a civilization at risk of destroying itself. Thus what is on the agenda is the competence and readiness of the world religions to assume the role of spokespeople and champions on issues affecting humankind: climate change, the plight of the poor and excluded and, not least, the *dignity* of ethnic, national and religious others.

Is Islam, Catholicism, Hinduism or Protestantism in a position to offer an inclusive post-socialist alternative to the world of capitalism with its reliance on economic growth and individual human rights? And, given the legacy of slavery, colonialism and imperialism, can any of these creeds hold out the prospect of dignity to our fellow human beings of the Third and Fourth Worlds? What contribution can the religions make to the world-historical process of civilizing civilization, and how can they demonstrate their humanity and modernity in the twenty-first century? This can be best illustrated in the case of the ethical core of climate change. This ethical core is neglected for the most part by ecological converts among both economic elites and political elites.

In the case of climate change, what is at issue, from a sociological perspective, is not just the weather, not just hurricanes, droughts, floods, streams of refugees and imminent wars. What is at issue is the fact that for the first time in history all populations, cultures, ethnic groups, religions and regions share a common present whose future is exposed to a danger that threatens everyone. In other words, we have to *include the excluded others in order to survive*. Climate politics become cosmopolitan politics, not as a matter of individualist conviction but from a spirit of realism, from a worldwide instinct of naked survival.

This will be no less true if the effects of global warming take different forms in different places and if they are interpreted in diametrically opposed ways against the backcloth of a radically unequal world. The fact that the expected climate catastrophe in the present will affect everyone does not mean that it is based on a common past and so it offers no guarantee of a common future. For all we know, a thriving agriculture will spring up in Alaska. People may well prance around in bikinis and Speedos at Christmas in New York and Munich. But what will happen to Africa? And what of the Middle East?

It is just as it was on the *Titanic*. The climate catastrophe is not democratic. Most of the *Titanic*'s victims were trapped in the cheaper accommodation on the lower decks and cabins, from which there was no escape. Whoever fails to stop climate change, or even reinforces it, attacks the poorest of the poor. Whoever tries to protect London, New York and Tokyo from the threat of rising water levels by building new embankments succumbs to the illusion that the social and political consequences of climate change can be resolved by individual countries going it alone. This is how people seek to evade the key question arising from the climate catastrophe. This question is: *How are we to achieve global justice?* At the level of detail that means asking whether the rich will reduce the level of their emissions so that the poor will still have growth opportunities. Technical innovations are not a sufficient response to such questions, although the mistaken belief in such solutions is still prevalent, even among ecologically literate members of the political parties and business. People imagine that such innovations could at least mitigate the consequences of climate catastrophe and thus eliminate the need to consider the question of global justice and to take the needs of cultural others into account in one's own decisions. Does this task not cry out for the intervention of the cosmopolitan voice of religious representatives and movements? Faced with the global threats of terrorism and war, climate change and poverty, as well as the slighted dignity of religious others, is it not they above all who are in a position to set nations of different beliefs on the 'common' path of justice? Or could they not at least raise their voices in the world's forums to demand contributions and so subvert their dogmatic tensions and disarm them pragmatically?

Perhaps this is what Pope Benedict XVI meant when he said that 'In addition to faith, the highest value of all believers should be reason not force.' Does he intend to uncouple faith and force by placing faith under the guardianship of reason and so 'civilizing' it? If so, I should like to add that this process also calls for the *guile* of reason. The task is to refrain from demonizing the individualization of religion because individualization makes it possible to practise the peaceable resolution of absolutist truths across religious frontiers. The same claim may be made in favour of a touch of 'God-selling'. It serves the purpose of rehearsing transnational and interdenominational religious tolerance. This still leaves open the question: How will the individual religions react to the individualization and cosmopolitization of faith? The answer must be reserved for another book-length poking around in the fog.

It is very clear that fundamentalists, maddened by their bloodthirsty love of violence, will not be impressed by these reflections, let alone stopped. But what would it take to achieve that happy outcome?

Bibliography

Adorno, Theodor W. (1979): 'Aberglaube aus zweiter Hand.' In: Adorno: *Soziologische Schriften I*, ed. Rolf Tiedemann. Frankfurt a.M.: Suhrkamp: 147–76.

Albrow, Martin (1996): *The Global Age*. Cambridge: Polity Press.

Albrow, Martin (1999): *Sociology. The Basics*. London: Routledge.

Anantharaman, Tanjore R. (2001): 'Leid, Wiedergeburt und Überwindung des Bösen im Hinduismus.' In: Koslowski, Peter (ed.): *Ursprung und Überwindung des Bösen und des Leidens in den Weltreligionen*. Munich: Fink: 63–95.

Angenendt, Arnold (2007): *Toleranz und Gewalt. Das Christentum zwischen Bibel und Schwert*. Münster: Aschendorff.

Anijar, Gil (2003): *The Jew, the Arab. A History of the Enemy*. Stanford: Stanford University Press.

Appiah, Kwame Anthony (2005): *Cosmopolitanism. Ethics in a World of Strangers*. New York and London: W.W. Norton & Company.

Arendt, Hannah (1967): *Men in Dark Times*. New York: Harcourt.

Asad, Talal (2006): 'French Secularism and the "Islamic Veil Affair."' In: *The Hedgehog Review* 8 (1/2). After Secularization: 93–106.

Assmann, Jan (2003): *Die mosaische Unterscheidung oder der Preis des Monotheismus*. Munich: Hanser.

Assmann, Jan (2007): '"Religio duplex." Zur europäischen Rezeption der ägyptischen Religion.' In: Simm, Hans-Joachim (ed.): *Die Religionen der Welt. Ein Almanach zur Eröffnung des Verlags der Weltreligionen*. Frankfurt a.M.: Verlag der Weltreligionen: 350–3.

Bainton, Roland H. (1964): *Hunted Heretic. The Life and Death of Michael Servetus 1511–1558*. Boston: Beacon Press.

Barker, Eileen (1989): *New Religious Movements. A Practical Introduction*. London: Her Majesty's Stationery Office.

Bauman, Zygmunt (1998): *Globalization*. Cambridge: Polity Press: Introduction and Chapter 1.

Bauman, Zygmunt (2007): *Liquid Times. Living in an Age of Uncertainty*. Cambridge: Polity Press.

Beck, Ulrich (1992): *Risk Society. Towards a New Modernity*, trans. Mark Ritter. London: Sage.

Beck, Ulrich (1993): *Die Erfindung des Politischen*. Frankfurt a.M.: Suhrkamp.

Beck, Ulrich (1997): *Was ist Globalisierung?* Frankfurt a.M.: Suhrkamp.

Beck, Ulrich (1999): *World Risk Society*: Cambridge: Polity Press.

Beck, Ulrich (2004): *Der kosmopolitische Blick oder Krieg ist Frieden*. Frankfurt a.M.: Suhrkamp.

Beck, Ulrich (2005): *Power in the Global Age*, trans. Kathleen Cross. Cambridge: Polity Press.

Beck, Ulrich (2007a): 'Beyond Class and Nation. Reframing Social Inequality in a Globalized World.' In: *British Journal of Sociology* 58 (4): 679–705.

Beck, Ulrich (ed.) (2007b): *Generation Global. Ein Crashkurs*. Frankfurt a.M.: Suhrkamp.

Beck, Ulrich and Beck-Gernsheim, Elisabeth (1995): *The Normal Chaos of Love*, trans. Mark Ritter and Jane Wiebel. Cambridge: Polity Press.

Beck, Ulrich and Beck-Gernsheim, Elisabeth (2002): *Individualization. Institutionalized Individualism and Its Social and Political Consequences*, trans. Patrick Camiller. London, Thousand Oaks, CA and New Delhi: Sage.

Beck, Ulrich; Bonß, Wolfgang; and Lau, Christoph (2001): 'Theorie reflexiver Modernisierung. Fragestellungen, Hypothesen, Forschungsprogramme.' In: Beck, Ulrich and Bonß, Wolfgang (eds): *Die Modernisierung der Moderne*. Frankfurt a.M.: Suhrkamp: 11–59.

Beck, Ulrich and Grande, Edgar (2004): *Kosmopolitisches Europa*. Frankfurt a.M.: Suhrkamp.

Beck, Ulrich; Holzer, Boris; and Kieserling, André (2001): 'Nebenfolgen als Problem soziologischer Theoriebildung.' In: Beck, Ulrich and Bonß, Wolfgang (eds): *Die Modernisierung der Moderne*. Frankfurt a.M.: Suhrkamp: 63–81.

Beck, Ulrich and Lau, Christoph (2005): 'Theorie und Empirie reflexiver Modernisierung. Von der Notwendigkeit und den Schwierigkeiten, einen historischen Gesellschaftswandel innerhalb der Moderne zu beobachten und zu begreifen.' In: *Soziale Welt* 56 (2/3): 107–35.

Beck, Ulrich and Sznaider, Nathan (2006): 'Unpacking Cosmopolitanism for the Social Sciences. A Research Agenda.' In: *British Journal of Sociology* 57 (1): 1–23.

Beck, Ulrich; Vossenkuhl, Wilhelm; and Ziegler, Ulf Erdmann (1995): *Eigenes Leben. Ausflüge in die unbekannte Gesellschaft, in der wir leben.* Munich: C.H. Beck: Chapters XII, XIII and XIV.

Beck, Ulrich and Willms, Johannes (2004): *Conversations with Ulrich Beck,* trans. Michael Pollack. Cambridge: Polity Press.

Beck-Gernsheim, Elisabeth (2002): *Reinventing the Family: In Search of New Lifestyles,* trans. Patrick Camiller. Cambridge: Polity Press.

Beck-Gernsheim, Elisabeth (2007): *Wir und die Anderen.* Frankfurt a.m.: Suhrkamp.

Beckford, James A. (2003): *Social Theory and Religion.* Cambridge: Cambridge University Press.

Beckford, James and Levasseur, Martine (1986): 'New Religious Movements in Western Europe.' In: Beckford, James (ed.): *New Religious Movements and Rapid Social Change.* London: Sage: 29–54.

Beer, Paul de (2007): 'How Individualized are the Dutch?' In: *Current Sociology* 55 (3): 389–413.

Bell, Daniel (1980): 'The Return of the Sacred? The Argument on the Future of Religion.' In: Bell: *The Winding Passage. Sociological Essays and Journeys.* New Brunswick, NJ: Transaction Books: 324–54.

Bellah, Robert N. (1970): *Beyond Belief. Essays on Religion in a Post-Traditional World.* New York: Harper & Row.

Bendikowski, Tillmann (2002): '"Eine Fackel der Zwietracht." Katholisch–protestantische Mischehen im 19./20. Jahrhundert.' In: Blaschke, Olaf (ed.): *Konfessionen im Konflikt. Deutschland zwischen 1800 und 1970: ein zweites konfessionelles Zeitalter.* Göttingen: Vandenhoeck & Ruprecht: 215–41.

Benedikt XVI (2006): *Glaube und Vernunft. Die Regensburger Vorlesung.* Freiburg, Basel and Vienna: Herder.

Berger, Klaus (2005): *Widerworte. Wieviel Modernisierung verträgt Religion?* Frankfurt a.M. and Leipzig: Insel.

Berger, Peter L. (1963): 'A Market Model for the Analysis of Ecumenicity.' In: *Social Research* (Spring): 77–93.

Berger, Peter L. (1969): *The Sacred Canopy. Elements of a Sociological Theory of Religion.* Garden City, NY: Doubleday/Anchor Books.

Berger, Peter L. (1979): *The Heretical Imperative. Contemporary Possibilities of Religious Affirmation.* Garden City, NY: Anchor Press/Doubleday.

Berger, Peter L. and Mathewes, Charles T. (2006): 'An Interview with Peter Berger.' In: *Hedgehog Review* 8 (1/2). After Secularization: 152–61.

Bielefeldt, Heiner (2003): *Muslime im säkularen Rechtsstaat. Integrationschancen durch Religionsfreiheit*. Bielefeld: transcript.

Blaschke, Olaf (2002): 'Der "Dämon des Konfessionalismus." Einführende Überlegungen.' In: Blaschke (ed.): *Konfessionen im Konflikt. Deutschland zwischen 1800 und 1970: ein zweites konfessionelles Zeitalter*. Göttingen: Vandenhoeck & Ruprecht: 13–69.

Blückert, Kjell (2000): *The Church as Nation. A Study in Ecclesiology and Nationhood*. Frankfurt a.M.: Peter Lang.

Bonus, Arthur (1911): *Zur Germanisierung des Christentums. Zur religiösen Krisis*, Vol. I. Jena: Eugen Diederichs.

Bosshart-Pfluger, Catherine; Jung, Josef; and Metzger, Franziska (eds) (2002): *Nation und Nationalismus in Europa. Kulturelle Konstruktion von Identitäten*. Frauenfeld, Stuttgart and Vienna: Huber.

Bourdieu, Pierre (1987): 'La dissolution des religieux.' In: Bourdieu: *Choses dites*. Paris: Éditions du Minuit: 117–23.

Boyarin, Daniel (1994): *A Radical Jew. Paul and the Politics of Identity*. Berkeley, Los Angeles and London: University of California Press.

Boyarin, Daniel (2004): *Border Lines. The Partition of Judaeo-Christianity*. Philadelphia: University of Pennsylvania Press.

Brannen, Julia and Nilsen, Ann (2005): 'Individualisation, Choice and Structure. A Discussion of Current Trends in Sociological Analysis.' In: *The Sociological Review* 53 (3): 412–28.

Brodie, Janine (2007): 'The New Social "isms": Individualization and Social Policy Reform in Canada.' In: Howard, Cosmo (ed.): *Contested Individualization. Debates about Contemporary Personhood*. New York: Palgrave Macmillan: 153–69.

Bruce, Steve (ed.) (1992): *Religion and Modernization. Sociologists and Historians Debate the Secularization Thesis*. Oxford: Oxford University Press.

Bruce, Steve (1999): *Choice and Religion. A Critique of Rational Choice Theory*. Oxford: Blackwell.

Bruce, Steve (2002): *God is Dead. Secularization in the West*. Oxford: Blackwell.

Bruce, Steve (2006): 'Secularization and the Impotence of Individualized Religion.' In: *The Hedgehog Review* 8 (1/2). After Secularization: 35–45.

Buisson, Ferdinand (1892): *Sébastien Castellion, sa vie et son oeuvre (1515–1563). Étude sur les origines du protestantisme libéral français*. Paris: Hachette.

Cardini, Franco (2000): *Europa and Islam*, trans. Caroline Beamish. Oxford: Wiley-Blackwell.

Casanova, José (1994): *Public Religions in the Modern World*. Chicago and London: University of Chicago Press.

Casanova, José (2006a): 'Rethinking Secularization. A Global Comparative Perspective.' In: *The Hedgehog Review* 8 (1/2). After Secularization: 7–22.

Casanova, José (2006b): 'Aggiornamenti? Katholische und muslimische Politik im Vergleich.' In: *Leviathan* 34 (3): 305–20.

Casanova, José (2007): 'Die religiöse Lage in Europa.' In: Joas, Hans and Wiegandt, Klaus (eds): *Säkularisierung und die Weltreligionen*. Frankfurt a.M.: Fischer: 322–57. [English translation: 'The Religious Situation in Europe.' In: Joas, Hans and Wiegandt, Klaus (eds): *Secularization and the World Religions*, trans. Alex Skinner. Liverpool: Liverpool University Press, 2009: 206–28.]

Certeau, Michel de and Domenach, Jean-Marie (1974): *Le christianisme éclaté*. Paris: Seuil.

Cheah, Pheng (2006): *Inhuman Conditions. On Cosmopolitanism and Human Rights*. Cambridge, MA and London: Harvard University Press.

Christmann, Gabriela B. (1996): 'Die "religioiden" Anteile im Denken von Umweltschützer/innen. Über Herkunfts- und Aufrechterhaltung umweltschützerischer Sinnelemente.' In: Gabriel, Karl (ed.): *Religiöse Individualisierung oder Säkularisierung. Biographie und Gruppe als Bezugspunkte moderner Religiosität*. Gütersloh: Chr. Kaiser Gütersloher Verlagshaus: 198–214.

Clarke, Peter (2006): *New Religions in Global Perspective. A Study of Religious Change in the Modern World*. London and New York: Routledge.

Cohen, Hermann (1966): *Religion der Vernunft aus den Quellen des Judentums*. Wiesbaden: Fourier.

Cohen, Roger (2007): 'The Merits of Secular Europe.' In: *Herald Tribune*, 24.12.

Cohen, Steven M. and Eisen, Arnold M. (2000): *The Jew within. Self, Family, and Community in America*. Bloomington: Indiana University Press.

Coleman, Simon and Collins, Peter (ed.) (2004): *Religion, Identity and Change. Perspectives on Global Transformations*. Burlington, VT: Ashgate.

Costa, Sérgio (2007): *Vom Nordatlantik zum "Black Atlantic". Postkoloniale Konfigurationen und Paradoxien transnationaler Politik*. Bielefeld: transcript.

Crook, Stephen; Pakulski, Jan; and Waters, Malcolm (1992): *Postmodernization. Change in Advanced Society.* London: Sage.

Dante Alighieri (1962): *The Divine Comedy,* 3 vols, trans. Dorothy L. Sayers. London: Penguin.

Dath, Dietmar (2006): 'Mein erstes Weihnachten.' In: *Frankfurter Allgemeine Zeitung,* 23.12.

Davie, Grace (1994): *Religion in Britain since 1945. Believing without Belonging.* Oxford and Cambridge, MA: Blackwell.

Davie, Grace (2000): *Religion in Modern Europe. A Memory Mutates.* Oxford and New York: Oxford University Press.

Davie, Grace (2002): *Europe: The Exceptional Case. Parameters of Faith in the Modern World.* London: Dartan, Longman and Todd.

Davie, Grace (2006): 'Is Europe an Exceptional Case?' In: *The Hedgehog Review 8* (1/2). After Secularization: 23–34.

Davie, Grace and Hervieu-Léger, Danièle (1996): *Identités religieuses en Europe.* Paris: Éd. la Decouverte.

Dellwing, Michael (2007): *Die entprivatisierte Religion. Religionszugehörigkeit jenseits der Wahl?* Wiesbaden: Deutscher Universitäts-Verlag.

Desai, Kiran (2007): *The Inheritance of Loss.* London: Hamish Hamilton.

Durkheim, Émile (1969): 'Individualism and the Intellectuals', trans. Steven Lukes. In: *Political Studies* 17 (1): 19–30.

Durkheim, Émile (2001): *The Elementary Forms of Religious Life,* trans. Carol Cosman. Oxford: Oxford University Press.

Eisenstadt, Shmuel N. (2006a): *Theorie und Moderne. Soziologische Essays.* Wiesbaden: VS Verlag für Sozialwissenschaften.

Eisenstadt, Shmuel N. (2006b): 'Multiple Modernen im Zeitalter der Globalisierung.' In: Schwinn, Thomas (ed.): *Die Vielfalt und Einheit der Moderne.* Wiesbaden: VS Verlag für Sozialwissenschaften: 37–62.

Elliott, Anthony (2002): 'Beck's Sociology of Risk. A Critical Assessment.' In: *Sociology* 36 (2): 293–315.

Elliott, Anthony and Lemert, Charles (2006): *The New Individualism. The Emotional Costs of Globalization.* London and New York: Routledge.

Emerson, Ralph Waldo (1982): *Emerson's Essays: First and Second Series,* ed. Irwin Edman. New York: Harper Perennial.

Esposito, John L.; Fasching, Darrell J.; and Lewis, Todd (2006): *World Religions Today.* New York and Oxford: Oxford University Press.

Faist, Thomas (2000): 'Jenseits von Nation und Post-Nation. Transstaatliche Räume und Doppelte Staatsbürgerschaft.' In: *Zeitschrift für internationale Beziehungen* 7 (1): 109–44.

Farrow, Douglas (ed.) (2004): *Recognizing Religion in a Secular Society. Essays in Pluralism, Religion, and Public Policy*. Montreal: McGill-Queen's University Press.

Fiorenza, Francis Schüssler (2006): 'Karl Rahner: A Theologian for a Cosmopolitan Twenty-First Century.' In: Skira, Jaroslav Z. and Attridge, Michael S. (eds): *In God's Hands. Essays on the Church and Ecumenism in Honour of Michael A. Fahey, S.J.* Leuven: Leuven University Press: 109–35.

Foucault, Michel (1972): 'The Discourse on Language,' appendix to the *Archaeology of Knowledge*, trans. A.M. Sheridan Smith. New York: Pantheon: 215–37.

Fraser, Nancy (2007): 'Justice in a Globalizing World.' In: Held, David and Kaya, Ayse (eds): *Global Inequality*. Cambridge: Polity Press: 252–72.

Frese, Hans-Ludwig (2002): *'Den Islam ausleben.' Konzepte authentischer Lebensführung junger türkischer Muslime in der Diaspora*. Bielefeld: transcript.

Frost, Rainer (2003): *Toleranz im Konflikt*, Frankfurt a.M.: Suhrkamp.

Fuller, Robert C. (2002): *Spiritual, But Not Religious. Understanding Unchurched America*. New York: Oxford University Press.

Furlong, Andy and Cartmel, Fred (1997): *Young People and Social Change. Individualization and Risk in Late Modernity*. Buckingham: Open University Press.

Gabriel, Karl (1992): *Christentum zwischen Tradition und Postmoderne*. Freiburg, Basel and Vienna: Herder.

Gabriel, Karl (ed.) (1996): *Religiöse Individualisierung oder Säkularisierung. Biographie und Gropper als Bezugspunkte moderner Religiosität*. Gütersloh: Chr. Kaiser Gütersloher Verlagshaus.

Gailus, Manfred and Lehmann, Hartmut (eds) (2005): *National-protestantische Mentalitäten. Konturen, Entwicklungslinien und Umbrüche eines Weltbildes*. Göttingen: Vandenhoeck & Ruprecht.

Gane, Nicholas (2001): 'Chasing the "Runaway World". The Politics of Recent Globalization Theory.' In: *Acta Sociologica* 44 (1): 81–9.

Gärtner, Christel (2000): 'Sinnsuche und das Phänomen der neuen religiösen Bewegung.' In: *Sociologia Internationalis* 38 (1): 87–113.

Gentz, Joachim (2007): 'Die religiöse Lage in Ostasien.' In: Joas, Hans and Wiegandt, Klaus (eds): *Säkularisierung und die Weltreligionen*. Frankfurt a.M.: Fischer: 376–434. [English translation: 'The Religious Situation in East Asia.' In: Joas, Hans and Wiegandt, Klaus (eds): *Secularization and the World Religions*, trans. Alex Skinner. Liverpool: Liverpool University Press, 2009: 241–77.]

Giddens, Anthony (1990): *The Consequences of Modernity*. Cambridge: Polity Press.

Gillies, Val (2005): 'Raising the "Meritocracy". Parenting and the Individualization of Social Class.' In: *Sociology* 39 (5): 835–53.

Glick Schiller, Nina; Çağlar, Ayşe; and Guldbrandsen, Thaddeus C. (2006): 'Beyond the Ethnic Lens.' In: *American Ethnologist* 33 (4): 612–33.

Göle, Nilüfer (2006): 'Islam in European Publics.' In: *The Hedgehog Review* 8 (1/2). After Secularization: 140–6.

Göle, Nilüfer and Ammann, Ludwig (eds) (2004): *Islam in Sicht. Der Auftritt von Muslimen im öffentlichen Raum.* Bielefeld: transcript.

Graf, Friedrich Wilhelm (2004): *Die Wiederkehr der Götter.* Munich: C. H. Beck.

Graf, Friedrich Wilhelm (2006): 'Religiöse Transformationsprozesse der Moderne deuten.' In: Mörschel, Tobias (ed.): *Macht Glaube Politik? Religion und Politik in Europa und Amerik*a. Göttingen: Vandenhoeck & Ruprecht: 49–60.

Gray, John (2007): *Black Mass. Apocalyptic Religion and the Death of Utopia.* London: Penguin Books.

Gross, Peter (2007): *Jenseits der Erlösung. Die Wiederkehr der Religion und die Zukunft des Christentums.* Bielefeld: transcript.

Guggisberg, Hans R. (1997): *Sebastian Castellio 1515–1568.* Göttingen: Vandenhoeck & Ruprecht.

Habermas, Jürgen (2001): *The Postnational Constellation*, trans. Max Pensky. Cambridge: Polity Press.

Habermas, Jürgen (2006): *Dialectics of Secularization*, trans. Brian McNeil. San Francisco: Ignatius Press.

Habermas, Jürgen (2007a): 'Die öffentliche Stimme der Religion.' In: *Blätter für deutsche und internationale Politik* 12: 1441–7.

Habermas, Jürgen (2007b): *Die Revitalisierung der Weltreligionen – Herausforderung für ein säkulares Selbstverständnis der Moderne?* Starnberg: Unpublished MS.

Habermas, Jürgen (2008): *Between Naturalism and Religion*, trans. Ciaran Cronin, Cambridge: Polity Press.

Hacker, Paul (1957): 'Religiöse Toleranz und Intoleranz im Hinduismus.' In: *Saeculum* 8: 167–79.

Haddad, Yvonne (2002): *Muslims in the West. From Sojourners to Citizens.* Oxford and New York: Oxford University Press.

Hahn, Alois (1982): 'Zur Soziologie der Beichte und anderer Formen institutionalisierter Bekenntnisse. Selbstthematisierung und Zivilisationsprozess.' In: *Kölner Zeitschrift für Soziologie und Sozialpsychologie* 34: 407–34.

Hamilton, Malcolm B. (2001): *The Sociology of Religion. Theoretical and Comparative Perspectives.* London and New York: Routledge.

Harris, Sam (2004): *The End of Faith. Religion, Terror, and the Future of Reason*. London: Free Press.

Haupt, Heinz-Gerhard and Langewiesche, Dieter (eds) (2001): *Nation und Religion in der deutschen Geschichte*. Frankfurt and New York: Campus.

Haußig, Hans-Michael (1999): *Der Religionsbegriff in den Religionen*. Berlin: Philo Verlagsgesellschaft.

Heelas, Paul (1996): *The New Age Movement*. Oxford: Blackwell.

Heelas, Paul (2006): 'Challenging Secularization Theory. The Growth of "New Age" Spiritualities of Life.' In: *The Hedgehog Review* 8 (1/2). After Secularization: 46–58.

Heelas, Paul; Woodhead, Linda; Seel, Benjamin; Szerszynski, Bronislaw; and Tusting, Karin (2005): *The Spiritual Revolution. Why Religion is Giving Way to Spirituality*. Oxford: Blackwell.

Hegel, Georg Wilhelm Friedrich (2008): *Lectures on Philosophy of Religion*, 3 vols, ed. Peter C. Hodgson. Oxford: Oxford University Press.

Herbert, Ulrich (ed.) (2002): *Wandlungsprozesse in Westdeutschland. Belastung, Integration, Liberalisierung 1945–1980*. Göttingen: Wallstein.

Herbert, Ulrich (2007): 'Europe in High Modernity. Reflections on a Theory of the 20th Century.' In: *Journal of Modern European History*. Special Issue 5 (1): 5–20.

Hervieu-Léger, Danièle (1990): 'Religion and Modernity in the French Context: For a New Approach to Secularization.' In: *Sociological Analysis* 51: 15–25.

Hervieu-Léger, Danièle (1999): 'Religiöse Ausdrucksformen der Moderne. Die Phänomene des Glaubens in den europäischen Gesellschaften.' In: Kaelble, Hartmut and Schriewer, Jürgen (eds): *Diskurse und Entwicklungspfade*. Frankfurt a.M. and New York: Campus: 33–161.

Hervieu-Léger, Danièle (2000): *Religion as a Chain of Memory*. Cambridge and Malden, MA: Polity Press.

Hervieu-Léger, Danièle (2004): *Pilger und Konvertiten. Religion in Bewegung*. Würzburg: Ergon.

Hervieu-Léger, Danièle (2006): 'In Search of Certainties. The Paradoxes of Religiosity in Societies of High Modernity.' In: *The Hedgehog Review* 8 (1/2). After Secularization: 59–68.

Hillesum, Etty (1981): *Das denkende Herz der Baracke: Die Tagebücher von Etty Hillesum 1941–1943*, ed. and introduced by J. G. Gaarlandt. Freiburg: F.H. Kerle. [English translation: *Etty: The Letters and Diaries of Etty Hillesum 1941–1943*, ed. Klaas A. D. Smelik, trans. Arnold J. Pomerans, Grand Rapids, MI/Cambridge:

William B. Eerdmans; St Paul University, Ottawa: Novalis, 2002.]

Hitzler, Ronald (1996): 'Orientierungsprobleme. Das Dilemma der Kirchen angesichts der Individualisierung der Menschen.' In: *Leviathan* 24 (2): 272–87.

Hobson, John M. (2004): *The Eastern Origins of Western Civilisation.* Cambridge: Cambridge University Press: Chapters 1 and 12.

Hoffmann, Johannes (ed.) (1994): *Universale Menschenrechte im Widerspruch der Kulturen.* Frankfurt a.M.: Suhrkamp.

Hoppe, Thomas (2002): *Menschenrechte im Spannungsfeld von Freiheit, Gleichheit und Solidarität. Grundlagen eines internationalen Ethos zwischen universalem Geltungsanspruch und Partikularitätsverdacht.* Stuttgart: W. Kohlhammer.

Horkheimer, Max (1972): *Gesellschaft im Übergang. Aufsätze, Reden und Vorträge 1942–1970,* ed. Werner Brede. Frankfurt a.M.: Fischer Athenäum.

Höver, Gerhard (ed.) (2001): *Religion und Menschenrechte. Genese und Geltung.* Baden-Baden: Nomos.

Howard, Thomas Albert (2006): 'American Religion and European Anti-Americanism.' In: *The Hedgehog Review* 8 (1/2). After Secularization: 116–26.

Höwelmeier, Gertrud (2006): *Nuns at the Airport: Cosmopolitans in Transethnic Religious Organizations.* Unpublished MS.

Huber, Wolfgang (1992): 'Menschenrechte/Menschenwürde.' In: *TRE* 22: 577–602.

Hübinger, Gangolf (1994): *Kulturprotestantismus und Politik.* Tübingen: Mohr.

Hunter, Shireen T. (ed.) (2002): *Islam, Europe's Second Religion. The New Social, Cultural, and Political Landscape.* Westport, CT: Praeger Publishers.

Iannaccone, Laurence R. (1992): 'Religious Markets and the Economics of Religion'. In: *Social Compass* 39: 123–31.

Iannaccone, Laurence R. (1997): 'Rational Choice. Framework for the Scientific Study of Religion.' In: Young, Lawrence A. (ed.): *Rational Choice Theory and Religion. Summary and Assessment.* New York: Routledge.

Iannaccone, Laurence R. (1998): 'Introduction to the Economics of Religion.' In: *Journal of Economic Literature* 36: 1465–95.

Inglehart, Ronald (1997): *Modernization and Postmodernization. Cultural, Economic and Political Change in 43 Societies.* Princeton, NJ: Princeton University Press.

Jagodzinski, Wolfgang and Quandt, Markus (1997): 'Wahlverhalten und Religion im Lichte der Individualisierungsthese.' In: *Kölner Zeitschrift für Soziologie und Sozialpsychologie* 49: 761–82.

Jakelič, Slavica (2006): 'Secularisation, European Identity, and "The End of the West".' In: *The Hedgehog Review* 8 (1/2). After Secularization: 133–9.

Jelen, Ted G. (2002): *Sacred Markets, Sacred Canopies. Essays on Religious Markets and Religious Pluralism.* Lanham, MD: Rowman-Littlefield.

Joas, Hans (2007a): 'Die Zukunft des Christentums'. In: *Blätter für deutsche und internationale Politik* 8: 976–84.

Joas, Hans (2007b): 'Gesellschaft, Staat und Religion. Ihr Verhältnis in der Sicht der Weltreligionen. Eine Einleitung.' In: Joas, Hans and Wiegandt, Klaus (eds): *Säkularisierung und die Weltreligionen.* Frankfurt a.M.: Fischer: 9–43. [English translation: 'Society, State and Religion. Their Relationship from the Perspective of the World Religions. An Introduction.' In: Joas, Hans and Wiegandt, Klaus (eds): *Secularization and the World Religions*, trans. Alex Skinner. Liverpool: Liverpool University Press, 2009: 1–22.]

Joas, Hans and Wiegandt, Klaus (eds) (2007): *Säkularisierung und die Weltreligionen.* Frankfurt a.M.: Fischer. [English translation: *Secularization and the World Religions*, trans. Alex Skinner. Liverpool: Liverpool University Press, 2009.]

Juergensmeyer, Mark (2000): *Terror in the Mind of God. The Global Rise of Religious Violence.* Berkeley, Los Angeles and London: University of California Press.

Juergensmeyer, Mark (2006): 'The Church, the Mosque, and Global Civil Society.' In: Kaldor, Mary; Albrow, Martin; Anheier, Helmut; and Glasius, Marlies (eds): *Global Civil Society 2006/7.* London: Sage: 144–59.

Jullien, François (1999): *In Praise of Blandness. Proceeding from Chinese Thought and Aesthetics*, trans. Paula M. Varsano. New York: Zone.

Kaldor, Mary (1998): *New and Old Wars.* Cambridge: Polity Press.

Kaldor, Mary; Albrow, Martin; Anheier, Helmut; and Glasius, Marlies (eds) (2006): *Global Civil Society 2006/7.* London: Sage.

Kallscheuer, Otto (2006): *Die Wissenschaft vom lieben Gott. Eine Theologie für Recht- und Andersgläubige, Agnostiker und Atheisten.* Frankfurt a.M.: Eichborn.

Kamphaus, Franz (2007): 'Wie werden Religionen friedensfähig?' In: *Frankfurter Allgemeine Zeitung* 299, 24.12: 7.

Kandora, Michael (2002): 'Homosexualität und Sittengesetz.' In: Ulrich, Herbert (ed.): *Wandlungsprozesse in Westdeutschland. Belastung, Integration, Liberalisierung 1945–1980.* Göttingen: Wallstein.

Kant, Immanuel (1964): 'Geheime Artikel zum Ewigen Frieden'. In: *Werke in zwölf Bänden*, Vol. XI. Frankfurt a.M.: Suhrkamp.

Kant, Immanuel (1970): *Political Writings*, ed. Hans Reiss, trans. H. B. Nisbet, Cambridge: Cambridge University Press.

Karam, Azza (ed.) (2004): *Transnational Political Islam. Religion, Ideology and Power.* London and Sterling, VA: Pluto Press.

Karcher, Tobias (ed.) (2007): *Religionen und Globalisierung.* Stuttgart: W. Kohlhammer.

Kermani, Navid (2003): *Dynamit des Geistes. Martyrium, Islam und Nihilismus.* Göttingen: Wallstein.

Kermani, Navid (2005): *Der Schrecken Gottes. Attar, Hiob und die metaphysische Revolte.* Munich: C.H. Beck.

Kermani, Navid (2008): 'Der Aufstand gegen Gott. Der persische Dichter Attar und seine Seelenverwandten. In: *Wespennest. Zeitschrift für brauchbare Texte und Bilder* 150: 61–7.

Keupp, Heiner (1998): 'Die Gemeinschaft der Selbstsucher. Sozialpsychologische Anmerkungen zur kulturellen Dynamik des Protestantismus.' In: Lade, Eckhard (ed.): *Christliches ABC Heute und Morgen*, Supplement No. 1: 441–62.

Kittel, Manfred (2002): 'Konfessioneller Konflikt und politische Kultur in der Weimarer Republik.' In: Blaschke, Olaf (ed.) *Konfessionen im Konflikt. Deutschland zwischen 1800 und 1970: ein zweites konfessionelles Zeitalter.* Göttingen: Vandenhoeck & Ruprecht: 3–297.

Klumpjan, Hans-Dieter and Klumpjan, Helmut (1986): *Henry D. Thoreau.* Reinbek bei Hamburg: Rowohlt.

Knoblauch, Hubert (1989): 'Das unsichtbare Neue Zeitalter. "New Age", privatisierte Religion und kultisches Milieu.' In: *Kölner Zeitschrift für Soziologie und Sozialpsychologie* 3: 504–25.

Knoblauch, Hubert (1991): 'Die Verflüchtigung der Religion ins Religiöse.' In: Luckmann, Thomas: *Die unsichtbare Religion.* Frankfurt a.M.: Suhrkamp.

Knoblauch, Hubert (1999): *Religionssoziologie.* Berlin and New York: de Gruyter.

Koch, Traugott (1991): 'Menschenwürde als Menschenrecht.' In: *Zeitschrift für Evangelische Ethik* 35: 96–112.

Koselleck, Reinhart (2004): *Futures Past. On the Semantics of Historical Time*, trans. Keith Tribe. New York: Columbia University Press.

Koselleck, Reinhart and Jeismann, Michael (eds) (1994): *Der politische Totenkult. Kriegerdenkmäle in der Moderne.* Munich: Fink.

Krüggeler, Michael (1996): ' "Ein weites Feld . . .". Religiöse Individualisierung als Forschungsthema.' In: Gabriel, Karl (ed.): *Religiöse Individualisierung oder Säkularisierung. Biographie und Gruppe als Bezugspunkte moderner Religiosität.* Gütersloh: Chr. Kaiser Gütersloher Verlagshaus: 215–35.

Küng, Hans (1990): *Projekt Weltethos*. Munich: Piper. [English translation: *Global Responsibility*, trans. John Bowden, London: SCM Press, 1991.]

Küng, Hans (2007): 'Die Globalisierung der Moral'. In: *Die Welt*, 28.12: 8.

Kurasawa, Fujuki (2007): *The Work of Global Justice*. Cambridge: Cambridge University Press.

Langewiesche, Dieter (2000): *Nation, Nationalismus, Nationalstaat in Deutschland und Europa*. Munich: C.H. Beck.

Langewiesche, Dieter (ed.) (2001): *Nation und Religion in der Deutschen Geschichte*. Frankfurt a.M.: Campus.

Lash, Scott (2002): 'Individualization in a Non-Linear Mode'. Preface in: Beck, Ulrich and Beck-Gernsheim, Elisabeth: *Individualization: Institutionalized Individualism and Its Social and Political Consequences*, trans. Patrick Camiller. London, Thousand Oaks, CA, and New Delhi: Sage: vii–xii.

Lenssen, Jürgen (2007): *Zukunft der Kirchen und Kirchenbauten in den kommenden Jahrzehnten*. Würzburg: unpublished MS.

Levitt, Peggy (2007): *God Needs no Passport*. New York: The New Press.

Ley, Michael with Graf, Wilfried (2005): *Zivilisationspolitik. Zur Theorie einer Weltökumene*. Würzburg: Königshausen & Neumann.

Locke, John (1963): *A Letter concerning Toleration, Works* (ed. 1823), Vol. 6. Aalen: Scientia Verlag.

Luckmann, Thomas (1967): *The Invisible Religion. The Problem of Religion in Modern Society*. New York: Macmillan.

Luhmann, Niklas (2000): *Die Religion der Gesellschaft*. Frankfurt a.M.: Suhrkamp.

Lüscher, Kurt (1994): 'Was heißt heute Familie?' In: Brauns-Hermann, Christa; Busch, Bernd M.; and Dinse, Hartmut (eds): *Verlorene Liebe – gemeinsame Kinder*. Reinbek: Rowohlt: 51–65.

McGrath, Alister (2004): *The Twilight of Atheism. The Rise and Fall of Disbelief in the Modern World*. London: Rider.

McLeod, Hugh (ed.) (1995): *European Religion in the Age of Great Cities, 1830–1930*. London and New York: Routledge.

McLeod, Hugh (1996): *Piety and Poverty. Working-Class Religion in Berlin, London and New York, 1870–1914*. New York and London: Holmes & Meier.

McLeod, Hugh (2000): *Secularisation in Western Europe, 1848–1914*. London: Macmillan.

McNeill, William H. (1986): *Polyethnicity and National Unity in World History. The Donald G. Creighton Lectures 1985*. Toronto, Buffalo, NY and London: University of Toronto Press.

Malcamson, Scott L. (1998): 'The Varieties of Cosmopolitan Experience.' In: Cheah, Pheng and Robbins, Bruce (eds): *Cosmopolitics. Thinking and Feeling beyond the Nation*. Minnesota: University Press of Minnesota.

Manuel, Paul Christopher; Reardon, Lawrence C.; and Wilcox, Clyde (eds) (2006): *The Catholic Church and the Nation-State. Comparative Perspectives*. Washington, DC: Georgetown University Press.

Marcuse, Ludwig (1981): *Das Märchen von der Sicherheit*, ed. and introduced by Harold von Hofe. Zurich: Diogenes.

Margalit, Avishai (2007): 'Human Dignity between Kitsch and Deification.' In: *The Hedgehog Review* 9 (3): 7–19.

Marquard, Odo (1995): 'Lob des Polytheismus.' In: Marquard: *Abschied vom Prinzipiellen*. Stuttgart: Reclam.

Martin, David (1978): *A General Theory of Secularization*. Oxford: Blackwell.

Martin, David (1990): *Tongues of Fire. The Explosion of Protestantism in Latin America*. Oxford: Blackwell.

Martin, David (2002): *Pentecostalism. The World Their Parish*. Oxford: Blackwell.

Martin, David (2005): *On Secularization. Towards a Revised General Theory*. Burlington, VT: Ashgate.

Martin, David (2007): 'Das europäische Modell der Säkularisierung und seine Bedeutung in Lateinamerika und Afrika.' In: Joas, Hans and Wiegandt, Klaus (eds): *Säkularisierung und die Weltreligionen*. Frankfurt a.M.: Fischer: 435–64. [English translation: 'The Relevance of the European Model of Secularization in Latin America and Africa.' In: Joas, Hans and Wiegandt, Klaus (eds): *Secularization and the World Religions*, trans. Alex Skinner. Liverpool: Liverpool University Press, 2009: 278–95.]

Mason, Mary Ann; Fine, Mark A.; and Carnochan, Sarah (2001): 'Family Law in the New Millennium. For Whose Families?', *Journal of Family Issues* 22: 859–81.

Mazrui, Ali A. (2006): *Islam between Globalization and Counterterrorism*, ed. Shalahudin Kafrawi, Alamin M. Mazrui and Ruzima Sebuharara. Oxford: James Currey.

Meyer, John W. (2009): *World Society. The Writings of John W. Meyer*, ed. Georg Krücken and Gili S. Drori. Oxford: Oxford University Press.

Milbank, John (2006): *Theology and Social Theory. Beyond Secular Reason*. Oxford: Blackwell.

Molendijk, Arie L. (1996): *Zwischen Theologie und Soziologie*. Troeltsch-Studien, Vol. 9. Gütersloh: Gütersloher Verlagshaus.

Moore, Robert L. (1994): *Selling God. American Religion in the Marketplace of Culture*. Oxford and New York: Oxford University Press.

Müller, Burkhard (1995): *Schlußstrich. Kritik des Christentums*. Lüneburg: zu Klampen.

Mythen, Gabe (2005): 'Employment, Individualization and Insecurity. Rethinking the Risk Society Perspective.' In: *The Sociological Review* 53 (1): 129–49.

Nakamura, Hajime (1970): 'Die Grundlehren des Buddhismus, ihre Wurzeln in Geschichte und Tradition.' In: Dumoulin, Heinrich (ed.): *Buddhismus der Gegenwart*. Freiburg: Herder: 9–34.

Nederveen Pieterse, Jan (2004): *Globalization and Culture. Global Mélange*. Lanham, MD: Rowman and Littlefield.

Nietzsche, Friedrich (1966): *Werke in drei Bänden*, Vol. 1, ed. Karl Schlechta. Munich: Hanser.

Nökel, Sigrid (2002): *Die Töchter der Gastarbeiter und der Islam. Zur Soziologie alltagsweltlicher Anerkennungspolitiken. Eine Fallstudie*. Bielefeld: transcript.

Norris, Pippa and Inglehart, Ronald (2004): *Sacred and Secular. Religion and Politics Worldwide*. Cambridge: Cambridge University Press.

Norris, Pippa and Inglehart, Ronald (2006): 'Sellers or Buyers in Religious Markets? The Supply and Demand of Religion.' In: *The Hedgehog Review* 8 (1/2). After Secularization: 69–92.

Novak, David (2006): 'Secularity without Secularism.' In: *The Hedgehog Review* 8 (1/2). After Secularization: 107–15.

Nurser, John S. (2005): *For All Peoples and All Nations. The Ecumenical Church and Human Rights*. Washington, DC: Georgetown University Press.

Pagels, Elaine (1995): *The Origin of Satan*. New York: Vintage Books.

Pally, Maria (2007): 'Leben und leben lassen. Was unterscheidet einen amerikanischen von einem europäischen Muslim?' In: *Die Welt*, 10.12.

Paret, Rudi (1970): 'Toleranz und Intoleranz im Islam.' In: *Saeculum* 21: 344–65.

Partner, Peter (1997): *God of Battles. Holy Wars of Christianity and Islam*. Princeton: Princeton University Press.

Poferl, Angelika (2006): 'Solidarität ohne Grenzen? Probleme sozialer Ungleichheit und Teilhabe in europäischer Perspektive.' In: Heidenreich, Martin (ed.): *Die Europäisierung sozialer Ungleichheit. Zur transnationalen Klassen- und Sozialstrukturanalyse*. Frankfurt a.M.: Suhrkamp: 231–52.

Pogge, Thomas (2007): 'Reframing Economic Security and Justice.' In: Held, David and McGrew, Anthony (eds): *Globalization Theory. Approaches and Controversies.* Cambridge: Polity Press: 207–24.

Pollack, Detlef (1996): 'Individualisierung statt Säkularisierung? Zur Diskussion eines neueren Paradigmas in der Religionssoziologie.' In: Gabriel, Karl (ed.): *Religiöse Individualisierung oder Säkularisierung. Biographie und Gruppe als Bezugspunkte moderner Religiosität.* Gütersloh: Chr. Kaiser Gütersloher Verlagshaus: 57–85.

Pollack, Detlef and Pickel, Gert (2008): 'Religious Individualization or Secularization? Testing Hypotheses of Religious Change – The Case of Eastern and Western Germany.' In: *British Journal of Sociology* 58 (4): 603–32.

Prantl, Heribert (2006): 'Grüß Gott – aber welchen?' In: *Süddeutsche Zeitung* 296, Christmas Issue: 4.

Raban, Jonathan (2008): 'Good News in Bad Times.' In: *The Guardian*, 5.1: 21.

Reinhardt, Wolfgang (1985): *Geschichte der europäischen Expansion*, Vol. 2: *Die neue Welt.* Stuttgart: W. Kohlhammer.

Riesebrodt, Martin (2000): *Die Rückkehr der Religionen. Fundamentalismus und der 'Kampf der Kulturen'.* Munich: C.H. Beck.

Riesebrodt, Martin (2007): *Cultus und Heilsversprechen. Eine Theorie der Religionen.* Munich: C.H. Beck.

Ritter, Henning (2004): *Nahes und fernes Unglück. Versuch über das Mitleid.* Munich: C.H. Beck.

Roberts, Kenneth; Clark, Stan C.; and Wallace, Claire (1994): 'Flexibility and Individualization. A Comparison of Transitions into Employment in England and Germany.' In: *Sociology* 28 (1): 31–54.

Robertson, Roland (1989): 'Globalization, Politics, and Religion.' In: Beckford, James A. and Luckmann, Thomas (eds): *The Changing Face of Religion.* London: Sage: 10–23.

Robinson, William I. and Harris, Jerry (2000): 'Towards a Global Ruling Class? Globalization and the Transnational Capitalist Class.' In: *Science & Society* 64 (1): 11–54.

Römhild, Regina (2007): 'Migranten als Avantgarde?' In: *Blätter für deutsche und internationale Politik* 5: 618–24.

Roof, Wade Clark (1999): *Spiritual Marketplace. Baby Boomers and the Remaking of American Religion.* Princeton: Princeton University Press.

Röthel, Anne (1999): 'Nichteheliche Lebensgemeinschaften – neue Rechtsfragen.' In: *Zeitschrift für Rechtspolitik* 12: 511–19.

Roy, Olivier (2004): *Globalised Islam: The Search for a New Ummah.* London: C. Hurst.

Roy, Oliver (2006): 'Islam in the West or Western Islam? The Disconnect of Religion and Culture.' In: *The Hedgehog Review* 8 (1/2). After Secularization: 127–32.

Sartre, Jean Paul (2003): *Being and Nothingness. An Essay on Phenomenological Ontology*, trans. Hazel E. Barnes. London: Routledge.

Schiffauer, Werner (2001): 'Islam in Deutschland.' In: *Der Bürger im Staat* 4: 1–17.

Schleiermacher, Friedrich Daniel Ernst (2003): *On Religion. Speeches to Its Cultured Despisers*, ed. Richard Crouter. Cambridge: Cambridge University Press.

Schreiner, Klaus (2003): 'Messianismus.' In: Hildebrand, Klaus (ed.): *Zwischen Politik und Religion. Studien zur Entstehung, Existenz und Wirkung des Totalitarismus*. Munich: Oldenbourg.

Sen, Amartya (1999): 'Global Justice. Beyond International Equity.' In: Kaul, Inge; Grunberg, Isabelle; and Stern, Marc A. (eds): *Global Public Goods. International Cooperation in the 21st Century*. New York and Oxford: Oxford University Press: 116–25.

Sen, Amartya (2006): *Identity and Violence. The Illusions of Destiny*. London: Penguin Books.

Sennett, Richard (1998): *The Corrosion of Character: The Personal Consequences of Work in the New Capitalism*. New York: Norton.

Simmel, Georg (1898): 'Zur Soziologie der Religion.' In: *Neue Deutsche Rundschau (Freie Bühne)*, Berlin: 111–23.

Simmel, Georg (1919): 'Die Persönlichkeit Gottes.' In: Simmel: *Philosophische Kultur*. Leipzig: Kröner: 187–204.

Simmel, Georg (1922): *Die Religion*, Frankfurt a.M.: Rütten und Loenig.

Simmel, Georg (1997): *Essays on Religion*, ed. and trans. by Horst Jürgen Helle in cooperation with Ludwig Nieder. New Haven and London: Yale University Press.

Skira, Jaroslav Z. and Attridge, Michael S. (eds) (2006): *In God's Hands. Essays on the Church and Ecumenism in Honour of Michael A. Fahey, S.J.* Leuven: Leuven University Press.

Sloterdijk, Peter (2006): Interview in: *die tageszeitung*, 24–26.12: 5f.

Sloterdijk, Peter (2009): *God's Zeal. The Battle of the Three Monotheisms*. Cambridge: Polity Press.

Smith, Anthony D. (1995): *Nations and Nationalism in a Global Era*. Cambridge: Polity Press.

Soeffner, Hans-Georg (1997): *The Order of Rituals*, trans. Maria Luckmann. New Brunswick, NJ: Transaction Publishers.

Sontag, Susan (2003): *Regarding the Pain of Others*. London: Penguin Books.

Soysal, Yasemin Nuhoglu (1998): 'Toward a Postnational Model of Membership.' In: Shafir, Gershon (ed.): *The Citizenship Debates. A Reader.* Minneapolis: University of Minnesota Press.

Spaemann, Robert (1996): 'Weltethos als "Projekt"'. In: *Merkur 50* (9/10): 893–904.

Stark, Rodney and Finke, Roger (2000): *Acts of Faith. Explaining the Human Side of Religion.* Berkeley, Los Angeles and London: University of California Press.

Sznaider, Natan (2008): *Gedächtnisraum Europa. Die Visionen des europäischen Kosmopolitismus: Eine jüdische Perspektive.* Bielefeld: transcript.

Taylor, Mark C. (2006): 'The Devoted Student.' In: *The New York Times*, 21.12.

Thoreau, Henry David (1993): *A Year in Thoreau's Journal, 1851*, ed. H. Daniel Peck. London: Penguin.

Thoreau, Henry David (2001): 'Civil Disobedience.' In: Thoreau: *Collected Essays and Poems.* New York: Library of America: 203ff.

Tietze, Nikola (2001): *Islamische Identitäten.* Hamburg: Hamburger Edition.

Tietze, Nikola (2002): 'Individualisierung und Pluralisierung im Islam.' In: *Sozialer Sinn* 2: 223–40.

Töllner, Axel (2007): *Eine Frage der Rasse? Die Evangelisch-Lutherische Kirche in Bayern, der Arierparagraf und die bayerischen Pfarrerfamilien mit jüdischen Vorfahren im 'Dritten Reich'.* Stuttgart: W. Kohlhammer.

Touraine, Alain (1995): *Critique of Modernity*, trans. David Macey. Oxford: Blackwell.

Troeltsch, Ernst (1910/11): 'Die Zukunftsmöglichkeiten des Christentums.' In: *Logos* 1: 165–85.

Troeltsch, Ernst (1913): 'Religiöser Individualismus und die Kirche.' In: Troeltsch: *Gesammelte Schriften*, Vol. 2. Tübingen: Mohr: 109–33.

Tyrell, Hartmann (1996): 'Religionssoziologie.' In: *Geschichte und Gesellschaft* 22: 428–57.

Ubbelohde, Julia (2002): 'Der Umgang mit jugendlichen Normverstößen.' In: Ulrich, Herbert (ed.): *Wandlungsprozesse in Westdeutschland. Belastung, Integration, Liberalisierung 1945–1980.* Göttingen: Wallstein.

Ulrich, Herbert (2002): 'Liberalisierung als Lernprozeß. Die Bundesrepublik in der deutschen Geschichte – eine Skizze.' In: Ulrich, Herbert (ed.): *Wandlungsprozesse in Westdeutschland. Belastung, Integration, Liberalisierung 1945–1980.* Göttingen: Wallstein: 7–52.

Weber, Max (1974): *The Protestant Ethic and the Spirit of Capitalism*, trans. Talcott Parsons. London: Unwin University Books.

Weber, Max (1988): 'Die Wirtschaftsethik der Weltreligionen.' In: Weber: *Gesammelte Aufsätze*, Vol. I. Tübingen: Mohr.

Weber, Max (2002): *Schriften 1894–1922*, selected by Dirk Kaesler. Stuttgart: Kröner.

Weidenfeld, Werner (2005): 'Die elementare Kraft religiöser Zeichen.' In: *Die Welt*, 20.12.

Weingardt, Markus A. (2007): *Religion macht Frieden. Das Friedenspotential von Religionen in politischen Gewaltkonflikten.* Stuttgart: W. Kohlhammer.

Wilde, Oscar (1973): 'De Profundis.' In Wilde: *De Profundis and Other Writings*, ed. Hesketh Pearson. London: Penguin: 89–214.

Wohlrab-Sahr, Monika (ed.) (1995): *Biographie und Religion. Zwischen Ritual und Selbstsuche.* Frankfurt a.M. and New York: Campus.

Wohlrab-Sahr, Monika (1996): 'Lösung eines deutschen Dilemmas. Maximaler Kontrast und innere Gefolgschaft als Struktur einer Konversion zum Islam.' In: Gabriel, Karl (ed.): *Religiöse Individualisierung oder Säkularisierung. Biographie und Gruppe als Bezugspunkte moderner Religiosität.* Gütersloh: Chr. Kaiser Gütersloher Verlagshaus: 150–70.

Wohlrab-Sahr, Monika and Krüggeler, Michael (2000): 'Strukturelle Individualisierung vs. autonome Menschen oder: Wie individualisiert ist Religion? Replik zu Pollack/Pickel: Individualisierung und religiöser Wandel in der BRD' (ZfS 6/99). In: *Zeitschrift für Soziologie* 29 (3): 240–4.

Woolf, Virginia (1984): *A Room of One's Own.* London: Hogarth Press.

Wuthnow, Robert (1978): *Experimentation in American Religion. The New Mysticisms and Their Implications for the Churches.* Berkeley: University of California Press.

Wuthnow, Robert (1998): *After Heaven. Spirituality in America since the 1950s.* Berkeley: University of California Press.

Zagorin, Perez (2004): *How the Idea of Religious Toleration Came to the West.* Princeton: Princeton University Press.

Zinser, Hartmut (2006): 'Der verkaufte Gott.' In: *WestEnd* 3 (1): 109–20.

Index